U.S. Defense Policy

Third Edition

CONGRESSIONAL QUARTERLY INC.
1414 22nd STREET, N.W.
WASHINGTON, D.C. 20037

Congressional Quarterly Inc.

Congressional Quarterly Inc., an editorial research service and publishing company, serves clients in the fields of news, education, business and government. It combines specific coverage of Congress, government and politics by Congressional Quarterly with the more general subject range of an affiliated service, Editorial Research Reports.

Congressional Quarterly publishes the *Congressional Quarterly Weekly Report* and a variety of books, including college political science textbooks under the CQ Press imprint and public affairs paperbacks designed as timely reports to keep journalists, scholars and the public abreast of developing issues and events. CQ also publishes information directories and reference books on the federal government, national elections and politics, including the *Guide to Congress*, the *Guide to the Supreme Court*, the *Guide to U.S. Elections* and *Politics in America*. The *CQ Almanac*, a compendium of legislation for one session of Congress, is published each year. *Congress and the Nation*, a record of government for a presidential term, is published every four years.

CQ publishes *The Congressional Monitor*, a daily report on current and future activities of congressional committees, and several newsletters including *Congressional Insight*, a weekly analysis of congressional action, and *Campaign Practices Reports*, a bimonthly update on campaign laws.

Editor: Michael D. Wormser
Major Contributors: Charles W. Corddry, Robert S. Mudge, Margaret
C. Thompson, Pat Towell
Cover: Richard A. Pottern
Graphics: Belle T. Burkhart, Bob Redding
Photo Credits: Cover — Department of Defense; p. 4 — James K. W. Atherton, *Washington Post;* pp. 116, 178, 201 — Department of the Army.
Indexer: Toni Gillas

Printed in the United States of America

Library of Congress Cataloging in Publication Data
Main entry under title:

U.S. Defense Policy.

Bibliography: p.
Includes index.
1. United States — Military policy. 2. United States — National security. I. Congressional Quarterly, inc. II. U.S. defense policy.
UA23.U18 1983   355'.033073'   83-7555
ISBN 0-87187-258-7

Table of Contents

Tables

PREFACE

In the three years since publication of the second edition of *Defense Policy*, the superpowers appeared to have entered a new era of "Cold War," the most immediate evidence of which was an acceleration of the arms race. The détente of the 1970s already had ended by the time Ronald Reagan took office as president in January 1981. But the military buildup he initiated decisively reflected the gulf that had arisen between the United States and the Soviet Union.

The attention given the president's dramatic increase in spending on defense tended to obscure his administration's acceptance of long-held U.S. defense policies. Reagan stuck to the nuclear deterrent strategy in effect since the 1960s, when the U.S.S.R. achieved nuclear parity with the United States.

It had been widely assumed that Reagan would break radically with the defense policies and programs of the Nixon, Ford and Carter administrations. But to the consternation of Reagan's most ideologically conservative advisers, the president eschewed calls for quick fixes to allay the perceived nuclear vulnerability of the United States, new ABM defenses and crash programs to increase weapons production and combat strength. The only exception was in the Navy.

For one thing, such a radical policy would have required the diversion of massive amounts of money, placing the U.S. economy almost on a war footing. Even among Reagan's Republican backers in Congress, there was little support for that approach.

To be sure, there was a significant speedup in defense spending. That change by itself presented enough of a departure from past policies to disrupt the federal government's domestic social and welfare policies that had been in place at least since Lyndon Johnson's "Great Society" era. More money for defense meant that funding for many of those popular programs had to be slashed.

The administration's defense and tax policies, along with a faltering economy, also exacerbated the federal budget deficit, although the gap between government revenues and spending would have widened no matter who had become president in 1981. The larger doses of money committed to defense did not, however, automatically reverse the military and foreign policy setbacks for which President Jimmy Carter was criticized.

Chapter 1 documents the Reagan military buildup through a detailed comparison of the defense budgets of both the Carter and Reagan administrations, and assesses the funding and policy changes made by Congress. Chapter 2 reviews the long history of U.S. strategic weapons policy since World War II. The chapter also discusses the détente era of the early 1970s and the efforts at arms control, begun by President Richard Nixon; the failure to achieve a SALT II arms treaty; and the nuclear "freeze" movement that sprung up in 1982 partly in reaction to public perception that the Reagan administration was not genuinely committed to reductions in nuclear arms.

Chapter 3 investigates the new importance the Reagan team attached to conventional (non-nuclear) warfare and a stronger NATO defense as well as its plan to build up the U.S. naval fleet to a 600-ship Navy. Chapter 4 traces the development of the Rapid Deployment Force initiated by President Carter soon after the Iranian revolution of 1979 and the hostage crisis that followed. The RDF was conceived as a mobile command made up of various air, land and sea forces that could quickly be deployed to world trouble spots, particularly in the Middle East.

Chapter 5 takes a look at the present state of the armed services: the active duty strength of the Army, Navy, Air Force and the Marines; their missions; recruitment and the adequacy of the all-volunteer concept; the number and location of U.S. troops stationed overseas; increases in basic pay and benefits under Reagan; and the role of women.

An appendix section provides a brief chronology of important dates in U.S. defense policy making since 1977, a glossary of defense terms and a comprehensive bibliography.

Pat Towell, a veteran Washington defense reporter for Congressional Quarterly, has written the chapter on the defense budget. In addition, much of the material covered in *Defense Policy*, third edition, is taken from his weekly coverage of Congress for the *Congressional Quarterly Weekly Report*. The chapter on the status of the armed services was written by Charles Corddry, Washington correspondent for *The Sun* (Baltimore). The chapters on strategic nuclear policy and the Rapid Deployment Force were written by Margaret C. Thompson, and the chapter on the role of conventional arms in U.S. military strategy by Robert Mudge. Both writers are on the CQ Book Department staff.

INTRODUCTION

In the second edition of this book the authors noted that "few military technologies are stable enough for defense planners to rely upon very far into the future." That "future" has been very short indeed. In the 33 months since the publication of that edition, a new administration and two different Congresses have tried to stay abreast of and plan for technological change in both strategic nuclear forces and conventional warfare. Of the Reagan administration's fiscal 1984 defense budget request of $273.4 billion, some $29.6 billion was earmarked for weapons research and development.

In the strategic nuclear arms area the Soviet Union appeared to have made the more dramatic advances in recent years, an unsettling fact to Americans and especially to a president who came to office determined to redress what he perceived to be a deteriorating U.S. defense posture.

The U.S.S.R. had achieved a rough parity with the United States in nuclear weapons long before the election of Ronald Reagan. Previous administrations did not look upon this fact as necessarily invalidating America's long-held national security policy based on nuclear deterrence. But Reagan and his conservative advisers believed the Russians had the technological momentum on their side, allowing them in the very near future to gain nuclear superiority over the United States. If not quickly closed, this "window of vulnerability" — allowing the Soviet Union theoretically to all but annihilate U.S. intercontinental (ICBM) missiles in a surprise attack — would expose the United States to nuclear blackmail, or worse, they warned.

How to regain a "credible" American deterrent became an overriding military concern of the Reagan administration. Reagan immediately was confronted by two salient facts, however. Weapons innovations were expensive and their value to national security uncertain and often fleeting.

A pertinent example of that reality was the proposed MX intercontinental missile, given the go-ahead by President Jimmy Carter in

June 1979. When Reagan took office, the price tag for that weapon system ranged from about $30 billion to $33 billion, depending on which of two Carter-proposed basing schemes were employed. Both plans presented scientific as well as economic, environmental, social and political obstacles. But the cost alone made the project prohibitive. And there was no certainty that the scheme would ever provide an adequate deterrence against Soviet missiles.

Reagan shelved the Carter MX plan, along with various expensive interim "crash" strategic weapons programs advocated by the president's hard-line defense advisers. Besides the enormous cost of MX, the problems involved in devising a launching system that would be invulnerable against an enemy attack became a technological quagmire. It took Reagan two years to select his own basing plan, called "dense pack." Its estimated cost was $22.9 billion. This, along with broad skepticism that the plan would work, quickly made it unacceptable to Congress. After further studies, it appeared by April 1983 that Reagan and Congress finally would settle on a compromise emplacing MX launchers in reinforced Minuteman missile silos, at an estimated cost of $19.9 billion.

The administration, however, conceded that placing the new missiles in reinforced Minuteman silos would not make them invulnerable to a Soviet attack. The April 1983 compromise plan thus demonstrated that, despite four years of intensive review, the Defense Department could not economically solve the technical problem of devising an invulnerable deterrent weapon.

The MX was just one example of planning a defense strategy based on very costly, sophisticated weaponry with no guarantee of success. Others that Reagan was counting on included the B-1 bomber, canceled by Carter because of its cost but revived in 1981, a radar-evading plane for the 1990s called "stealth" and improved sea-launched Trident missiles.

Finally, the president himself added to the uncertainty about the worth of today's war-making technology by suggesting that national security in the next century may be based on a "Star Wars" system of laser-guided anti-missile missile defenses.

Reliance on expensive technology did not end with nuclear weaponry, however. Reagan's first secretary of state, Alexander M. Haig, Jr., had said in April 1982 that without nuclear superiority a policy based on massive retaliation no longer was credible. The changing military balance, he warned, had cast "a shadow over every significant geopolitical decision. . . . It influences the management of international crises and the terms on which they are resolved." As a result, the United States could deter future Soviet threats or outright aggression only by matching Moscow's vast land and air forces and expanding its sea power.

Three programs for conventional forces reflected the Reagan administration's approach: a push to increase the Navy's fleet from about 450 warships to more than 600; a move to accelerate development and procurement of exotic battlefield weapons and to increase the stockpiles of war materiel that would be needed in a protracted conflict in Europe; and a still undefined and imprecise plan to pressure peripheral Soviet interests around the world in order to gain military leverage in other areas of critical interest to the United States.

Of the three initiatives, a larger Navy was by far the most ambitious and costly. President Reagan succeeded in persuading Congress to approve construction of two additional nuclear-powered aircraft carriers, at a cost of $6.8 billion. The carrier request was symbolic of the president's acceptance of the growing consensus among U.S. military planners that conventional forces were becoming more crucial than at any time since the Soviet Union achieved nuclear parity. This belief reflected Haig's grim assessment of a growing conventional war threat to the United States and its NATO allies from Soviet and other communist forces.

Without trivializing the military threats to the United States, congressional critics feared that Reagan's approach would be self-defeating. Their concern resulted in new ideas about weapons procurement as well as innovations in battlefield strategy, particularly for defending Europe.

And at the more mundane level, some defense-oriented members criticized the armed services' apparent infatuation with expensive and technologically complex weaponry, particularly in the Army and the Air Force.

Michael D. Wormser
May 1983

Chapter 1

BUDGETING FOR DEFENSE

When Congress spent the first five months of 1983 debating the
size of President Ronald Reagan's defense budget, it was a fitting
example of the way Congress usually considers defense policy, at least
since the mid-1970s.

The air was thick with sweeping proposals to kill off expensive
weapons programs and more or less radically alter U.S. defense strategy.
But the only specific action Congress took — at least in the first round of
the annual budget battle — was to trim about 5 percent from the amount
requested by the president for Defense Department programs and
operations. The Pentagon and its allies on the congressional defense
committees were left to allocate the reductions according to their own
priorities.

That illustrates the general rule: Congress deals with U.S. defense
policy in terms of overall dollars, asking in effect, "How much is
enough?"

The Congressional Imprint

At least since the end of U.S. involvement in Vietnam, Congress
rarely has changed the direction of the chief executive's defense program.
And on the few occasions when Congress has left its imprint on policy, it
usually has done so in monetary terms: by varying slightly the overall level
of military spending or by altering the Pentagon's spending priorities. Its
influence on the details of military programs seldom makes much
difference in the long run.

There are exceptions, a few of which have had an important impact
on the nation's defense programs. In 1982, for instance, a vast amount of
time was expended over what kind of large cargo planes should be
bought for the Air Force: the administration's preference — the

5

Lockheed C-5, built in Georgia — or the Boeing 747, built in the state of Washington.

Policy vs. Politics

Complex technical arguments were bandied about on all sides of the issue. However, to all intents and purposes they were irrelevant to the outcome of the legislative fight, which turned largely on the question of whose constitutents would get the thousands of new jobs in the economically strapped aircraft industry. (Lockheed won that test of strength.)

It was a big battle in Congress, but no fundamental issues of military policy were at stake. Regardless of who got the contract, the U.S. fleet of transport planes for carrying combat units overseas was going to be substantially enlarged.

On the other hand, Congress sometimes makes seemingly insignificant alterations that cast a long shadow over defense strategy. For example, in 1982 the Pentagon was concerned that its plans for the defense of Europe might be seriously affected by Congress' refusal to approve several minor items costing a total of less than $100 million — a very small amount in the context of the Defense Department's annual budget.

Some of the money was earmarked for equipping West German reservists assigned to provide transportation and supply support to U.S. combat units stationed in Western Europe. Another slice was allocated for additional tanks and other heavy weapons and machinery needed to equip an extra Army division. U.S. defense plans relied on having the capability to quickly fly in a division of U.S. troops in the event of a major East-West crisis.

Congress rejected these funds, at least in part to signal its dissatisfaction with the level of defense spending of most of America's allies in Europe. Most Western European countries spent a much smaller proportion of their annual budget on defense, a longstanding sore point with Congress.

But such examples are the exceptions. Normally, congressional consideration of defense policy is confined to its influence over the gross amount of money available to the Pentagon.

Vietnam and Détente

There is no single answer to the question "How much is enough?" for defense, partly because the question has had a different political meaning to members of Congress at different times.

In the early 1970s, the first groups of senators and representatives who saw U.S. involvement in Vietnam as the symptom of a dangerous overextension of U.S. military commitments were, for the most part, liberal and moderate lawmakers. They generally favored higher federal spending on domestic social programs, such as those that were established under President Lyndon B. Johnson's "Great Society" agenda. The U.S. military commitment in Southeast Asia had jeopardized that policy.

The sense that U.S. military efforts could be relaxed seemed to gain political momentum after the 1972 Moscow summit meeting between President Richard Nixon and Soviet President Leonid I. Brezhnev. It appeared to many Americans that U.S.-Soviet relations had moved into an era of reduced tension — an era of détente, to use the fashionable word.

Through most of the Nixon presidency, the question: "How much is enough?" seemed to translate politically into a referendum on whether the Pentagon should be reined in. And the predominant answer on Capitol Hill was "yes." That approach reached its high watermark in 1975, when Congress cut some $7.4 billion from President Gerald R. Ford's defense budget request of $104.7 billion.

1970s Soviet Buildup

Even as the 1975 (fiscal 1976) Pentagon budget was being cut by Congress, however, supporters of a U.S. military buildup and a tougher policy toward Moscow were rallying behind Ronald Reagan's 1976 presidential candidacy and giving the "how much" question a new twist.

Citing the Soviets' growing involvement in Africa and the Middle East, and the steady expansion of their military forces at home, they rephrased the question to: "How fast a rate of growth in the defense budget will signal U.S. willingness to stand up to Russian pressure around the world?"

Jimmy Carter came to the White House in 1977 as the heir to the "no-more-Vietnams" tradition of the early 1970s. In his election campaign, he pledged to make significant cuts in the defense budget, withdraw U.S. combat troops from South Korea and negotiate a new nuclear arms treaty with Moscow. But by the time he was inaugurated, the political momentum was shifting rapidly to the defense hard-liners.

By the end of 1978, a year before Russia invaded Afghanistan, the defense debate in Congress had reversed direction; the issue had become one of how fast the budget should grow.

Reagan's victory in 1980, however, appeared to be the high watermark of the "how fast can we grow" approach to defense policy. Even in the new administration's initial changes in the defense budget, submitted to Congress barely a month after Reagan took office, another turn in the debate was foreshadowed.

Budgetary Limitations

Partly masked by his combative campaign rhetoric about the need to stand up to the Russians was the fact that President Reagan's $26 billion addition to Carter's January 1981 defense budget made very few major changes in what the Pentagon planned to defend, how it planned to fight and, accordingly, what it planned to buy.

And Reagan's overall increase was substantially smaller than that proposed by some conservative defense specialists who had advised Reagan during the 1980 campaign. The level of defense spending was restrained to some degree, particularly when compared to the dire warnings of candidate Reagan. This was not because the president suddenly changed his view of Moscow but rather because of early projections of unexpectedly high budget deficits. And before the first year of his term was over, these budgetary restraints — what the Pentagon sometimes called the "affordability" level — forced Reagan to retrench from his original defense plans. His initial $26 billion supplement to Carter's final defense budget was cut back by some $8 billion.

The problem of skyrocketing budget deficits was the result of a combination of factors: the administration's defense buildup, inflation, Reagan's record 1981 tax cut and Congress' refusal to cut domestic programs as deeply as the president wanted.

By the time Reagan presented his third budget to Congress in January 1983, "How much?" once again clearly meant to large majorities in both houses of Congress, "How much can we afford?"

Post-Vietnam Defense Budgets

A confrontation with Congress over President Ford's 1975 defense budget laid the foundation for the post-Vietnam era of defense spending disputes between the legislative and executive branches.

Ford's secretary of defense, James R. Schlesinger, warned Congress repeatedly that any reduction in the Defense Department's $104.7 billion

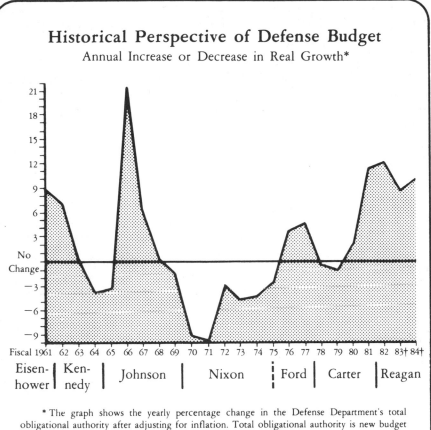

Historical Perspective of Defense Budget

Annual Increase or Decrease in Real Growth*

Fiscal 1961 62 63 64 65 66 67 68 69 70 71 72 73 74 75 76 77 78 79 80 81 82 83† 84†

| Eisen-hower | Ken-nedy | Johnson | Nixon | Ford | Carter | Reagan |

*The graph shows the yearly percentage change in the Defense Department's total obligational authority after adjusting for inflation. Total obligational authority is new budget authority plus several hundred million dollars for programs not requiring annual appropriations.

† The fiscal 1983 figure is projected and the fiscal 1984 figure is the budget request proposed by President Reagan in January 1983.

request for fiscal 1976 would place the United States second to the Soviet Union in military power before the decade was out.

Ford Budgets: The Pendulum Turns

Besides sounding the alarm about a Soviet military buildup, Schlesinger pointed to the erosion of "real" purchasing power in the defense budget caused by inflation. He argued that after allowing for the cost of inflation, the military budget was lower than it had been before the Vietnam War buildup. *(Chart, this page)*

If that trend were not reversed immediately, he warned, the Soviet Union would achieve military "preponderance" by about 1978. But congressional critics of Schlesinger's spending plans met the defense secretary head-on, questioning whether it was necessary for the U.S. military to continue to play the global role given it through the Vietnam period. "We may have gotten to the crossroads where the United States does not have to be first in every aspect of defense," Sen. John C. Culver, D-Iowa (1975-81), a member of the Armed Services Committee, told Schlesinger early in the year, "particularly if it is not first in the quality of life for our own people."

Despite Schlesinger's pleas, Congress sliced $7.4 billion from the administration's $97.9 billion defense appropriations request.

The funding cut was less an endorsement of the foreign policy arguments presented by Culver than of Congress' intense desire to control federal spending. That tight-fisted approach was buttressed by implementation on a limited basis of new federal budget procedures established by the Congressional Budget and Impoundment Control Act of 1974. *(Glossary of budget process terms, pp. 16-17)*

Despite the size of Congress' 1975 cut — nearly 7.5 percent of Ford's request for programs funded by the annual Defense Department appropriations bill — it was spread among hundreds of items rather than in a few selected programs. For instance, $1.3 billion of the reduction was for military aid to South Vietnam, which had fallen under communist control that April, months before Congress acted on the bill. The only major weapon not funded that year, a nuclear-powered frigate costing a quarter of a billion dollars, foundered less on budgetary restraints than on a disagreement between the Senate and House Armed Services committees over the wisdom of building nuclear-powered surface ships.

Nevertheless, when the House Appropriations Committee, on which Ford once had served, took the first step in cutting the defense budget, Schlesinger accused the panel of making "deep, savage and arbitrary cuts," to Ford's acute embarrassment.

The president already was at odds with his defense chief over a White House effort to squeeze some $28 billion from the projected fiscal 1977 federal budget. Schlesinger began a semi-public campaign to keep 1977 defense funding at $117 billion, the amount Ford initially planned to submit to Congress. Subsequently, it was reported that the president had decided on a Pentagon budget of about $107 billion as part of his budget cutting.

Schlesinger and Rumsfeld. Ford had been uncomfortable with Schlesinger's pedantic style. Now, angered by what he regarded as the secretary's political clumsiness in attacking a powerful House committee, and his disloyalty in fighting Ford's budget reduction effort, the president fired Schlesinger in early November. Former U.S. representative Donald Rumsfeld succeeded Schlesinger.

Ford recognized that Schlesinger was popular with congressional conservatives, who distrusted the policies of Secretary of State Henry A. Kissinger. To try to placate his critics, Ford linked Schlesinger's dismissal with the appointment Lt. Gen. Brent Scowcroft as head of the National Security Council, replacing Kissinger, who continued as secretary of state.

At the same time, Vice President Nelson A. Rockefeller, another lightning rod for conservative criticism, announced he would not be Ford's running mate in the 1976 election. But foreign policy hardliners were enraged nevertheless at the sacking of Schlesinger, who was viewed as a counter-weight to Kissinger's arms control and détente-oriented policies toward the Soviet Union.

Meanwhile, Rumsfeld engaged in a much-publicized and largely successful battle with the Office of Management and Budget to fix the fiscal 1976 defense budget at $112.7 billion. That restored a little more than half the amount for which Schlesinger had gone down fighting.

1976 Budget Increases. Rumsfeld's $112.7 billion budget was sent to Congress in January 1976. The amount was about $8 billion more than Ford had sought a year earlier and $14.4 billion more than Congress approved. Allowing for inflation, the new request represented an estimated $7.2 billion increase in real purchasing power for defense.

In addition to the increase needed to compensate for the cost of inflation, the administration insisted that substantial real growth was needed to offset the steady rise in Soviet military expenditures.

The largest increase in defense funding was earmarked for procurement, up 38 percent over the previous year to $29.3 billion. This included funds to begin production of the controversial B-1 bomber as a replacement for the aging B-52, the Trident missile-launching submarine and the F-16 fighter plane.

Defense Department planners said the procurement surge was needed to make up for shortfalls that occurred during the Vietnam War years. They argued that many new programs were deferred because of the cost of that war.

Congress was far more amenable to Ford's 1976 request than it had been in 1975. It reduced the $108 billion sought in the fiscal 1977 defense appropriations bill by only 3.3 percent, less than half the rate at which it had cut the previous year's bill.

A final decision on producing the B-1 bomber was put off until after the 1976 election. The purchase of some warships was deferred, partly because of a running dispute on whether to build nuclear-powered or conventional-powered surface ships and partly because funding in the bill had reached a congressionally imposed budget ceiling.

Hardening U.S. Attitude

Three factors blocked any serious congressional challenge to the Ford administration's argument that U.S. global commitments required an expansion of and improvement in both nuclear and conventional forces:

Skepticism About Soviet Aims. The perception of a rising Soviet military threat was fueled by growing congressional suspicion of Soviet intentions. This hardening attitude followed a sequence of Soviet political and military activities in the Middle East and Africa, including incitement of the Arab combatants in the 1973 war against Israel and diplomatic and financial support of leftist revolutionary movements in Angola and elsewhere in southern Africa. The congressional concern also was caused by a new Soviet crackdown against Russian dissidents and Jews wishing to emigrate to Israel.

Reinforcing the skepticism about Soviet aims were broader concerns triggered by the collapse of U.S. policy in Southeast Asia. Many members of Congress, particularly those who had supported the Vietnam War, were anxious to demonstrate to America's allies and adversaries that the United States did not lack the will to maintain its other commitments. One result of that attitude was widespread congressional support for the president's swift recourse to military force when Cambodian gunboats seized the U.S. merchant ship *Mayaguez* in 1975. Because of the widespread belief that the size of the defense budget was a symbol of U.S. global determination, the embarrassment of Saigon's fall also helped the administration to stave off sizable cuts in defense funding.

Growing Military Imbalance. The administration's warnings of growing Soviet military power were buttressed by three government analyses of the Soviet military buildup:

● The "dollar model." The CIA in February 1976 estimated that it would cost the United States about $114 billion (in 1974 dollars) to buy the quantity of weapons Moscow had bought in 1975 — 40 percent more than the United States actually spent on defense that year. If the costs of military pensions were disregarded, the defense "dollar gap" was 50 percent in favor of the Soviet Union. The study concluded that, in real terms, Soviet military spending had increased by nearly 3 percent annually since 1965, while U.S. spending had declined.

● The "ruble model." Roughly 15 percent — twice the amount of an earlier estimate — of the Soviet Union's estimated $900 billion annual gross national product (GNP) went to military purposes, according to another CIA study. The U.S. military effort consumed about 6 percent of its $1.5 trillion GNP.

● A Library of Congress study. "The quantitative military balance since 1965 had shifted substantially in favor of the Soviet Union," according to a Library of Congress study released Feb. 11, 1976, by the Senate Armed Services Committee. The study concluded that "U.S. qualitative superiority never compensated completely and, in certain respects, was slowly slipping away." The analysis, requested by Sen. Culver, listed Soviet advantages over the United States in the numbers of military personnel (4.8 million to 2.1 million), tanks (35,000 to 9,000) and armored personnel carriers (40,000 to 19,000).

Doubting Détente. In 1976, as in 1972, U.S. relations with the Soviet Union were a central issue in the presidential election campaign, but the focus was different. In 1972 the policy of détente — Secretary of State Henry A. Kissinger's cultivation of a web of U.S.-Soviet cooperative ties

was the centerpiece of President Nixon's carefully crafted image of statesmanship. Four years later, there was great concern in both major parties about what détente might be costing the United States in its competition with the Soviet Union for political and military influence in the world.

Conservatives of both parties had never been entirely comfortable with détente. In 1972 they raised objections to the sale of 400 million bushels of wheat to the Soviet Union on favorable financing terms and to the strategic arms agreement (SALT I) that gave the Soviet Union a numerical superiority in land-based and sea-based ballistic missiles. By late 1975, evidence of a large-scale Soviet arms buildup as well as continuing direct Soviet military and political support to various leftist forces in the developing world had fostered a suspicion of Soviet intentions that was not limited to the political right wing in the United States.

13

These suspicions were reflected in the presidential campaigns of Sen. Henry M. Jackson, D-Wash., and Republican hopeful Ronald Reagan. Both were uncompromising opponents of the kind of overly eager accommodation with the Soviet Union that they saw as the fruit of détente; both attacked the Ford administration for permitting what they viewed as the erosion of the nation's military strength.

Early in the campaign, Reagan began denouncing détente as "a one-way street," telling a New Hampshire audience that the United States had received no benefits more substantial than "the right to sell Pepsi-Cola in Siberia." Citing U.S. estimates of Soviet military production, he challenged administration claims that U.S. military strength was second to none. Jackson hit at the same theme, calling the Nixon-Ford policy toward the U.S.S.R. "a coverup for the gross mismanagement of the foreign policy of the United States."

Ford's response was to emphasize his determination to avoid "nuclear holocaust," implying that a harder line in foreign policy could have catastrophic results. He stressed his experience in foreign affairs and lamented that "nitpicking" challenges to the administration's policies were not helpful to the country.

Although Ford was adamant in defense of his policies, there was evidence of a hardening of the administration's line on U.S.-Soviet relations. Liberal critics charged that major areas of national security policy, including negotiations on a new strategic arms limitation (SALT) agreement with the Soviet Union, were being sacrificed to the president's renomination strategy. To avoid any last-minute alienation of the Republican Party's right wing, Ford acquiesced in changes in the party's 1976 campaign platform — drafted by Reagan delegates — that repudiated aspects of the Kissinger foreign policy.

Supplemental Ford Requests. In April 1976 Ford requested an additional $317 million to procure 60 Minuteman III intercontinental ballistic missiles and to equip them with a new, larger and more accurate warhead, the Mark 12A. Production of the missile had been scheduled to end in September 1976, but the administration warned in January that it might request funds to continue Minuteman production if arms limitation talks with the Soviet Union bogged down. Congressional Democrats charged that the supplemental request, which was made four days before the Texas presidential primary election, was aimed less at the diplomatic intransigence of the Soviet Union than at the political success of Ford's Republican challenger for the presidential nomination. Reagan repeatedly accused Ford of allowing U.S. military strength to deteriorate. Despite some opposition, Congress approved the additional funds.

On May 4, three days after the Texas primary in which Reagan overwhelmed Ford, the administration again amended its request by adding $974 million for five more warships — four antiaircraft escorts and an oiler — and $200 million for Navy research on vertical takeoff and landing combat aircraft, thus obviating the need for giant aircraft carriers.

Administration spokesmen denied Democratic charges that the additional request was politically motivated, insisting that it was based on a high-level study that had been under way for months and that the specific request was decided on by Ford at a White House meeting May 2, the day of the Texas primary.

In August, after Congress had refused to fund two warships in the initial fiscal 1977 budget and the four escort ships in the amended request, the president submitted a supplemental appropriations request of $1.1 billion for the six ships. But the House Democratic leadership insisted the request could not be considered because it exceeded the federal budget ceiling already approved by Congress. On Sept. 27 the House Armed Services Committee rejected the supplemental.

In the campaign for the Democratic nomination, the hard line on national security policy was muted by the early failure of Jackson's campaign (the Washington senator withdrew from the race after losing to Jimmy Carter in the April 27 Pennsylvania primary). But the party showed no desire in 1976 to challenge Ford on defense spending or on any other major aspect of the administration's national security policy.

Carter's Defense 'Savings.' The party's campaign platform adopted at its national convention in July called for a reduction of $5 billion to $7 billion in "present defense spending" — the figure used by Carter in the primaries. But in the fall election campaign, Carter was careful always to emphasize that the reductions would be made by cutting fat and waste from the Pentagon budget rather than by reducing force levels or procurement programs.

Throughout the presidential campaign, independent candidate Eugene J. McCarthy essentially was alone in his position that "it's not the fat [in the defense spending] that worries me; it's the lean that is causing all the trouble."

Whether as a cause or an effect of the campaign oratory, public support of higher defense spending, as reflected in the Gallop and Harris polls, showed a clear increase over the previous years. The same Harris

Glossary of Common Terms . . .

The Constitution gave Congress the power to decide what taxes the federal government may levy and how revenues received through taxation are spent. Through action on the president's annual budget, usually submitted in late January or early February, Congress determines the level of funding for each federal department and agency on a yearly basis. The federal government's **fiscal year** begins on Oct. 1 and continues through Sept. 30 of the following year.

In its detailed legislative consideration of the defense requests contained in the president's annual budget, Congress deals directly only with **budget authority** — the amount made available to the Defense Department for a particular ship or a year's worth of production of a particular airplane, and so forth. But that amount will be turned over to the weapons manufacturer only in stages, as the contractor reaches certain thresholds in the production process. Only at that point does the budget authority become an **outlay** — money that actually is spent by the government. At this point, defense spending will become part of the federal budget **deficit** — if there is one. The lag between budget authority and outlays can be up to three years for airplanes and more than seven years for large warships.

Congress adopts its own budget for the federal establishment in the form of two **concurrent budget resolutions**. The **first budget resolution**, which is supposed to be approved by May 1 of each year, sets overall goals for **revenue, budget authority, outlays** and the federal **deficit**; amounts are broken down among major budget categories or functions, such as national defense or health. A **second budget resolution**, having a deadline of Sept. 15, sets binding budget figures. (Congress never considered a second resolution in 1982. Instead, the first resolution was made binding, although Congress could revise the figures.)

Before Congress can consider the budget for most federal programs, it must pass authorizing legislation. The House has a rule which says that "no appropriation shall be reported in any . . . bill for any expenditure not previously authorized by law. . . ." An **authorization** is an act of Congress that establishes or continues government programs. It defines the scope of the programs and sets a ceiling on how much money can be spent. Authorizations do not actually provide the money for any program. That requires passage of a separate appropriations bill. Although most federal programs must be authorized before money can be appropriated for them, there are exceptions, including a portion of the defense budget. Approximately 80 percent of the Defense Department's budget requires prior authorization.

The **appropriations** bill provides money for programs, within the limits established in the previously approved authorization bills for those programs. An appropriation may be for a single year, a specified period of years, or an

... Used in the Budget Process

indefinite number of years, according to the restrictions Congress wishes to place on spending for particular purposes. The appropriations bills generally are made up of budget authority amounts rather than outlays since federal agencies cannot neatly tailor their spending requirements to a congressional session or a 12-month period. Amounts actually spent or obligated during a year may be drawn partly from the budget authority conferred by Congress in the year in question and partly from budget authority conferred in previous years.

For defense programs, there are three sets of parallel **authorization** and **appropriations** measures that Congress considers each year: the largest in terms of the number of programs and the amount of money involved are the Department of Defense authorization and appropriations bills covering weapons research, development and procurement and operations and maintenance of the armed services. (Military pay and benefits are not covered by the annual authorization bills but are included in the DOD appropriations measure. The pay of the Pentagon's 1 million civilian employees, however, must be both authorized and appropriated since it is included in the funding requested for both the research and development and the operations and maintenance accounts.) The next largest are the military construction bills covering projects as diverse as servicemen's housing and air base runways; finally, there are the Department of Energy authorization and appropriations measures. The Energy Department funds all nuclear weapons research and production.

Congress occasionally includes mandatory spending requirements in an authorization bill in order to earmark spending for a particular program.

Continuing appropriations resolutions, legislation enacted by Congress to provide budget authority for specific ongoing activities in cases where the regular appropriation has not been enacted by the beginning of the fiscal year, have been used with increasing regularity in recent years. The continuing resolution usually specifies a maximum rate at which the agency may incur obligations, based on the rate of the previous year, the president's budget request or an appropriations bill passed by either or both houses of Congress but not yet cleared and sent to the president. The fiscal 1983 appropriations for the Defense Department was included in a continuing resolution funding several other government departments. It was passed in December and covered the remainder of the fiscal year.

At least one **supplemental appropriations** measure is necessary each year. Normally, these are passed after the regular (annual) appropriations bills, but before the end of the fiscal year to which they apply. A supplemental that included additional funding for defense for fiscal 1982 was enacted over President Reagan's veto in September 1982.

poll showed a narrow plurality (38 percent to 43 percent) rejecting a $5 billion to $7 billion cut in military spending.

Defense Spending Under Carter

Soon after winning the presidency, Jimmy Carter began to stress that his somewhat vague campaign promise to achieve savings of $5 billion to $7 billion in defense spending would be realized gradually through reductions in the rate at which defense spending would increase, rather than through an outright reduction in the $110.2 billion that had been appropriated in Ford's last year.

Reductions — Real and Symbolic

Three days before the end of his term, Ford submitted a defense budget for fiscal 1978 of $123.1 billion. On Feb. 22 Carter reduced that request by $2.8 billion.

The largest part of the reduction came from funding for 11 major weapons Carter wanted either to cancel (such as a tanker-version of the DC-10 jetliner) or purchase at a much slower rate. Among the slowdowns proposed were those in:

● Development of the MX intercontinental missile ($134 million compared with Ford's $294 million).

● Purchase of the B-1 bomber (five planes at a cost of $1.3 billion instead of eight planes at $1.8 billion).

A dramatic break with Ford's defense policies came later, on June 30, 1977, when Carter canceled production of the B-1 altogether. The president said the existing B-52 bomber fleet would still be able to threaten Soviet targets if they were armed with accurate cruise missiles — little jet-powered drones designed to hit within tens of yards of a target 1,500 miles distant.

In the main, Carter's defense funding priorities were sustained, though the House approved the B-1 decision by a relatively narrow margin. But during the year, three issues emerged that helped to galvanize the hard-line critics of Carter's defense plan:

Arms Control Complications. The battle lines were drawn over nuclear arms policy even before Carter's inauguration, when the president-elect selected former Air Force Secretary Harold Brown as secretary of defense.

Former Defense Secretary Schlesinger and Sen. Jackson, among others, believed that Moscow was driving toward numerical and qualitative superiority in strategic nuclear weapons — especially in land-based missiles (ICBMs) — that would give it a dangerous political advantage over the United States.

Brown, a nuclear physicist with more than two decades of experience in the U.S. defense program, was widely thought to hold a contrary view: That a nation could not gain diplomatic leverage by threatening to use nuclear weapons because the threat would not be taken seriously; no one would believe that a nuclear war could be fought in a controlled way and "won."

Brown's nomination sailed through the Senate with little opposition. But Jackson and his Senate allies decided to challenge Carter's choice of Paul Warnke to be chief U.S. arms control negotiator and head of the Arms Control and Disarmament Agency (ACDA). For years Warnke had been a forceful advocate of the position on nuclear arms attributed to Brown, and he had opposed the development of various weapons systems.

After occasionally rancorous hearings and four days of debate, the Senate confirmed Warnke for the SALT job by a 58-40 vote.

The administration then caught its hard-line critics off guard by proposing an arms control treaty that would have slashed the number of Soviet ICBMs that could threaten U.S. missiles. Jackson had regarded this presumed threat as one of the most crucial arms control issues. But when the Russians dismissed the proposals out of hand, the hard-liners resumed their campaign to ensure that no treaty would be ratified that could yield even an apparent advantage to the Soviet Union.

Troop Withdrawal Promise. Carter's second irritant in the eyes of the defense hard-liners was his order to the Defense Department, within a few months of taking office, to implement a campaign pledge to withdraw the 32,000 U.S. ground combat troops stationed in South Korea. The proposal drew strong opposition from foreign policy hard-liners and many senior military officers and also from some liberals, including Sen. Hubert H. Humphrey, D-Minn. (1949-64, 1971-78).

The issue came to a head in May when Maj. Gen. John K. Singlaub, the third-ranking U.S. Army officer in Korea, flatly predicted to *The Washington Post* that a U.S. withdrawal would lead to war in Korea.

When the president ordered Singlaub home, Carter's opponents in Congress used the incident to focus attention on the troop withdrawal issue. The administration appeared taken aback at the force of pro-Singlaub reaction on Capitol Hill. But Carter nevertheless reaffirmed his intention to carry out the withdrawal.

Hard on the heels of the U.S. troops issue, Carter decided to cancel production of the B-1 bomber in favor of equipping existing B-52s with long-range cruise missiles.

Cruise Missile, B-1 Decisions. There were technical dimensions to Carter's decision to use cruise missiles as replacements for, rather than supplements to, manned bombers. For instance, one had to weigh the long-term prospects of thwarting Soviet radars through the cruise missile's small size compared to the bomber's use of powerful radar jamming devices.

Such issues had been raised repeatedly in the long debate on the B-1. But such technical questions had been overwhelmed by the plane's irresistible potential as a political symbol. The plane had become a target for liberal critics of higher defense budgets. Capitalizing on its $100 million-a-copy price tag and its failure to meet some of its more extravagant design goals, the opponents ridiculed the B-1 as a plaything for generals.

Foreign policy hard-liners now argued that Carter's decision to kill the plane was a dramatic embodiment of a basic hostility toward defense and a fixation on the cost of the weapon to the exclusion of concern for the plane's importance to national security.

Carter's second year in office was a good one for the president, at first glance. Both the Senate and House rejected decisively several moves by dissidents to the left and the right of Carter to raise or lower his $126 billion defense budget request for fiscal 1979. And by unexpectedly large margins, Congress supported Carter's position not to produce the B-1 bomber or build a fifth nuclear-powered aircraft carrier.

The political drift toward a tougher defense posture was unmistakable, however. This was reflected, in part, in the battles that Carter chose not to fight during the year. These included his failure to follow up on his campaign pledge to pull U.S. ground troops out of South Korea or to complete the SALT II negotiations with the Soviet Union. In each case, Carter stayed his hand, in part because of the vehement congressional opposition. (In the case of the SALT treaty, Carter felt he had to keep dickering with Moscow for a tougher treaty.)

Commitment to 3 Percent Growth

Even Carter's success in 1978 in protecting his defense budget came in the context of an unconditional commitment to increase funding for the Defense Department. He pledged his administration to an annual real growth rate (after factoring in inflation) of 3 percent in defense spending, a policy agreed upon by all NATO members.

To some degree, even Carter's victories in the B-1 and nuclear carrier fights illustrated how the political atmosphere had changed since the early post-Vietnam years.

In both fights, Carter argued that he was opposing a weapon whose time was past in order to invest in other projects that would do the job more effectively — cruise missiles and smaller, more numerous carriers. The immediate effect was to reduce defense spending, but the alternatives backed by Carter eventually would have cost about as much as the weapons they were to replace.

In the case of the B-1, Carter had the advantage of strong support from ranking military leaders, including then-Air Force Chief of Staff Gen. David C. Jones. Jones had fought hard to sell Carter on the plane. But when Carter decided to kill the program, Jones decided it was doomed and opposed an effort by some lawmakers to keep the program alive by spending $462 million dollars to build two prototype B-1s. The Air Force position was that it would rather spend the money on other programs.

The Navy had campaigned vigorously for a fifth nuclear-powered aircraft carrier, and the Senate and House Armed Services committees had approved it as part of the annual Defense Department authorization bill. But Carter vetoed the bill and easily turned aside an effort to override the veto in the House.

Many observers felt that the Navy's case for the ship was undermined by long-festering problems with cost-overruns and delays in its shipbuilding program.

Defense Spending Pressures

Proponents of a faster defense buildup consolidated their grip on Pentagon programs in 1979. Ironically, it was Carter's effort to ratify the SALT II arms control treaty that created the political pressure for higher spending on defense.

By the end of the year, Carter and Congress had agreed to a fiscal 1980 defense budget of approximately $142.6 billion — an increase of almost $15 billion over the previous year. And Carter was forced to pledge that he would seek future and real increases for defense of 5 percent annually. The Senate already had approved a buildup at that rate.

SALT II Politics. Carter by 1978 had begun to lobby for the SALT II treaty almost exclusively in terms of the military advantages it would bring the United States.

In contrast to Nixon's campaign for SALT I, in which the president had argued that the 1972 treaty would have a calming effect on U.S.-Soviet tensions, the Carter team insisted that SALT II should be weighed only in terms of its impact on the U.S.-Soviet military balance. On those grounds alone, the administration maintained, the treaty clearly was beneficial to the United States since it limited several ongoing Soviet weapons, while imposing no significant limit on any planned U.S. arms programs.

Because of the way the Carter administration chose to defend the treaty, the Senate hearings on SALT II became a forum for reviewing the U.S.-Soviet military balance and assessing the adequacy of Carter's defense policies.

The Joint Chiefs of Staff were firm in their endorsement of the treaty. But the hearings gave them a much wider audience than usual for their warnings of gaps in the U.S. arsenal. And defense hard-liners seized on the chiefs' recommendation of a 5 percent annual real growth rate as evidence that the earlier 3 percent increase that Carter had proposed was inadequate.

Soviet Pressures. The image that the Soviet military was gaining the upper hand over U.S. forces was reinforced by reports in late August 1979 that a Soviet combat brigade was stationed in Cuba. And in November this issue was overshadowed by an even more disturbing indication of slipping U.S. influence in the world: the seizure by Iranian militants of the the U.S. Embassy in Tehran.

In the wake of these events, the American public backed a more assertive U.S. international posture. By mid-December Carter had committed himself to a 5 percent annual increase in defense spending, at least partly as a tactic to win the two-thirds Senate majority needed to ratify the SALT II treaty.

The Congressional Factor. The Soviet invasion of Afghanistan on Dec. 27 ended any remaining hope that the Senate would approve the treaty. And several other Carter policies aimed at reducing global military tensions already were dead or indefinitely shelved:

● Carter had been forced to further delay his campaign promise to withdraw U.S. ground combat troops from South Korea.

• Two nuclear weapons that Carter originally had opposed — the mobile MX intercontinental missile and medium-range missiles able to strike Soviet territory from launchers in Western Europe — now were solidly ensconced in the administration's defense plans.

• Efforts by the administration to negotiate a treaty with Moscow to remove military forces from the Indian Ocean region — in effect making it a nuclear-free zone — came to naught. The hostage crisis with Iran led to the stationing of a large U.S. naval fleet in the Arabian Sea, and, after the Soviet invasion of Afghanistan, administration officials announced that two aircraft carrier task forces would stay in the area for the foreseeable future.

• By margins of better than two-to-one, both houses of Congress voted to substitute a fifth *Nimitz*-class nuclear-powered aircraft carrier for the slightly less expensive oil-powered version Carter reluctantly had requested. Events in the Persian Gulf demonstrated that the Navy's carrier fleet still was an important instrument of U.S. military policy and diplomacy.

• During a December preview of his 1980 budget request, Carter announced a $10 billion plan (stretching over several years) to train and equip U.S. forces to be able to move quickly to countries in the Persian Gulf region at the request of local governments. This became the so-called Rapid Deployment Force (RDF). *(Details, see Rapid Deployment Force chapter.)*

1980: Events Overwhelm Policies

Carter's January 1980 budget earmarked $161.8 billion for the Pentagon in fiscal 1981. This already represented an increase of almost $34 billion over the amount Congress approved the previous year (not counting enactment of a defense supplemental bill for fiscal 1980). But when the budget was submitted, Defense Secretary Brown noted that it had been drafted before the Soviet invasion of Afghanistan, and he promised a supplemental funding request to keep pace with events.

The supplemental, forwarded to Congress in March 1980, added $2.9 billion to the fiscal 1981 request and $2.3 billion to the budget for fiscal 1980, the year already well under way. The administration also asked permission to reallocate to certain Pentagon programs $2.5 billion previously appropriated for other defense purposes.

Persian Gulf Buildup. The additional funding contained in Carter's supplemental request was allocated by the Pentagon for higher than anticipated costs of fuel ($5.4 billion) and inflation ($1.3 billion) and to begin a large expansion of the U.S. military presence in the Persian Gulf/Indian Ocean area ($1 billion).

Some of that extra money went to pay for the operation of two Navy task forces, each led by an aircraft carrier. The rest was to begin organizing and equipping the proposed RDF. Although this did not involve any new battalions or squadrons, the additional money was needed to organize a headquarters that could plan how existing U.S. forces might be trained and sent to the Middle East or any other area where, unlike Western Europe and Japan, there were no U.S. forces.

RDF-related funds also were used for construction of runways and supply depots at bases in Southwest Asia and to expand the U.S. fleet of transport ships and airplanes.

Military Pay Issue. In May, Carter faced yet another budgetary quandary. Congress was about to approve a substantial boost in military compensation, on top of the other increases it appeared bent on making in the president's defense budget.

At issue was a package of increases in various fringe benefits and in special wages and bonuses for certain miltary job specialties. Crafted by Senate Armed Services Committee members Sam Nunn, D-Ga., and John Warner, R-Va., the package was directed at senior enlisted personnel, who were leaving the services in alarming numbers for higher paying civilian jobs.

After a vigorous, though apparently futile, lobbying campaign against the Nunn-Warner proposal, Carter suddenly announced his support of the $700-million package during a welcoming home ceremony for the crew of the aircraft carrier *Nimitz*, which was ending its tour in the Indian Ocean. (The *Nimitz* was the first carrier sent to the region after the U.S.S.R. invaded Afghanistan.)

Soon thereafter, however, the president urged Congress to reject a congressional move to set the fiscal 1981 defense budget at $171.3 billion. His own revised request of $164.7 billion was adequate and had the approval of the Joint Chiefs of Staff, Carter said. But it did not include the $700 million Nunn-Warner pay package. Carter's sudden switches on Nunn-Warner, combined with his insistence that his own request was sufficient, generated a firestorm of criticism. The chairman of the Senate Budget Committee, Ernest F. Hollings, D-S.C., called Carter a "hypocrite."

A subcommittee of the House Armed Services Committee summoned the Joint Chiefs of Staff to inquire into the adequacy of Carter's request. All five service chiefs said they needed more money than Carter had requested. And they said they had not been consulted before Carter invoked their authority to condemn the higher $171.3 billion congressional defense budget recommendation.

Congress Leads the Way. By Carter's last year in office, then, it was apparent that congressional alarm over the U.S.-Soviet military balance had reached a new level of intensity. And for the first time in 13 years Congress in 1980 approved a defense appropriation that was higher than the amount the chief executive had requested. That year's final defense bill was $5.2 billion above Carter's original request.

Despite the congressional consensus favoring a "tougher" defense stand, there were signs of some underlying disagreements. The House in 1980 backed a much smaller defense increase than did the Senate, and there were differences over some programs. Funds for development of a new cargo plane for the Rapid Deployment Force were curtailed sharply. Moreover, there appeared to be political limits as to how far Congress would be willing to go to boost military preparedness. This became evident during debate on Carter's proposal to resume mandatory registration of men for the military draft. (The draft law had been allowed to expire July 1, 1973, and President Ford on April 1, 1975, suspended the obligation of 18-year-old males to register for the draft.)

A Senate effort to block draft registration showed only modest strength. But it delayed enactment of the plan long enough to rob it of the symbolism of national unity Carter had hoped it would provide. At the same time, the House approved registration by only a narrow margin, partly because of opposition by some conservatives, who accused Carter of using it as window dressing to cloak the absence of a really tough policy toward Moscow.

Defense Peak: Election of Reagan

By nearly all accounts, the lagging economy dominated the 1980 presidential campaign, but defense issues, particularly the size of the defense budget, also were the subject of contentious debate by the major candidates.

Usually, congressional consideration of defense issues turns on images rather than substance. Carter portrayed himself as tough but sensible, anxious to negotiate arms agreements with Moscow yet willing to oppose Soviet adventurism through a boycott of the Olympic Games, a cutoff of sales of American grain to the U.S.S.R. and the resumption of military draft registration.

Carter painted Reagan as belligerent, confrontational, eager for an arms race and casual, at best, about the risks of nuclear war.

Reagan portrayed himself as an uncompromising foe of communism, committed to preserving the peace but determined to restore what he called the nation's military "margin of safety."

Carter's administration was characterized by Reagan as one of weakness and vacillation, and Carter himself as a naive appeaser obsessed with avoiding provocation of the Soviet Union.

Reversing 'Decline' in Defense

Carter, who ran for president in 1976 on a promise to cut the defense budget, in 1980 boasted during the campaign that he had "reversed the Republican decline in defense" spending.

Reagan talked in general terms of spending more for defense, but he avoided specific commitments, apart from contrasting Carter's requests with the more ambitious five-year defense plan Ford had proposed the day before he left office in January 1977.

Independent candidate John B. Anderson implied that he would hold down the defense budget. His platform warned against "simplicities which hold that spending more money will itself provide a solution to our security problems." But Anderson was no more specific than the other two candidates about how much was enough for defense.

The nearest the election campaign came to specifics about defense policy was in the treatment of two symbolically charged weapons projects: the B-1 bomber and the MX missile.

Reagan sharply attacked Carter's 1977 decision to cancel production of the B-1, although he avoided a firm commitment to resuscitate the program if elected. As a Republican representative from Illinois, Anderson had supported cancellation of the plane.

Both Reagan and Anderson attacked as unworkable and unduly complex Carter's initial proposal for basing the MX, which involved shuttling at random 200 missiles among 23 launch sites so that Soviet missiles would have to attack some 4,600 missile silos to have any chance of destroying the whole MX fleet. *(Details of MX controversy, see Strategic Nuclear Policy chapter, p. 82)*

Reagan also charged that Carter's proposed MX plan would not offset the alleged vulnerability of U.S. missiles quickly enough. But he did not propose an alternative until almost a year after he was elected.

Reagan's Defense Buildup

Reagan's first defense funding request, announced in March 1981, proposed a substantial, though far from drastic, increase in the budget Carter had submitted in January. After an initial surge in fiscal 1981 and 1982, Reagan's plan for fiscal 1983 through 1986 called for increases in the Pentagon's budget of about 7 percent annually in real purchasing power (after adjusting for inflation). Carter's last defense budget projected annual real increases of about 5 percent, but Carter's real growth estimates were based on higher inflation assumptions than Reagan used.

Five-Year Spending Plan. The following table lists the presidential budget requests for new budget authority (BA) for defense for fiscal 1982 and projected requests for fiscal years 1983-86 as recommended by Carter in January 1981 and by Reagan in March *(amounts in billions of dollars)*:

	1982	1983	1984	1985	1986
Carter	$196.4	$224.0	$253.1	$284.3	$318.3
Reagan	222.2	254.8	289.2	326.5	367.5

Reagan also added $6.5 billion to a $6.3 billion fiscal 1981 supplemental defense appropriation Carter requested shortly before leaving office.

Legislative Agenda. The only immediate force increase projected by Reagan's 1981 budget amendments was for the Navy. Senior admirals and critics of Carter's defense plans wanted to increase the fleet by about 150 ships, from 450 ships to about 600. Of the $25.8 billion Reagan added to Carter's proposed fiscal 1982 defense budget, $4.2 billion was earmarked for new ships and for refurbishing some older ones then in mothballs. This was to be the first step toward expanding the Navy to 15 carrier task forces instead of the 12 then in the fleet.

In his additions to the fiscal 1981 supplemental and to the fiscal 1982 budget request, Reagan nearly doubled — to $2.5 billion — the funds for the RDF and related programs.

Another $2.5 billion went to continue the development of a new strategic bomber. Reagan's choice, the B-1 bomber, was not announced until October 1981. But the 1977 decision to cancel the B-1 was high on

27

the list of items in the hard-liners' indictment of Carter; it had been widely anticipated that Reagan would try to resurrect that program.

Reflecting his often-expressed commitment to an all-volunteer military, Reagan in mid-1981 proposed an extraordinary 5.3 percent military pay hike — costing $2.3 billion — in addition to an automatic cost-of-living increase beginning Oct. 1. (The October increase came to 9.1 percent.)

Reagan also asked for an extra $2 billion in the 1981 supplemental and $13.7 billion in fiscal 1982 to buy more warplanes, missiles, tanks and communications equipment. In nearly every case, the Reagan plan merely accelerated purchases to which Carter theoretically already was committed. The Reagan changes allowed for the purchase of almost 150 more airplanes, 55 more helicopters, 151 more tanks and 136 more armored troop carriers than Carter requested.

Radical Departures Avoided. During the 1980 presidential campaign, and in the intervening weeks before Reagan was inaugurated, conservative defense analysts long committed to Reagan predicted the new administration would break radically with the defense policies of the Nixon, Ford and Carter administrations. But when Reagan's defense budget appeared in March 1981, what was immediately apparent was the new administration's disregard of the defense recommendations and theories put forward by some of Reagan's hard-line defense advisers.

The first clear indication of the direction Reagan would take had come nearly a month before the administration took office, when Defense Secretary-designate Caspar W. Weinberger abruptly dismissed Reagan's Pentagon transition team headed by William R. Van Cleave, Reagan's defense adviser during the campaign.

Personal animosities between Weinberger and Van Cleave reportedly contributed to the break. But the basic issue was Van Cleave's three-year-old campaign for a program of expensive "quick fixes" to immediately strengthen the U.S. nuclear arsenal. One Van Cleave proposal was to modify existing U.S. ICBMs so they could be fired from movable launchers.

Van Cleave's package was intended primarily to close the so-called "window of vulnerability" Reagan had warned about during the campaign. The phrase referred to the period during which, according to Reagan's advisers, Soviet missiles theoretically would be able to destroy most U.S. ICBMs in a surprise attack.

Even among Republican defense experts, only a minority of

strategic arms specialists shared Van Cleave's view of the critical importance of the technical details of the strategic military balance. But the decisive blow to the quick-fix package was its cost. Early on, it became clear that Reagan's budget increases would force the Pentagon to make painful choices among alternatives. Most senior military officers and hard-line defense analysts placed a much higher priority on improving U.S. conventional forces than on developing new strategic programs (except for the symbolically important B-1 bomber).

Deterrence and ABM System. Another popular course advocated by some military analysts but rejected by the Reagan administration in 1980-81 was a renewed emphasis on an anti-missile (ABM) defense system.

A group of senators led by conservative Republicans from Western states maintained that a nuclear attack could be deterred by an ABM system able to shoot down Soviet missiles and bombers, obviating the need to threaten a massive retaliatory attack.

Their basic premise was that technical developments held out the possibility of a virtually "leak-proof" defense protecting U.S. territory. New anti-missile missiles would be much more effective than the system deployed briefly in 1976, they maintained. And within a decade, they argued, laser-armed space satellites could be developed that would destroy Soviet missiles soon after they were launched.

Most senior Pentagon scientists and military brass were skeptical, warning that new ABM weapons would require years to develop and deploy. Despite some favorable references to new defense techniques, Reagan in his first two years in office did not request a significant increase in strategic defense funds. *(1983 ABM proposal, see box, p. 46)*

Selective Force Increases. The administration also eschewed calls for a crash program to speed up the production of weapons and, except for the Navy, did not recommend any substantial increase in the number of combat units on active duty.

In February 1980 a group of staff aides employed by various conservative senators and representatives drafted a memorandum called "A Program for Military Independence." It called for a doubling of the production rates of several kinds of combat planes, armored vehicles and warships and an expansion of U.S. forces by five ground divisions, four carrier task forces and nine tactical airwings. The plan also included Van Cleave's "quick fixes" and an energetic research and development program on strategic defenses.

Using cost estimates that were widely regarded as understated, the group maintained that their plan would require $226.6 billion more than the $1 trillion Carter projected for defense in fiscal years 1981-85. For fiscal 1981 alone, the projected cost of the "Independence" program was $198.7 billion, compared to Carter's initial request of $161.8 billion.

Just over a year later, in March 1981, Reagan was projecting a $184.4 billion increase in Carter's five-year defense program. Reagan called for defense funding of $1.46 trillion in fiscal 1982-86 compared with Carter's $1.276 trillion. For fiscal 1982 Reagan's increase was $26 billion. But even these increases would buy only a modest increase in the number of tanks and planes. And in September, Reagan's original request was pared back because of the ballooning federal deficit.

Warning Signals for Reagan

Developments in late 1981 raised the possibility that Reagan might encounter serious challenges in subsequent stages of his ambitious defense program:

Burgeoning Budget Deficits. By late 1981 some Republican leaders in Congress insisted that any further cuts in domestic programs be accompanied by restraint in the growth of defense spending. This new resistance to Reagan's policies came only after these lawmakers had accepted the president's March budget, which boosted funding for defense by 14.6 percent over the level Carter had recommended and cut spending for virtually all controllable domestic programs. But by late August, it was becoming apparent that "Reaganomics" was not having the psychological impact on the economy the president had predicted and on which his budgetary policies were based. Interest rates soared and stock prices dropped in response to projections that the fiscal 1982 federal budget deficit would far outstrip Reagan's $42.5 billion estimate.

David A. Stockman, the director of the Office of Management and Budget (OMB), and some senior White House aides called for cuts of up to $30 billion in projected Pentagon outlays (actual spending) for the fiscal 1982-84 period. (Because appropriations approved by Congress in any given year for weapons procurement are spent over a period of several years, much larger cuts in appropriations usually are necessary for any plan intended to reduce outlays — and thus budget deficits — by a particular amount.)

Recognizing the need for some budgetary corrections, Reagan announced on Sept. 11 that he would cut slightly his 1981 defense buildup program for fiscal 1982-84 — by $13 billion in outlays — $2 billion of which would come out of the fiscal 1982 budget. To achieve that $2 billion outlay cut, Reagan in October proposed an $8 billion cut in his $222 billion 1982 defense appropriations budget request.

Several influential GOP senators told the White House that the Defense Department should take a larger share of the cuts needed to control the budget deficit. These included Senate Majority Leader Howard H. Baker Jr. of Tennessee, Budget Committee Chairman Pete V. Domenici of New Mexico and Defense Appropriations Subcommittee Chairman Ted Stevens of Alaska. House Minority Leader Robert H. Michel of Illinois joined them.

Echoing the demand for greater restraint in defense spending were several prominent "Boll Weevils" — Southern Democrats who had backed Reagan's economic plan. But Reagan resisted further cuts in his defense plan and, in the end, most of his complaining allies relented. The only sizable group of defectors from among his original supporters were one or two dozen so-called "Gypsy Moths" — liberal and moderate Republicans from the Northeast and Midwest who had been unhappy from the outset with the severity of the cuts in domestic programs that were important to their regions.

In acting on the defense appropriations bills in late December 1981, Congress actually cut less than $1.5 billion from Reagan's overall request of $208.2 billion.

Arms Control Policies. The second portent of growing resistance to Reagan's defense plans was rising public anxiety over the administration's approach to strategic nuclear weapons and its commitment to arms control.

The administration was not yet two months old when National Security Council staff member Richard Pipes, a Harvard historian, was reported to have said that there was little likelihood of coexistence with Moscow unless the Soviet system were radically transformed. "Soviet leaders would have to choose between peacefully changing their Communist system in the direction followed by the West or going to war," Pipes told the Reuters news service. "There is no other alternative, and it could go either way."

In another widely quoted interview, appearing in *The Los Angeles Times* in January 1982, Deputy Under Secretary of Defense T. K. Jones said of a U.S.-Soviet nuclear war: "Everybody's going to make it [through a U.S.-Soviet nuclear war] if there are enough shovels to go around."

31

Long an advocate of broadening the U.S. civil defense program, Jones was arguing that deterrence would be improved if the U.S. urban population were trained to protect itself against nuclear fallout by evacuating the cities and digging improvised fallout shelters in the countryside. He subsequently insisted that the quotation was taken out of context.

Such statements by relatively junior Reagan appointees took on added political significance because Reagan's seemingly casual comments on questions of nuclear strategy nourished the widespread belief that neither he nor Weinberger had a working knowledge of the subject.

When European demonstrations erupted in the fall of 1981 against the NATO decision to station U.S. Pershing II missiles in Western Europe, Reagan spoke publicly, and blandly, of a "limited" nuclear war without linking it to the underlying purpose of nuclear deterrence or expressing much discomfort at the prospect of what an actual nuclear exchange might mean.

Reagan Commitment Questioned. The administration's rhetoric, along with a delay in renewing the dialogue with the Soviets on arms control issues, contributed to public concern about the direction of U.S. nuclear planning.

"The public senses we are about to enter into a period of greater instability in the superpower relationship," former Secretary of State Edmund S. Muskie told the Council on Foreign Relations in March 1982. And he noted that the period was "one in which the arms race — for the first time in a dozen years — is not accompanied by the restraining influence of serious arms control talks."

Despite the criticism of U.S. nuclear policies, the Reagan administration remained adamant in its opposition to SALT II, though it announced that its own strategic weapons plans would remain consistent with that treaty's restrictions.

Reagan publicly addressed the issue of nuclear arms control only after opposition to U.S. strategic policies sprung up in West Germany and other European countries during the summer of 1981.

On Nov. 18 he proposed the so-called "zero option" plan for U.S. and Soviet medium-range missiles in Europe. If Moscow destroyed its existing force of several hundred missiles aimed at targets in Western Europe from bases inside Russia, the United States would abandon plans to deploy several hundred Pershing II and cruise missiles in the NATO countries.

1982: 'Staying the Course'

Reagan's fiscal 1983 defense request of $263 billion held firmly to the program of modernizing virtually every facet of the U.S. military arsenal. Also in prospect was a slight increase in the size of U.S. ground and air combat forces and a substantial increase in naval forces.

Fiscal 1983 was a key year for several weapons programs crucial to the Reagan plan. Funding was requested for the first seven production-line models of a revised version of the controversial B-1 bomber ($4 billion), the first nine production versions of the MX missile ($1.5 billion) and the two additional nuclear-powered aircraft carriers ($6.8 billion) that formed the core of the administration's naval expansion.

From the outset, the request came under heavy fire from both conservatives, who were alarmed at the prospect of a budget deficit that was expected to run far above the administration's figure of $91.5 billion, and liberals, who were outraged that the Pentagon's budget was being expanded by 13.1 percent in real terms while many popular domestic programs were being slashed.

But the Defense Department went on the offensive, insisting in its presentations to the congressional Armed Services and Appropriations committees that management improvements and cost-reduction initiatives made by Frank C. Carlucci, the deputy defense secretary, already had wrung the budget dry of unnecessary spending and waste.

Carlucci and other DOD officials argued that their tight management had saved $7.4 billion in the fiscal 1983 budget and would save a total of $51.5 billion through fiscal 1987, though critics immediately pointed out that a governmentwide pay cap on federal employees, rather than any specific Pentagon policy, would account for more than half of those total projected savings.

Carlucci also maintained that the 1983 defense budget would result in savings over the long run. The administration argued that by spending a little more in the beginning — by taking account of more realistic, and thus higher, estimates of the cost of inflation and buying some weapons in large lots — it would save on the unit price of each weapon through economies of scale.

The most dramatic instance of this "spend now to save later" approach was the decision to buy two *Nimitz*-class nuclear carriers in a single package. According to the Navy, this would save $754 million and allow for delivery 21 months sooner than by using the usual procedure of contracting for the ships separately, three or four years apart.

33

Critics Dismiss Defense Cuts. Most galling to Pentagon critics was the administration's position that defense cuts could provide little help in reducing the overall federal budget deficit without jeopardizing the nation's security. There were two factors to consider here, according to the administration:

● Substantial reductions in the requests for military personnel and for operations and maintenance would yield immediate cuts in outlays, but would risk sharp cutbacks in the number and combat-readiness of units in the field.

● Reductions in the weapons procurement accounts — which were the primary target of most liberal critics of the Reagan-induced level of defense spending — would yield relatively small outlay reductions in fiscal 1983. For instance, according to Carlucci, fiscal 1983 outlays would drop by only $5 billion even if Congress refused to appropriate the entire $19.5 billion requested for the B-1 bomber, MX missiles, two nuclear-powered carriers, two Trident submarines and the cruise missile program. This was because the total projected cost of each weapon would be appropriated in one fiscal year, but it actually would be paid to contractors only gradually, over the several years the equipment would be under construction.

Defense Budget Compromises. Congress and the White House were deadlocked over Reagan's overall budget proposals until May 1982, when Senate GOP leaders worked out a budget deal with the White House that included $95 billion in tax hikes, $40 billion in unspecified savings in Social Security and a $22 billion reduction in defense outlays (not counting a cap on military pay increases) over a three-year period.

Subsequent negotiations with Congress yielded further defense cuts in the final version of the concurrent budget resolution (S Con Res 92) enacted in June. That left Congress committed — with administration concurrence — to a reduction in fiscal 1983 defense outlays of almost $9 billion below the level projected in Reagan's initial budget. (Since the battle over the defense budget was dominated by the budget deficit issue, most of the battles were fought over the level of defense spending.)

With the annual defense authorization bill already on the Senate floor at the time of the final negotiations on the budget, the Armed Services Committee proposed a $2.8 billion reduction in new military appropriations; this was on top of a $3.3 billion cut the Senate panel had made during committee markup of the bill.

The House Armed Services Committee, which had trimmed some

$3.2 billion from its version of the authorization bill, recommended additional cuts of $3.2 billion when the bill was debated by the House. This was accepted, bringing the lower defense spending level negotiated with Reagan within reach. And the House took a symbolic swipe at the Pentagon by also approving an across-the-board cut of 1 percent, amounting to $1.7 billion in budget authority (new appropriations).

The final version of the defense authorization bill for fiscal 1983, passed in August 1982, provided $177.9 billion in new spending authority, $5.59 billion less than Reagan originally requested for those portions of his defense budget requiring annual authorization by Congress. The Congressional Budget Office (CBO) estimated that this $5.59 billion reduction would cut about $2.6 billion from estimated defense outlays in fiscal 1983. The cap on pay and reductions in other defense-related bills brought the total estimated reduction in defense outlays to about $4.6 billion by the time the Appropriations committees began to consider the defense bill.

Appropriations Levels. Actions taken in 1982 by the Senate Defense Appropriations Subcommittee resulted in additional cuts in the spending levels for defense funding envisioned in the enacted fiscal 1983, $177.9 billion Defense Department authorization bill. But Senate floor action on the appropriations measure was delayed by a disagreement between the subcommittee and Secretary Weinberger over how deep an outlay reduction the administration had agreed to in June.

At issue was a provision in Congress' fiscal 1983 budget resolution that was separate from the funding ceilings established in that measure for defense and other budget functions. It required each federal agency to absorb, from its own budget, half of the cost of the 4 percent cost-of-living pay hike granted to all federal civilian and military employees, beginning Oct. 1, 1982.

The Defense Appropriations Subcommittee insisted this required a reduction of $8.7 billion in the outlays for defense contained in the president's budget request. Weinberger balked at what he insisted was an additional $1.2 billion cut beyond the level he previously had agreed to. The impasse eventually was broken simply by deferring the pay raise question, though the subcommittee declared its intention to make the additional cut.

As approved by the Senate Appropriations Committee in September, the bill slashed $12.1 billion from Reagan's original request for new budget authority. It was from this reduction that the panel then

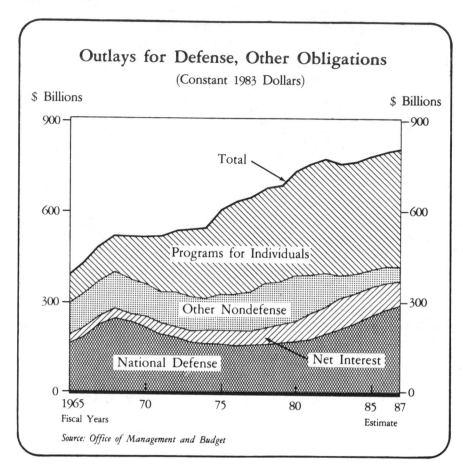

Outlays for Defense, Other Obligations
(Constant 1983 Dollars)

$ Billions $ Billions

Total

Programs for Individuals

Other Nondefense

National Defense   Net Interest

900 — —900
600 — —600
300 — —300
0 — —0

1965   70   75   80   85   87

Fiscal Years   Estimate

Source: Office of Management and Budget

calculated that the cut in actual outlays (spending) on defense would come to $8.7 billion for the year.

In the post-election session in November-December 1982, the defense bill was passed by the Senate essentially in the form it was approved by the Appropriations Committee. During the floor debate, an amendment that would have reduced budget authority for procurement and research by an additional $5.6 billion was rejected 52-45, with members splitting generally along liberal-conservative lines.

The House-passed version of the appropriations measure was $17.99 billion below Reagan's request. That amounted to a 7.2 percent cut, the largest made by either house in a defense bill in many years.

The final version totaled $232 billion in new spending authority. By

CBO's estimate, this put outlays for all defense activities in fiscal 1983 at $212.4 billion — $8.7 billion lower than the administration's budget request. For the Defense Department alone, the outlay total was projected at $206.6 billion, down from an initial request of $215.9 billion. *(Annual defense legislation, see budget glossary, box pp. 16-17)*

Few Weapons Feel the Pinch. Despite the size of the reduction made by Congress in 1982, most of it was achieved by relatively inconsequential trimming in hundreds of programs rather than in dramatic austerity moves that changed the shape or direction of Reagan's defense policies.

The bulk of the cut came from various kinds of bureaucratic belt-tightening, including a $2.3 billion reduction in the size of the annual pay hike. A substantial portion was the result of fortuitous changes in the state of the economy since the budget was drafted in late 1981. For example, a continuing decline in petroleum prices permitted an $833 million cut in funds for fuel purchases for the armed services.

Although nearly $9 billion was cut in budget authority for weapons procurement, with few exceptions — the MX and Pershing II missiles and new chemical warfare weapons — major programs were subjected to only minor slowdowns in the planned rate of production. None was canceled or terminated. Liberal critics of Reagan's defense spending policies had targeted several new Army weapons — the M-1 tank, the M-2 armored troop carrier and the Apache anti-tank helicopter — for major cutbacks, contending they were too complex and too costly. However, none of them suffered serious program cuts. *(Details, see Conventional Warfare chapter.)*

Nor was there a major challenge to the Navy buildup, which was probably the most visible symbol of the Reagan defense buildup. With the two additional nuclear carriers fully funded at year's end, John F. Lehman Jr., the administration's aggressive, and even abrasive, Navy secretary, could boast that the "600-ship Navy" was well along to becoming an accomplished fact.

A minor cloud on the Navy's horizon was Congress' refusal to provide a $94 million down payment on the conversion of a third battleship to carry long-range cruise missiles. But the first of the converted ships, the *New Jersey*, was recommissioned on Dec. 28, 1982, and $301 million was allocated in the Pentagon's fiscal 1983 appropriation to complete the conversion of the second, the *Iowa*.

Only minor changes were made in the president's requests for combat aircraft, except for the controversial A-10 tank-hunting bomber.

In a wrestling match redolent with the aroma of the pork barrel, an authorization requested by the administration for 20 of the planes was denied by the Senate Armed Services Committee. Nevertheless, Congress went ahead and appropriated funds for their procurement, but with the proviso that the money could be spent only in the unlikely event that both Armed Services panels approved it.

The most heated 1982 debate of the whole defense funding cycle on Capitol Hill — apart from the MX missile fight — involved some of the country's giant aircraft manufacturers. The prize was a new long-range transport plane for the armed forces. *(Details, box, pp. 160-161)*

Except for the Navy, Reagan's plans to increase the size of U.S. combat forces were deferred in the course of the budget-cutting negotiations with Congress. But most of the proposed increases would not have occurred before the mid-1980s in any case.

Defense Buildup Assessment

By the end of 1982 it was apparent that Congress had slowed the momentum behind Ronald Reagan's defense buildup.

● His original $263 billion request for fiscal 1983 was reduced, but not altered in any basic way. Nevertheless, the prospect of massive budget deficits forced Congress to make an unprecedentedly large reduction of nearly $19 billion in budget authority, an overall cut of 7.27 percent.

● Congress' refusal to approve initial production funds for the MX intercontinental missile marked the first time since the Vietnam War that Congress had denied funds for a major weapon requested by a president; that action represented a deferral, however, rather than an outright cancellation of the missile. A final congressional decision on the MX appeared to be in sight by May 1983. *(Details, pp. 92-93)*

● In early August the House fell three votes shy of calling for a nuclear arms freeze the administration had spent much political capital in opposing. This followed by only two weeks a House vote against production of a new form of lethal chemical weapons called binary warheads. *(Nuclear "freeze" movement, p. 107)*

In each of those battles some Republicans and conservative Democrats defected from the administration's position. At a time when budget deficits were reaching historically high levels, Reagan's war cry on behalf of higher and higher defense spending coupled with austerity for domestic social programs no longer was able to win majority support.

Another contributing factor was the administration's occasional insensitivity to the fine line between "toughness" and politically unpalatable bellicosity.

Compounding the administration's political problems was an apparently widespread suspicion that neither Reagan nor Defense Secretary Weinberger had a firm personal hold on defense policy. That belief was linked to complaints that there was no underlying purpose to the administration's defense buildup, that the armed services simply had been allowed to go on uncoordinated buying sprees.

And the apprehension was widespread in Washington and among America's European allies that the administration's outlook was too rigid to reach any type of nuclear arms control agreement with the Soviet Union.

The MX intercontinental missile containing 10 independently targeted nuclear warheads.

Chapter 2

U.S. STRATEGIC DEFENSE POLICY

Today, not only the peace but also the chances for real arms control depend on restoring the military balance. We know that the ideology of the Soviet leaders does not permit them to leave any western weakness unprobed, any vacuum of power unfilled. . . . Yet, I believe the Soviets can be persuaded to reduce their arsenals — but only if they see it as absolutely necessary. Only if the Soviets recognize the West's determination to modernize its own military forces will they see an incentive to negotiate a verifiable agreement establishing equal, lower levels [of nuclear arms]. And, very simply, that is one of the main reasons why we must rebuild our defensive strength.

—President Ronald Reagan, March 31, 1983, to the Los Angeles World Affairs Council.

President Reagan was elected on a platform that sounded a call to arms against what he viewed as a dire and immediate danger — an accelerating Soviet threat to America's national security. The communist adversaries in Moscow, he said in his first presidential news conference (Jan. 29, 1981), had "more than once repeated . . . their determination that their goal must be the promotion of world revolution and a . . . communist state"; they "reserve unto themselves the right to commit any crime, to lie, to cheat, in order to attain that [goal]."

More than two years later, the president remained distrustful of the détente in U.S.-Soviet relations pursued by both Republican and Democratic administrations during the 1970s. He considered that policy disastrous because to him it ignored the harsh realities of Soviet expansionism and failed to deter the balance of strategic nuclear arms from tipping alarmingly in Moscow's favor. In response, Reagan committed his administration to a rapid buildup of U.S. military forces and to large increases in spending for defense. Nevertheless, the president recognized — reluctantly and belatedly, according to his critics — the need to move forward in controlling weapons of mass destruction. Although he continued to criticize the arms limitation agreement (SALT II) pursued by his Democratic predecessor, Jimmy Carter, Reagan submitted his own arms control proposals to drastically reduce the levels of both intercontinental and intermediate-range strategic missiles and bombers.

Costs of Nuclear Preparedness

The weapons at stake and the money involved in producing them were staggering. For Americans to comprehend a defense budget that surpassed two hundred billion dollars annually was difficult enough. It was harder still for the average citizen to visualize the destructive might of the arsenal these funds supported: a military force that included thousands of nuclear weapons of varying types, sizes and destructive power. Just one of the largest nuclear missiles in the U.S. arsenal in 1983 had a thousand times the lethal power of the bombs that demolished Hiroshima and Nagasaki in 1945, killing 250,000 and maiming untold numbers through the effects of radiation.

From a rather crude atomic bomb that nonetheless could wipe out an entire city, nuclear weapons systems have been refined to such an extent that today they can be targeted with almost pinpoint accuracy; their firepower has been increased drastically; and the time it takes to launch them is measured in seconds, not hours or even minutes.

Although it comprises a relatively small fraction of defense spending, amounting to 10.3 percent of the Defense Department's total fiscal 1984 request of $273.4 billion, the U.S. strategic nuclear defense program — the arsenal of land- and submarine- launched intercontinental missiles (ICBMs), land- and air-launched cruise missiles and long-range, missile-carrying bombers — received the most attention in the initial years of President Reagan's military buildup. These weapons accounted for $28.1 billion of the fiscal 1984 request, a 30.1 percent increase over fiscal 1983 in terms of real purchasing power (after taking inflation into account).

Opposition to Arms Buildup

Although many Americans agreed with Reagan's emphasis on confronting the Soviet threat, by 1982 the administration's policy of insisting on large increases in defense expenditures at a time of high unemployment, cutbacks in government social programs and high federal budget deficits was met by growing resistance in Congress and the nation. And in 1983 Congress seriously challenged the president's defense buildup by demanding a slowdown in the 10 percent annual rate of growth in the defense budget sought by Reagan in his fiscal 1984 budget.

Opposition to the administration's defense policies was centered on Reagan's strategic nuclear weapons development programs and his arms control record. Critics accused the president of embarking upon a new, more dangerous and expensive arms race with the Soviet Union.

Efforts to prod the administration to speed up negotiations on strategic nuclear weapons took many forms, the most visible being the so-called nuclear freeze movement that gathered momentum early in 1982. The House in August of that year narrowly defeated a resolution — vigorously opposed by the president — calling for an immediate mutually verifiable freeze on the testing, production and further deployment of nuclear weapons systems, approving instead a watered-down version acceptable to the administration. But in May 1983 the solidly Democratic House, after numerous delays forced by Republicans, passed a freeze resolution that was similar to the defeated 1982 measure.

The Republican leadership in the Senate, though uneasy with the size of Reagan's defense buildup, was reluctant to open up a potentially divisive debate in which the administration would come under attack from both liberals who favored the freeze and hard-line conservatives who demanded that the White House take an even tougher stance toward Moscow on strategic arms issues. The Senate took no action on the House initiative in 1982, and the Republican leadership vowed to oppose it in the 98th Congress.

Congressional ambivalence toward the freeze initiative mirrored public confusion about and divisions over nuclear arms policy in general. Though Americans wanted an end to the arms race, they remained profoundly suspicious of the Soviet Union.

Reagan and the Soviet Threat

During his 1980 campaign for the presidency, Ronald Reagan emphasized the need to strengthen America's strategic nuclear defenses to counter what he perceived to be a most serious Soviet military threat. He insisted that only a policy of preparing the United States to wage a nuclear war if challenged would deter war and deny Moscow the diplomatic leverage it might extract from a perception of Soviet nuclear superiority.

Reagan charged that President Jimmy Carter had not done enough to shore up the country's nuclear war capability and military readiness in the face of the Soviet buildup.

Reagan denounced the U.S.-Soviet strategic arms limitation treaty (SALT II) negotiated by Carter, but never approved by the Senate, as "fatally flawed"; basically, this was because the treaty, according to Reagan, gave the Soviet Union certain military advantages over the United States. Responding to charges that his emphasis on a U.S. military buildup and opposition to SALT II would provoke a new round in a dangerous nuclear competition with the U.S.S.R., Reagan in August 1980 said, "We're already in an arms race, but only the Soviets are racing."

Despite some criticism that Reagan was intractable in his opposition to any U.S.-Soviet accord on nuclear arms, his position during the election campaign struck a responsive chord with a majority in Congress and with a public disillusioned with the meager successes of the U.S.-Soviet détente so eagerly sought by Republican and Democratic administrations alike since the 1960s. For one thing, a series of international reverses in the late 1970s had eroded support for arms control as a solution for easing East-West tensions.

Détente was a casualty of the rapid Soviet defense buildup, undertaken initially while the United States had begun to slow down its military spending toward the end of the Vietnam War. That development gradually fed apprehension in Washington that Moscow would be emboldened to take political and military advantage of America's loss of nuclear hegemony. Despite such fears, the United States continued to lag behind the U.S.S.R. through the remainder of the 1970s in its commitment to defense.

Toward the end of that decade, Soviet influence in the Middle East and the oil-rich Persian Gulf increased, particularly after the U.S.S.R. invaded Afghanistan in December 1979. Then in December 1981 the communist government of Poland imposed martial law, an action generally believed to have been dictated by the Soviet Union.

Reagan's defense planners concluded that one reason Moscow was acting with increased boldness was the improvement and modernization of its strategic nuclear arsenal.

Search for an 'Equitable' Balance

By the middle of Reagan's second year in office, there was increasing public anxiety that administration policies were increasing the risks of nuclear war with the Soviet Union. Reagan was forced to modify his position somewhat, agreeing to resume U.S. efforts to reach an arms control accord with the Soviet Union. He offered to begin a new round of talks with the Soviet Union, labeled the strategic arms reduction talks (START). They were to begin on May 9, 1982. But the president and his defense advisers were quick to declare that the talks would be grounded in more "realistic" proposals than those submitted at the SALT II negotiations under Carter. Any arms agreement, the president emphasized, would have to preserve an "equitable" balance between the two superpowers. The goal, he said, was not simply to freeze but to reduce the deployment of weapons capable of nuclear destruction without endangering U.S. security.

Reagan's START proposal included substantial cuts in the existing stockpiles of U.S. and Soviet intercontinental ballistic missiles (ICBMs) and submarine-launched ballistic missiles (SLBMs). Each side would be allowed to deploy the same number of these weapons. *(Major features of proposal, p. 69)*

Nonetheless, the administration continued to maintain that a concerted U.S. arms buildup was the only way to deter Soviet military threats and prod the Russians to negotiate actual arms reductions. That required not only the means to retaliate massively against any Soviet aggression, but the capacity to respond "selectively" and "appropriately" to all forms of Soviet military and political pressure around the globe.

Peace Through Nuclear Strength

Many defense experts relied upon by Reagan for advice argued that the U.S. nuclear arsenal needed to be strengthened and at the same time diversified so it could resist any military challenge in constantly changing crisis situations. In other words, the United States had to consider how to *fight* a nuclear war successfully as well as how to *deter*, or avoid, one.

The two objectives were not mutually exclusive in the minds of Reagan's military planners. By being able to respond to a limited act of aggression, they reasoned, the United States would be more likely to avoid a nuclear holocaust. This was one of the arguments marshaled by the administration in its campaign to deploy the controversial MX (missile experimental) land-based intercontinental ballistic missile in the United States and the intermediate-range Pershing II and ground-launched cruise missiles (small, pilotless drone jets carrying nuclear warheads) in Western Europe.

Reagan's Futuristic Approach: . . .

In a nationally televised address billed as the first in a series of statements intended to dramatize the magnitude of the Soviet strategic threat and to win support for deploying new missile systems, President Reagan March 23, 1983, held out the possibility of a radical break with post-World War II strategic defense concepts.

Instead of the current policy of deterrence — threatening massive nuclear retaliation as a means of discouraging a Soviet attack on the United States — Reagan proposed development of anti-missile weapons that could destroy missiles launched by the U.S.S.R. before they hit the United States. According to Reagan, such a shift in policy held out "the promise of changing the course of human history."

Reagan did not give any details about the plan in calling on the scientific community to undertake "a long-term [missile defense] research and development program to begin to achieve our ultimate goal of eliminating the threat posed by strategic nuclear missiles." Administration officials acknowledged that the project would take decades to reach fruition, with no guarantee of success. Moreover, Reagan did not propose to commit additional funds for the project.

As of 1983, approximately $1 billion annually was being spent on developing land- and space-based ballistic missile defense (BMD) systems in the United States. Greater amounts already were being spent by Moscow, according to Pentagon officials.

The president's futuristic proposal encountered a mixed reception. The feasibility of such a system was questioned, and many members of Congress expressed concern about the potentially destabilizing impact it would have on the arms race. Sen. Edward M. Kennedy, D-Mass., called the proposal a "reckless Star Wars scheme." Possession by one side of a system thought to be a foolproof missile defense might lead an aggressor to feel it could launch a nuclear surprise attack against the other side while being confident that a retaliatory blow could be stopped or deterred with its own offensive missiles.

A number of European commentators maintained that emphasizing a U.S. missile defense system aimed primarily at Soviet intercontinental ballistic missiles (ICBMs) would "decouple" Western Europe from the U.S. security umbrella.

Denouncing the proposal as "irresponsible," Soviet leader Yuri Andropov said it would "open the floodgates to a runaway race for all types of strategic arms, both defensive and offensive." Andropov added that in embarking on arms control negotiations the two superpowers had "agreed that there is an inseverable interrelationship between strategic offensive and defensive weapons." He said it was "not by chance" that the 1972 Anti-Ballistic Missile (ABM) Treaty was signed simultaneously with the treaty limiting strategic arms (SALT I). He

. . . Missile Defense in Space

warned that "the Soviet Union will never allow" the development of ABM systems that could render its ICBMs impotent.

Some American observers contended that Reagan's proposal would violate the terms of the 1972 ABM treaty, under which each party agreed "not to deploy ABM systems for a defense of the territory of its country." (Each side originally was allowed to construct two ABM systems; this subsequently was reduced to one.) According to Gerard C. Smith, who was the chief U.S. negotiator to the SALT I negotiations, the only objective interpretation of the treaty was that "any exotic system is banned." Reagan acknowledged the problems associated with an ABM system. "I clearly recognize that defensive systems have limitations and raise certain problems and ambiguities," he said in his speech. "If paired with offensive systems, they can be viewed as fostering an aggressive policy and no one wants that."

The president's emphasis on a defense system echoed the call sounded for a number of years by a small but energetic band of military experts, scientists and conservatives. Its leading spokesman in Congress was Sen. Malcolm Wallop, R-Wyo., who claimed that new breakthroughs in anti-missile technology made Reagan's proposal feasible. "As a practical matter, in order to minimize the number of Soviet warheads reaching the U.S., we are going to have to build systems to destroy Soviet missiles in flight," Wallop wrote in *The Washington Post* Feb. 6, 1983. "I believe a variety of good defenses against ballistic missiles is possible. . . . The technology of space-based lasers gives substantial hope that attacking Soviet missiles could be defeated, or at the very least severely thinned, just after they rose out of the atmosphere."

Proponents of the so-called "defense dominance" school estimated that by 1990 the United States could field satellites able to destroy Soviet missiles shortly after they were launched. An article appearing in the Post on March 27, 1983, cited a classified study made by the General Accounting Office for the Pentagon in 1981 that was critical of the low level of funding for high-energy laser weapons in outer space. The GAO study, according to the article, predicted a laser weapon could be tested by 1993, and that the full system would cost $30 billion.

But in congressional testimony, Pentagon officials had recommended against extra funding for laser research, contending that such a system would cost $50 billion to $100 billion.

Despite the skepticism, Defense Secretary Caspar W. Weinberger said at a news conference a week after Reagan's speech that he was "confident" U.S. scientists could develop an anti-ballistic missile defense. And he said the administration might redirect some funding to lasers and other space weapons.

In addition to the land-based ICBMs, the administration emphasized the need to upgrade the U.S. submarine-launched missile force and its strategic nuclear weapons-carrying aircraft. The three comprised the so-called "triad" of strategic weapons systems representing the basic elements of U.S. strategic defense policy.

By the late 1970s and early 1980s those weapons — and their Soviet counterparts — had become both symbols and concrete evidence of the changing U.S.-Soviet strategic balance. And they were part of the larger debate by defense planners as well as arms controllers over what type of nuclear weapons would provide the best security for the nation and how much nuclear capability was needed.

Deterrence and Strategic War

"Strategic war is something new in the world," wrote Thomas Powers, author of *Thinking About the Next War*, in an article published in the November 1982 issue of *The Atlantic Monthly*.

"A strategy, in its traditional military sense, is a broad theory of how to defeat an enemy.... Strategic war in its current sense retains the notion of striking at the sources of enemy strength, with the added meaning of striking from long range. A strategic weapon is now generally defined as one that can go from our country, or our submarines at sea, to their country. Strategic war, then, is a kind of mighty hammering, across oceans and continents, at an enemy's whole capacity to wage war...."

In a major address to the nation on arms policy Nov. 22, 1982, Reagan asked, "What do we mean when we speak of 'nuclear deterrents'? Certainly, we don't want such weapons for their own sake. We don't desire excessive forces or what some people have called 'overkill.' Basically, it's a matter of others knowing that starting a conflict would be more costly to them than anything they might hope to gain.

"And, yes, it is sadly ironic that in these modern times, it still takes weapons to prevent war.... I intend to search for peace along two parallel paths: deterrents and arms reductions. I believe that these are the only paths that offer any real hope for an enduring peace."

Deterrence, according to Webster's dictionary, rests on one's ability to discourage an unwanted action by instilling fear, anxiety and/or doubt. In the context of strategic doctrine, deterrence involves the capability to shape an opponent's calculations as to the probable outcome if he chooses to commit aggression.

The ability to deny an adversary any gain from aggression is perhaps the surest way to deter him. Put another way, deterrence entails a nation's ability to convince the enemy that he is likely either to be defeated if he attacks, or that "winning" will exact an unacceptable price.

"Deterrence is not, and cannot, be bluff," cautioned President Reagan's Commission on Strategic Forces in a report reviewing the role of the MX missile and the strategic balance made public April 11, 1983. "In order for deterrence to be effective, we must not merely have weapons, we must be perceived to be able, and prepared, if necessary, to use them effectively against the key elements of Soviet power," said the commission, which was established by President Reagan to determine the best way to base the MX missile. "Deterrence is not an abstract notion amenable to simple quantification. Still less is it a mirror image of what would deter ourselves. Deterrence is the set of beliefs in the minds of the Soviet leaders, given their own values and attitudes, about our capabilities and our will. It requires us to determine, as best we can, what would deter them from considering aggression, even in a crisis. . . ."

Making Deterrence Work

A central question of the nuclear war strategy debate has always been: What is needed for deterrence to work?

One answer to the first question is that deterrence, if employed by both sides, is automatic. Neither superpower is willing to start a nuclear war because of the sheer destruction that would result. But the Reagan administration — like its Republican and Democratic predecessors in the 1970s — has answered the question differently. It argues that deterrence depends on a detailed analysis of how effectively each superpower plausibly can respond to any move of the other, whether against cities, military targets or allies.

From that policy follows the Reagan administration's position on two of the most controversial nuclear arms issues today:

● First, how can the United States deter a Soviet missile attack that could, theoretically, destroy most of America's ICBMs on the ground before they could be launched, thus leaving the vast bulk of the U.S. population hostage to a second Soviet strike? In order to deter such an attack, according to administration defense planners, U.S. nuclear forces must be able to carry out very accurate and narrowly confined attacks (surgical strikes, in the Pentagon's jargon) on targets of great importance to the Soviet leadership, such as the U.S.S.R.'s land-based ICBMs, the bulk of its nuclear forces and its military command and industrial headquarters, without causing huge Soviet civilian casualties.

● Second, the Reagan administration maintained that the threat of a Soviet move against military targets in Western Europe was best deterred by deploying U.S. intermediate-range missiles — the Pershing II — that would be able to hit Soviet targets from launchers based in Western Europe.

From these two assessments, the administration concluded that the United States must attain a capability that presumes nuclear war is "thinkable," that it can be fought in such a way and "won" at an acceptable cost in U.S. lives and destruction.

However improbable these scenarios of so-called limited war might appear, and many administration defense advisers themselves acknowledged that it would be difficult to prevent a U.S.-Soviet military exchange from escalating to a general nuclear holocaust, Reagan administration officials insisted that failure to prepare for nuclear war contingencies would foster perceptions of relative Soviet military superiority that would cast a heavy shadow across the noncommunist world.

"Put simply, our own vulnerability to nuclear blackmail, as well as the susceptibility of our friends to political intimidation, depends on our ability and willingness to cope credibly with any Soviet threat," said then-Secretary of State Alexander M. Haig Jr. in April 1982. This required a broad range of deterrent capabilities, according to Haig. Without such flexibility, a U.S. threat to retaliate by attacking Soviet cities would not be a credible policy, meaning the Russians would not take it seriously and thus would not be deterred. Both governments would realize that Washington would shrink from carrying out such an attack for fear that Moscow then would turn its remaining missiles against American cities. To avoid that trap, according to this theory, Washington had to be able to meet any Soviet military move with a response that:

● Denied Moscow a military outcome that the Soviets could regard as advantageous to them.

● Was at the lowest feasible level of destruction, in the hope of reducing the risk of an even more destructive Soviet countermove.

As Haig stated the administration's position, "War, and particularly nuclear war, can be deterred, but only if we are able to deny an aggressor military advantage from the action, and thus ensure his awareness that he cannot prevail in any conflict with us. A strong and credible strategic posture enhances stability by reducing for the Soviets the temptations toward adventurism at the same time that it strengthens our hand in responding to Soviet political-military threats."

Strategic Doctrines

The basic component of America's deterrent force long has been its strategic nuclear arsenal. Since the 1960s these forces have consisted of ICBMs launched from underground silos or surface sites, submarine-launched ballistic missiles (SLBMs) and long-range bombers, the B-52s. A principal purpose of maintaining this triad of strategic systems is to provide a hedge against Soviet technological breakthroughs that might nullify or limit the effectiveness of any one leg of that force.

By diversifying its weapons systems, the United States has sought to enhance the survivability of a sufficient portion of its missiles so that even if Moscow were to destroy a substantial number of missiles or planes in one or even two of the strategic systems, the United States still would retain enough weapons to retaliate.

In addition to these long-range strategic nuclear forces, the United States has deployed tactical nuclear weapons, designed for short-range support on the battlefield, along with tanks, guns and men. A third category of nuclear weapons, scheduled for deployment in Western Europe in late 1983, are the so-called "theater" nuclear forces — intermediate-range missiles capable of reaching targets within one theater, or specific geographic area, of military operations.

U.S. Nuclear Superiority

Although America's strategic weapons in the early 1980s were much more sophisticated, accurate, destructive and diversified than those produced during the early years of the nuclear age, it was debatable whether additional improvements in these weapons actually provided a significant increase in the national security of either the United States or the Soviet Union. Throughout the postwar era, weapons refinements made by one side soon were matched by the other.

The first atomic bombs of the 1940s were large, unwieldy and not very accurate. By today's standards, they took a long time to assemble and transport. Moreover, there were not many of them (the United States had stockpiled about 100 atomic bombs by 1948). Given the nature of those weapons and the United States' monopoly over them, defense planners envisaged that the bombs would be used primarily to threaten to carry out a devastating strike against major Soviet population and industrial centers, in effect laying waste to much of the U.S.S.R. The deterrent value of those weapons was based on the assumption that Moscow would not risk a major military provocation when faced with a response of that magnitude. Thus only as a last resort would such bombs ever have to be used.

By the early 1950s the situation had changed. Although general confidence in America's nuclear superiority remained, the development of the hydrogen bomb by both the United States and the U.S.S.R. forced a re-evaluation of the concept of deterrence. By this period, both sides were vulnerable to massive destruction by the other.

From this strategic standoff and intense mutual suspicion emerged the Cold War doctrine of "massive retaliation," propounded by President Dwight D. Eisenhower's secretary of state, John Foster Dulles. Dulles argued that to maintain a credible deterrent in the face of overwhelming Soviet conventional superiority, the United States had to be willing and able to initiate a devastating nuclear strike against the U.S.S.R. at the first provocation, before Moscow could launch its own weapons. The Dulles policy prevailed at that time because the United States still retained a nuclear superiority. The Soviet Union had only a small number of nuclear bombs, and its planes could not return home without refueling.

'Mutual Assured Destruction'

By the early 1960s the United States had acquired an arsenal of more than 7,000 strategic warheads, while the U.S.S.R. had fewer than 500. Meanwhile, technological advances continued to upgrade the firepower and accuracy of nuclear weapons on both sides. And the Russians' success in launching the first orbiting satellite, Sputnik, in 1957 had provided dramatic evidence that Moscow might be drawing even or possibly pulling ahead of the United States in technological know-how, thus achieving solid superpower status.

By the end of the decade, the Soviet Union had begun to develop long-range bombers and ICBMs. U.S. strategic doctrine had to be modified to take account of the new nuclear equation. What emerged was the concept of "mutual assured destruction" (MAD), or the state of mutual balance of terror. According to this theory, the Soviet Union would be deterred from launching a first strike against America by the certain knowledge that the United States had sufficient capability to retaliate, even after absorbing a Soviet nuclear attack.

The MAD strategy was advanced by Robert S. McNamara,

secretary of defense under Presidents John F. Kennedy and Lyndon B. Johnson. It achieved its purpose in the Cuban missile crisis of October 1962, but only because the United States still retained a substantial lead in nuclear weapons development.

The crisis arose when U.S. intelligence agencies indicated that the U.S.S.R. was attempting to sneak missiles into Cuba to compensate for America's advantage in ICBMs. Kennedy responded by ordering a naval blockade and threatening a nuclear attack on the Soviet Union if the weapons were not withdrawn. The threat succeeded, but it also made Soviet and American policy makers and the public acutely aware of the very real danger of nuclear war in any confrontation between the superpowers. That awareness gave considerable impetus to efforts aimed at easing East-West tensions.

As a result of the Cuban missile crisis, the United States and the U.S.S.R. in 1963 signed the Nuclear Test Ban Treaty and set up a Washington-Moscow "hot line." It was hoped that these measures would foster a relaxation of East-West tensions and lessen the chances of the superpowers stumbling into a nuclear war.

.Five years later, the two countries were signatories to the Nuclear Non-Proliferation Treaty, which was approved by the Senate in 1969. The era of "peaceful coexistence" had begun, but the United States continued to build up its strategic forces. By the mid-1960s it had deployed about 1,000 land-based ICBMs and 41 nuclear submarines carrying more than 650 submarine-launched ballistic missiles (SLBMs). Soon after that, it began to replace its older liquid fuel Atlas and Titan missiles with the solid fuel land-based Minuteman and submarine-launched Polaris that could survive a Soviet nuclear strike and then launch a retaliatory attack.

'Flexible Response'

During his tenure as defense secretary, McNamara also formulated the policy that came to be known as "flexible response." That concept already had been discussed in the 1950s by such well-known defense experts as Paul H. Nitze, who later served on the SALT I arms limitation negotiating team. "[I]t is to the West's interest, if atomic war becomes unavoidable, that atomic weapons of the smallest sizes be used in the smallest area and against the most restricted target systems...," Nitze had written in the January 1956 issue of *Foreign Affairs* magazine. "We should limit ourselves to military objectives, primarily to those which are necessary to achieve control of the air. We should not initiate the bombing of industrial or population centers."

"Nuclear war should be approached in much the same way that more conventional military operations have been regarded in the past," McNamara stated in a widely circulated address at the University of Michigan in June 1962. He said weapons should be aimed at a variety of targets to ensure that the United States would be able to deter a number of different kinds of threats. A policy of mutual annihilation of populations, by itself, was losing its credibility as a defense policy, and the United States needed to develop other options that included the means to zero in on Soviet military targets.

Détente and 'Essential Equivalence'

Adherence to the doctrines of flexible response and MAD continued into the late 1960s and early 1970s. The basic tenets of America's nuclear strategy during Richard Nixon's presidency were contained in National Security Decision Memorandum 242 of January 1974. That report stated that U.S. forces should have the capability to inflict limited damage to selected military or economic targets so that if a president faced a Soviet provocation less cataclysmic than a massive nuclear strike on U.S. cities he could threaten a less than cataclysmic retaliation. If deterrence failed, nuclear weapons would be used in a selective way, according to the memorandum, in order "to seek early war termination . . . at the lowest level of conflict feasible."

At the same time, Nixon's defense planners moved toward acceptance of a policy of strategic nuclear weapons parity with the Soviet Union. Allowing a situation of U.S.-Soviet weapons equivalence to exist would inject a stabilizing factor into the arms race, they reasoned. Instead of superiority, the United States should strive to maintain "nuclear sufficiency," or "essential equivalence." In a March 4, 1973, appearance on Capitol Hill, Nixon's defense secretary, James R. Schlesinger, explained: "What it means is, first, that we do not plan to have our side a mirror image of their strategic forces. We do not have to have a match for everything in their arsenal. But in the gross characteristics of the forces, in terms of overall number and overall throw weight or payload, there should be some degree of equivalence between the two."

Because both superpowers appeared to be reaching parity, Nixon and Henry A. Kissinger, the president's national security adviser and secretary of state, began to press for an arms control treaty. The development of orbiting spy satellites that could monitor Soviet military activities reduced the problems of verifying compliance with an arms agreement.

Arms Control Under Nixon

The first round of U.S.-Soviet arms control discussions, the strategic arms limitations talks, or SALT I, was initiated by the Nixon administration in the fall of 1969. That effort culminated in the signing in Moscow on May 26, 1972, of two major arms agreements: a treaty limiting strategic missile defense (ABM) systems and an agreement setting ceilings on the number of offensive nuclear weapons each side could stockpile.

The treaty, which easily won Senate approval, limited the United States and the Soviet Union to two anti-ballistic missile (ABM) sites — one for the defense of each nation's capital and the other for the defense of an ICBM facility in each country. Subsequently, in 1974, the two sides signed a protocol restricting each nation to one ABM site. In 1976 the United States abandoned its effort to deploy its ABM system, called Safeguard.

The second pact under SALT I was a five-year interim agreement limiting offensive missile launchers — land-based silos and submarine missile tubes — to those under construction or deployed at the time of the signing. The Soviet Union had a greater number of missile launchers than the United States in 1972, but the United States had a numerical superiority in warheads and strategic bombers.

Largely because the agreement on the number of launchers allowed the Soviet Union to retain considerably more offensive missiles than the United States had deployed, the interim agreement proved to be controversial. In the Senate, Henry M. Jackson, D-Wash., succeeded in adding an amendment to the pact stating that any permanent strategic arms treaty should "not limit the United States to levels of intercontinental strategic forces inferior to" those of the Soviet Union, but rather should be based on "the principle of equality." The House and the Nixon administration later accepted the amendment.

Almost as soon as SALT I was signed, talks began on a SALT II treaty, which was to take effect when the interim agreement limiting offensive nuclear missiles expired in October 1977. Those negotiations took an upward turn Nov. 24, 1974, when President Gerald R. Ford and Soviet leader Leonid I. Brezhnev met in the Siberian port of Vladivostok and reached tentative agreement on guidelines for an arms pact limiting through 1985 the numbers of offensive strategic nuclear weapons and delivery systems.

Nixon's policy of relaxing tensions with the Soviet Union received widespread public approval, and the Ford administration carried on essentially the same policies.

Carter and the Defense Balance

If the 1970s opened with some optimism about the advantages of a policy of deterrence, East-West stability and arms control, it closed with considerable gloom. By mid-1972 it generally was believed by U.S. defense experts that Moscow had gained the lead in the number of missiles deployed: about 2,000 compared to 1,700 for the United States. Each side's missiles were about equal in accuracy and reliability, but the Soviets' ICBMs were able to carry a larger payload (explosive charge).

While members of the NATO alliance, including the United States, had adopted a policy of arms restraint and reduced their overall military expenditures, the Soviet Union's defense budget showed a steady increase, according to Defense Department estimates. The Pentagon projected Soviet spending for defense at about 12 to 14 percent of the U.S.S.R.'s annual Gross National Product. This compared to 5.9 percent for the United States and considerably less for the other members of NATO. Partly in reaction to the heavy Vietnam-War era defense expenditures and partly because many U.S. officials continued to believe in the efficacy of détente, the United States cut back on weapons procurement and delayed or canceled the deployment of new strategic weapons such as the cruise missile and supersonic B-1 bomber.

Soviet Technological Advances

Stability was strained not only by a numbers imbalance but also by U.S. and Soviet technological advances that undermined predictability, and thus deterrence. Increased missile accuracy, for example, meant that an enemy's nuclear arsenal could be hit without inflicting unacceptable damage on the civilian population. This was thought to make a nuclear first strike more tempting.

A major innovation in the early 1970s was the development of warheads called multiple independently targeted re-entry vehicles, or MIRVs. This enabled a single missile to carry several nuclear warheads, each of which could be aimed at a different target. Accurate MIRVs that could be launched in minutes changed the numbers game dramatically.

With MIRVs on each superpower's missiles, a few launchers could deliver a devastating blow to the other side's ability to retaliate, and the attacker still would retain enough warheads to attack a second time.

President Jimmy Carter faced some difficult defense choices upon taking office in January 1977. The U.S.S.R. already had begun to deploy its SS-18s, the largest Soviet intercontinental missile (and considerably larger than anything in the U.S. missile arsenal). The SS-18 was equipped with a warhead having up to 10 MIRVs.

Moscow also had begun to deploy intermediate-range ballistic missiles, its SS-20s. Able to fly 3,000 miles, these weapons, most of which were based near the U.S.S.R.'s border with the East European communist countries, easily could hit targets in Western Europe. The United States and the NATO allies had no counterpart to the SS-20. Instead, they continued to rely on the U.S. strategic triad of ICBMs, SLBMs and long-range bombers. By the late 1970s, however, the triad appeared to be somewhat shaky, particularly its ICBM leg.

SALT II Failure/Defense Buildup

When Carter took office in 1977 he already had committed himself to the goal of nuclear disarmament. "[W]e will move this year toward our ultimate goal — the elimination of all nuclear weapons from this earth," he declared in his Jan. 20, 1977, inaugural address.

Two months later, Secretary of State Cyrus R. Vance went to Moscow with a hastily formulated proposal for deep arms cuts in the nuclear arsenal of both countries. The Soviets immediately rejected the plan. However, talks resumed subsequently in private on terms more acceptable to Moscow, and what finally emerged after two years of negotiation still resembled the Vladivostok proposal in its major features.

The SALT II treaty, signed at a summit meeting in Vienna on June 18, 1979, set the following basic numerical limits on intercontinental missiles and bombers (which were to be in effect beginning on Jan. 1, 1981, and running until 1985):

● Of 2,250 weapons allowed each country, no more than 1,320 could be missiles with MIRVed warheads or strategic bombers carrying long-range cruise missiles.

● Of those 1,320, no more than 1,200 could be missiles equipped with MIRVed warheads.

● Of those 1,200, no more than 820 could be land-based intercontinental missiles (ICBMs).

Additional restrictions that were placed on mobile ICBMs and on cruise missiles launched from land or ships were to be in effect only through Dec. 31, 1981.

In a speech outlining the treaty to a joint session of Congress, Carter June 18 emphasized the pact's constraints on Soviet strategic programs. "Under this new treaty, the Soviet Union will be held to a third fewer strategic missile launchers and bombers by 1985 than they would have simply by continuing to build at their present rate," he said.

On the other hand, he pointed out, the agreement allowed the United States to develop the mobile MX intercontinental missile. The treaty therefore ensured that the MX would be a militarily viable weapon. "Without the SALT II limits," Carter warned, "the Soviet Union could build so many [missile] warheads that any land-based system, fixed or mobile, could be jeopardized."

The argument that the treaty would be militarily advantageous to the United States was one of two main contentions the administration pressed upon lawmakers in bid for Senate approval. The second, closely linked to the argument made for SALT I in the early 1970s, was that partial limits on expansion of the strategic arms race — within which limits the race would continue — were of such vital importance that they should be considered on their own merits, regardless of various ongoing U.S.-Soviet conflicts.

Assault on SALT II

Opponents of SALT II had mounted a two-pronged attack against the agreement even before it was signed. Their main objections were twofold. First, they maintained that the treaty would not prevent a substantial Soviet strategic arms buildup and thus would leave Moscow capable, theoretically, of destroying the entire U.S. Minuteman intercontinental ballistic missile force by 1982.

Second, they argued that SALT II could endanger U.S. security by anesthetizing Congress and the American public to the need for increased defense efforts at home and greater resistance to Soviet adventurism abroad.

As part of his campaign to convince the Senate's defense hard-liners and wavering members that the treaty would protect U.S. military options, President Carter reaffirmed his commitment to the development of the MX missile. But that commitment did not quiet Senate objections. The treaty's impact on three other weapons issues, as well as

Intercontinental Ballistic Missiles
(March 1983)

United States: 1,049 ICBMs operational; 2,152 warheads

● 550 Minuteman IIIs. Length: 18.2 meters (m). Range: 14,000 kilometers (km). Carries 3 MIRV (multiple independently targeted re-entry vehicle) warheads of 200 kilotons (kt) each; 300 retrofitted with Mark 12A improved warheads, 330 kt each.

● 456 Minuteman IIs. Length: 18 m. Range: 12,500 km. Carries one re-entry vehicle (rv) warhead of 1-2 megatons (mt).

● 43 Titan IIs. Length 30 m. Range: 12,000 km. Carries a single rv warhead of 5-10 mt. Scheduled to be retired by 1987.

● 100 MX missiles requested by President Reagan and recommended by the President's Commission on Strategic Forces. Length: 21.6 m. Range: 11,000 km. Carries 10 MIRV Mark 21 warheads, 330 kt each. Scheduled to be operational in 1986.

Soviet Union[1]: 1,398 ICBMs operational; 5,158 warheads

● 330 SS-19s. Length: 25 m. Range: more than 9,000 km. Each carries 4-6 MIRVs, about 200 kt each. Reload capability.

● 308 SS-18s. Length: 35 m. Range: 11,000 km. Each can carry one rv of 18-25 mt (and possibly up to 50 mt), or 8-10 MIRVs of 2 mt each. Reload capability.

● 150 SS-17s. Length: 24 m. Range: 10,000-11,000 km. Each carries one rv of 5 mt or 4 of 900 kt. Reload capability.

● 60 SS-13s. Length: 20 m. Range: 8,000-10,000 km. Each carries one rv of 1 mt.

● 550 S-11s. Length: 20 m. Range: 10,000-11,000 km. Each carries one rv of 1-2 mt or 3 of 100-300 kt. Reload capability

● Under development: 2 solid propellant ICBMs, one equivalent to MX deployed in silos; the other a smaller missile designed for mobile deployment. Testing expected in 1983.

[1] *All figures for Soviet ICBMs are U.S. Government estimates.*

Source: Secretary of Defense, *Annual Report to the Congress*, fiscal 1984 (Washington, D.C.: U.S. Government Printing Office, 1983); Joint Chiefs of Staff, *United States Military Posture*, fiscal 1984 (Washington, D.C.: Government Printing Office, 1983); Department of Defense, *Soviet Military Power* (Washington, D.C.: U.S. Government Printing Office, March 1983); *Jane's Weapon Systems, 1982-83*, ed. Ronald T. Pretty (London: Jane's Publishing Co. Ltd., 1982)

its procedures for verification of Soviet compliance, also were sharply criticized by SALT opponents.

The treaty allowed the Soviet Union to retain 326 of its largest ICBMs, the SS-18s, which carried up to 10 MIRVed warheads. Because of their pinpoint accuracy, the SS-18s by themselves would be able to destroy the U.S. ICBM Minuteman force, the critics maintained, thereby holding in reserve the more than 1,000 other Soviet land-based missiles in case they were needed to deter a U.S. retaliation.

Missile Size, Range Issues. Another target of treaty opponents was a provision prohibiting the development of any new missiles as large as the SS-18 (all existing U.S. missiles were smaller); the result was to prevent U.S. deployment of a missile comparable in size to the SS-18.

In response, the Carter administration argued that, because the MX would have 10 warheads powerful enough to destroy any target, it would be the equivalent of the larger Soviet SS-18, even though the Soviet missile could carry more megatonnage in its payload. Administration officials also stressed that since the treaty limited to 10 the number of warheads that could be mounted on any land-based missile, SALT II guaranteed that the SS-18 could not become any more dangerous than it was already.

Criticism of the treaty also focused on the Soviets' insistence on excluding its new Backfire bomber from the SALT II limitations. The Backfire, in operation since 1974, was capable of performing nuclear strikes, conventional attacks and anti-ship and reconnaissance missions. Although the Soviets said it was designed to be used against targets in Western Europe and China, it also was capable of reaching targets in North America, SALT critics repeatedly emphasized.

The treaty did not place any limits on the 3,000-mile-range Soviet SS-20 missile, which was capable of reaching civilian and military targets in Western Europe from bases in the Soviet Union. To offset that weapon, some NATO defense officials lobbied for development of a long-range U.S. cruise missile that could hit Soviet territory from Western Europe. But the pact limited (through 1981 only) any ground- or sea-launched cruise missile to a 375-mile target radius.

Verification Issue. A major concern of many treaty critics was verification of Soviet compliance. Each side agreed, as in SALT I, not to interfere with the other's means of ensuring that the weapons limits were being observed.

The verification procedure itself was not verifiable, treaty opponents charged. Other specific provisions critics claimed might not be verifiable were the proposed limitation on the number of new types of ICBMs that could be tested by each side and a prohibition on testing rapid-reloading systems (launchers that can be fired and quickly used again), particularly for ICBMs.

By the fall of 1979 it was becoming increasingly apparent that the treaty would not be approved by the Senate. Carter nevertheless continued to express support for the agreement on its merits, reiterating that it did not depend on Soviet trust. But after the Soviet invasion of Afghanistan in late December 1979, he formally requested postponement of Senate action. Throughout 1980 Carter emphasized the need to adhere to the SALT II limitations even though the treaty remained in limbo.

'Countervailing Strategy'

Concern about maintaining the parity with the U.S.S.R. in strategic weapons had surfaced well before the final demise of SALT II. According to administration defense planners, disparities between the superpowers in nuclear weaponry that could be perceived as making Soviet strategic forces more powerful than their U.S. counterparts would not be accepted.

Carter officials began to emphasize the need for planning for a nuclear war as well as for deterring one. This shift in thinking was contained in Presidential Directive 59, issued in July 1980.

The directive was similar to the memorandum President Nixon had issued in January 1974. Both documents stressed the need to have sufficient forces capable of providing a credible deterrence against a nuclear attack and, if deterrence failed, to have forces invulnerable and accurate enough to be able to conduct selected nuclear attacks, particularly against protected, or "hardened," Soviet military targets. The Carter document pointed to an urgent need to upgrade the U.S. command, control, communications and intelligence systems, particularly if a war were to be fought over a period of several months.

Highlights of PD 59 were made public by Defense Secretary Harold Brown in an Aug. 20, 1980, speech at the Naval War College. Brown called for strengthening the U.S. war-fighting capability in order to provide an added measure of deterrence by demonstrating America's ability to respond in credible fashion without having to escalate immediately to an all-out nuclear war. The goal of U.S. nuclear defense strategy, he said, was to convince the Soviets "that no . . . use of nuclear weapons — on any scale of attack and at any stage of conflict — could lead to victory, however they may define victory."

Brown also acknowledged that it was "very likely" that the use of nuclear weapons by either superpower at any level would escalate into all-out nuclear warfare.

The objectives of U.S. defense policy — deterrence through what the Carter administration termed a countervailing strategy (a second strike capability), weapons stability and essential equivalence, or balance, in nuclear arms between the superpowers — were summarized in the Defense Department's Jan. 29, 1980, annual report.

Successful deterrence, according to the report, required the United States to have an adequate second-strike force, that is, one that could attack a comprehensive set of targets, including those having major political, military and economic value, after having sustained a nuclear attack by the Soviet Union. In addition, the United States had to have the capability to:

● Delay or withhold retaliation against selected targets.

● Continually cover a sizable percentage of the Soviet economic base with U.S. nuclear weapons so that such targets could be destroyed, if necessary.

● Employ an adequate reserve force for a substantial period after a nuclear attack.

Although the 1980 Pentagon report acknowledged that MAD — the capability to devastate Soviet industries and cities, even if Moscow struck first — remained "the bedrock of nuclear deterrence," it said an assessment of the range of nuclear attacks the Soviets might launch and the targets the United States should attack in retaliation was equally important. "We have concluded that if deterrence is to be fully effective, the United States must be able to respond at a level appropriate to the type and scale of Soviet attack . . . while retaining an assured destruction capacity in reserve."

The statement sought to refute the "myth" that the United States had "suffered a major loss of leverage because of the Soviet nuclear buildup." However, the report added, "We must ensure that Soviet leads or advantages in particular areas are offset by U.S. leads or advantages in others." Essential equivalence had to be maintained "to prevent the Soviets from gaining political advantage from a real or perceived strategic imbalance."

By the time he left office, Carter himself was considerably less confident about existing U.S. defense capabilities, particularly in light of the SALT II breakdown. That unease was nowhere more apparent than in the administration's attempt to reverse the downward trend in defense spending. *(Details, see Budgeting for Defense chapter.)*

Reagan's Nuclear Strategy

The Reagan administration generally agreed with its predecessor that maintaining essential equivalence with the Soviet Union in nuclear weapons was essential for ensuring the nation's security.

Both administrations pursued a strategic policy based on the development of the most advanced land-based nuclear missiles. And both placed particular importance on the theoretical ability of Moscow's very accurate MIRVed ICBMs to destroy America's land-based missiles during a period in which U.S. nuclear weapons, according to some defense analysts, posed no equivalent threat to heavily protected Soviet missile silos embedded in tons of concrete and rock.

Throughout his first two years in office, Reagan emphasized the need to modernize and strengthen the U.S. strategic nuclear triad. But with demands increasing for presidential action to contain the arms race, Reagan also initiated programs to eliminate nuclear weapons in Europe and to reduce the superpowers' arsenal of intercontinental nuclear weapons:

● In a Nov. 18, 1981, speech, Reagan announced his "zero option" proposal. Under that plan, the Soviet Union would eliminate its previously deployed European-targeted intermediate-range ballistic missiles (IRBMs). In return, the United States would refrain from deploying its new Pershing II IRBMs and ground-launched cruise missiles (GLCMs) in Western Europe; deployment was scheduled to begin in December 1983. U.S.-Soviet talks on European theater nuclear forces (TNF) began in Geneva two weeks later. Moscow, however, quickly rejected the zero-option plan.

● Also in his November 1981 address, Reagan said the administration was developing proposals for "substantial" reductions in U.S.-Soviet arsenals of long-range ICBMs and SLBMs. The new round of arms control talks was labeled START, for strategic arms reduction talks, to distinguish them from the previous SALT negotiations.

● On May 9, 1982, Reagan announced that the administration was ready to begin arms reduction talks with the Soviet Union based on his START proposals. The plan called for an equal and verifiable reduction in the two nations' arsenals of long-range ICBMs and SLBMs. Negotiations to limit those weapons opened in Geneva on June 29.

● Facing an impasse in the U.S.-Soviet TNF talks, Reagan on March 30, 1983, suggested an interim compromise to his "zero option" plan that would reduce, rather than eliminate, the number of Soviet IRBMs already in place and limit the number of U.S. intermediate-range Pershing IIs and cruise missiles to be deployed in Europe.

At the same time, Reagan reaffirmed his commitment to a defense buildup so that the United States would not come to the bargaining table from what he considered a strategically inferior position.

'Window of Vulnerability'

The Reagan administration viewed the existing nuclear balance generally as much more favorable to Moscow than did Carter and his defense advisers. Reagan repeatedly warned that Soviet strategic advantages might encourage Moscow to step up political confrontations and even risk military actions jeopardizing vital interests of the United States and its NATO allies. At a March 31, 1982, press conference, Reagan himself presented this view even more starkly. "On balance, the Soviet Union does have a definite margin of superiority, enough so that there is risk and there is . . . a window of vulnerability," he said. The president and his military planners frequently used the "window" metaphor to describe the overall U.S.-Soviet nuclear relationship. The other side of the so-called U.S. window of vulnerability was the Soviets' "window of opportunity," either real or perceived, that, according to Reagan, might provide a vista for the Soviets to attempt political or military initiatives that would adversely affect the United States or its allies.

Administration officials implied that part of the alleged danger in the existing nuclear balance of forces was one of diplomatic perceptions of the relative momentum of U.S. and Soviet nuclear arms programs. They pointed to the steady deployment of new Soviet nuclear arms during the 1970s, when U.S. nuclear weapons advances were much less dramatic. The military balance casts "a shadow over every significant geopolitical decision," said Secretary of State Haig in an April 6, 1982, speech at Georgetown University's Center for Strategic and International Studies. "It affects on a day-to-day basis the conduct of American diplomacy. It influences the management of international crises and the terms on which they are resolved."

Some defense experts, including administration officials, were skeptical that the "window" was as large as Reagan and others had described. Among them were members of the Presidential Commission on Strategic Forces, appointed to recommend an adequate MX missile deployment plan in light of the current strategic balance. Although the panel said that some deployment of MX missiles was needed, the members also concluded that, viewed in its entirety, the U.S. strategic system of ICBMs, SLBMs and long-range bombers continued to provide an effective deterrent against a successful Soviet attack.

Diversity, Flexibility, Endurance

The president outlined his views on nuclear strategy in a Nov. 22, 1982, address to the nation. In it, he stressed two fundamental premises on which he based his strategic arms policy:

● Peace depended on a nearly symmetrical balance of U.S. and Soviet forces, especially in land-based ICBMs.

● The Soviet Union could be persuaded to reduce its nuclear arsenals only if confronted by unequivocal indications that the United States would match Soviet military advances in the absence of an arms control agreement.

"What we are saying to them is this," Reagan summed up. "We will modernize our military in order to keep the balance for peace, but wouldn't it be better if we simply reduced our arsenals to a much lower level?"

In shaping the U.S. nuclear defense force for the 1980s, the administration incorporated three principles adopted by its predecessors:

● Diversity. The administration maintained the longstanding U.S. dependence on a triad of nuclear weapons launchers (ICBMS, SLBMs and B-52 bombers), accepting the assumption that no two of these forces would be wiped out by a Soviet attack. To guarantee that at least part of the U.S. nuclear force would remain invulnerable, Reagan officials argued that the triad needed to be modernized and reinforced. For example, they insisted that the decision to begin production immediately of the controversial B-1 bomber, canceled by Carter in 1977, was based on an assessment that the B-52 bombers could not be relied on to penetrate continually improving Soviet air defenses during the several years it would take to develop a radically new type of aircraft designed to evade Soviet air defenses by new "stealth" techniques *(B-1 issue, p. 99)*

● Flexibility. The U.S. nuclear arsenal needed to be flexible; that is, it had to contain weapons that could be used to cover the gamut of possible Soviet targets under various scenarios of "limited" as well as all-out nuclear war. Accordingly, the Reagan administration retained the Carter commitment to deploy, by 1986 if feasible, the MX intercontinental missile designed to destroy even the most heavily armored Soviet military targets.

The administration also planned to go ahead with deployment in December 1983 of intermediate-range Pershing II and ground-launched cruise missiles (GLCMs) in Western Europe. This force was intended to deter or, if necessary, counter any attack on the NATO countries by Soviet intermediate-range ballistic missiles (IRBMs) or conventional forces.

● Endurance. Reagan defense planners believed the U.S. nuclear force must be designed to survive a Soviet strike and still have enough missiles in reserve to mount a devastating retaliatory attack. In addition to missiles, according to the administration, an adequate defense required better radar capability to warn of impending attacks and an improved communications, command and control network that could function after a war had begun. A number of defense specialists maintained that the U.S. command structure — the organizational and technical network providing direction for American strategic forces — might not be able to survive a Soviet attack.

The Reagan administration also accelerated development of a new version of the submarine-launched ballistic missiles (SLBMs) carried by U.S. Trident missile-launching submarines. The modified version, the Trident II (D-5), scheduled to be deployed by 1989, would be carried by a new, larger class of Trident submarines, the *Ohio* class. ICBMs carried by submarines were considered nearly invulnerable to attack since they were difficult to locate. Nevertheless, Soviet tracking capabilities, according to the Pentagon, were improving.

The longer-range Trident II missile was expected to be nearly as accurate as the MX and powerful enough to destroy hardened Soviet missile silos and other vital targets. The administration planned to continue building Trident submarines at the rate of one per year and to equip anti-ship submarines with nuclear-armed cruise missiles able to reach targets deep inside the Soviet Union.

A major controversy over deployment of the MX missile during the Carter and Reagan administrations dealt with the question of how the MX and its launching sites could be adequately protected against Soviet attack. It was largely this concern that prompted Congress in 1982 to delete funds for production of the MX from the administration's fiscal

1983 defense budget and to direct Reagan to come up with a better plan for basing the missile.

On Oct. 2, 1981, Reagan announced a five-part, $180 billion long-term program to modernize the U.S. strategic arsenal. The plan called for deployment of the MX; procurement of 100 modified versions of the B-1 bomber; continued development of a new "stealth" bomber; continued production of Trident missile-launching submarines, with deployment by 1989 of the larger Trident II missile; construction of new ground-based radars, AWACS (airborne warning and control system) radar planes and F-15 jet interceptors; and more sophisticated communications systems and mobile command posts.

Divergences From Carter Policy

Reagan's nuclear program broke with the Carter approach in two important respects. First, Reagan's concept of deterrent credibility — being able to survive a Soviet attack with enough remaining nuclear warheads to inflict heavy damage on the Soviet Union — placed more emphasis than Carter's on the need to build up defensive systems to wipe out incoming Soviet missiles and to minimize the civilian damage that would be incurred by a Soviet strike. The latter concern was evident in the Reagan administration's blueprint for a seven-year, $4.2 billion civil defense program providing for the evacuation of most large U.S. cities in case of a severe crisis with the Soviet Union.

Reagan's plan protected, theoretically, about 90 percent of the U.S. population against a Soviet attack. Reagan officials contended that the program would contribute to deterrence by making the resort to war a more "credible" U.S. option. The administration emphasized that the Soviets' civil defense effort was substantially greater than the United States'. But a skeptical and cost-conscious Congress slashed $100 million of the $254 million requested for civil defense planning in the fiscal 1983 budget.

Reagan also accelerated development of defensive systems designed to provide early warning of incoming Soviet warheads. As of 1983, according to the Pentagon, the United States had fewer than 120 ground radar systems and AWACS planes, no surface-to-air missiles (SAMs) deployed to defend North America, fewer than 300 interceptor aircraft (most of which were of 1950s' vintage) and no anti-ballistic missile (ABM) defense capability. By contrast, Moscow had made heavy investments in defensive systems. The Pentagon estimated that the

Soviets had more than 7,000 air defense radars, 2,500 interceptor planes, 10,000 SAM launchers (including a SA-10 system that could attack and destroy more than one aircraft simultaneously at any altitude) and 32 ABM launchers.

The anti-missile defense plans initially designed by Reagan emphasized systems that could protect only very heavily armored military targets (such as MX missile launchers). In this, Reagan's policy did not differ from Carter's. Congress, though, was less than enthusiastic about the program. In 1982 it slashed $350 million from the budget request of $727 million for anti-missile research. In 1983 the administration requested $709.3 million for research and development on missile defenses, including new ground-based radars, AWACS radar planes and F-15 interceptors to defend U.S. territory.

In a major address on defense policy on March 23, 1983, Reagan called for new efforts by America's scientific community to develop space-based missile defense systems. But he did not commit additional federal funds to the program. Administration officials conceded that implementing such a system was far in the future. Moreover, critics of Reagan's initiative maintained that elaborate earth- and space-based defense systems would violate the 1972 U.S.-Soviet ABM treaty and also inject a new element of instability into the nuclear balance.

Reagan's Approach to Arms Control

A judgment that the U.S.S.R. was gaining an edge in nuclear capabilities molded Reagan's view of arms control agreements in his defense strategy. Reagan strongly suggested there was little point to any agreement that would not substantially reduce the Soviet arsenal of large ICBMs, since the administration considered those weapons the most destabilizing element in the arms balance.

"The main threat to peace posed by nuclear weapons today is the growing instability of the nuclear balance," Reagan said in a May 9, 1982, speech at Eureka College in which he said the United States had developed concrete proposals for the START negotiations. "This is due to the increasingly destructive potential of the massive Soviet buildup in its ballistic missile force. Therefore," he added, "our goal is to enhance deterrence and achieve stability through significant reductions in the most destabilizing nuclear systems, ballistic missiles, and especially the giant intercontinental ballistic missiles, while maintaining a nuclear capability sufficient to deter conflict, to underwrite our national security and to meet our commitment to allies and friends."

In Reagan's view, Moscow would agree to a treaty reducing its nuclear arsenal only if the United States demonstrated its willingness to match the Soviet force. "Let's not fool ourselves," Reagan said during a radio broadcast April 17, 1982. "The Russians will not come to any conference table bearing gifts. . . . To achieve parity, we must make it plain that we have the will to achieve parity by our own effort."

The initial phase of the START negotiations, the third major American initiative in U.S.-Soviet arms control negotiations in a decade, began June 29 in Geneva. Coloring the Reagan administration's approach to the negotiations was its belief that the SALT process had bred a euphoria about the overall state of U.S.-Soviet relations that ignored the threat posed by various Soviet weapons developments. As a result, Reagan officials argued, the Nixon, Ford and Carter administrations gave too much away in their negotiations with Moscow and significantly underfunded both nuclear and non-nuclear American defense programs.

Initially, President Reagan said his administration would "refrain from actions which would undercut" the SALT I and II agreements, provided the Soviet Union did likewise. Nevertheless, he continued to assert that SALT II was flawed: that its weapons restrictions were unfair to the United States. One of his major objections was that it placed ceilings only on the number of strategic weapons launchers, that is, on the devices from which ICBMs and SLBMs are fired, and on the number of strategic bombers. It did not place any limits on the number of warheads each side could retain, even though the growing nuclear instability, in Reagan's view, was caused largely by the superpowers' development of more powerful and accurate warheads, particularly the refinement that allowed a number of these warheads to be carried on a single missile. (The SALT II treaty, however, did limit to 10 the number of MIRVs that could be installed on a single missile.)

In announcing his START proposal for a "practical, phased reduction" in U.S. and Soviet nuclear forces, Reagan May 9, 1982, said both superpowers must "reduce significantly the most destabilizing systems — ballistic missiles, the number of warheads they carry and their overall destructive potential."

START's Weapons Limits

In contrast to the SALT approach, Reagan's START plan focused on restricting each country's total number of ballistic missile warheads, as well as the number of deployed missiles. Reagan argued that such restrictions provided a more accurate measure of strategic capability than launchers alone. The START proposal set the following approximate limits, to be reached over a period of five to 10 years:

● No more than a total of about 5,000 warheads on ICBMs and submarine-launched missiles (SLBMs). Administration officials said there were about 7,500 such warheads in each country's arsenal as of 1982.

● No more than about 850 ICBMs and SLBMs. The administration placed the inventories at about 2,500 for the Soviet Union and 1,700 for the United States.

● A limit of 2,500 on the number of ICBM warheads on each side. The totals in 1982 were 5,500 for the Soviet Union and 2,152 for the United States, according to the administration.

Though Reagan did not propose ceilings on bombers and cruise missiles in this first stage of START, Secretary of State Haig told the Senate Foreign Relations Committee in May 1982 that those weapons still might be included in a first-phase START treaty. In the interim, he said, the United States would go forward with development of the modified B-1 bomber and with the so-called stealth plane. The Pentagon also was working on improvements in air-, ground-, and sea-launched cruise missiles.

As a second step in the START process, Reagan intended to seek equal limits on total throw weight — the weapons-carrying capacity of long-range missiles — at a lower level than the existing U.S. throw-weight total. Hard-line U.S. defense analysts had condemned the SALT II treaty for limiting the number of weapons launchers, but not missile throw weight, a measure by which Moscow enjoyed an advantage of nearly three-to-one over the United States. However, adherence to throw-weight limits was more difficult to verify than limits on the number of missiles and warheads. At this stage, Reagan's plan also called for equal limits on both countries' strategic weapons not covered by the first phase of START, such as bombers and cruise missiles.

Reactions to START Plan

Reagan's proposal generally received a favorable reception in Congress. A number of members said the plan, though portending long, tough sessions with the Soviets, was a serious and negotiable proposal. Nevertheless, START encountered many of the same objections raised against SALT II. Opponents, who included some of the same defense hard-liners who had opposed Carter's plan, said Moscow would retain an advantage in missile throw weight and warhead power, at least in the first phase, even if an initial START treaty set equal ceilings on the U.S. and Soviet ICBM arsenals. That was because all existing Soviet ICBMs were larger than the U.S. Minuteman missiles, and the Soviet SS-18 was larger than the projected MX.

Like SALT II, the START plan also was criticized because it limited the number of deployed missiles only, rather than the total missile stockpile. Unlike U.S. launchers, some Soviet missile launchers could be reloaded within a few days. Thus Moscow could continue to stockpile a large number of missiles that could be fired from reusable launchers. However, Secretary Haig had given assurances that large stockpiles of such missiles would be barred by "mutual understandings" under START.

Some defense experts objected to the START proposal (and to the preceding SALT agreements) because they felt its underlying assessment of the nuclear balance was misleading. It was not so much the number of warheads and the throw weight of the missiles that mattered, these critics said, but rather their accuracy and invulnerability. Various estimates placed the total throw weight of Soviet missiles at about 11 million pounds and of U.S. missiles at 4 million pounds. (Total U.S. megatonnage reached a peak of approximately 8 million pounds in about 1960 and then was deliberately allowed to decline as defense planners emphasized technological improvements over throw weight.)

Unlike the initial Carter proposal, Reagan's START plan was not summarily rejected by Moscow. Nonetheless, it was clear that the U.S.S.R. would not accept it as proposed. "The most obvious problem with the Reagan proposal is that it will not be accepted by the Soviets without major modification and compromise," wrote Jan Lodal, senior staff member of the National Security Council from 1973-75, in the Fall 1982 issue of *Foreign Policy*. "The provisions of phase two would require a massive restructuring of Soviet forces, obliging Moscow to abandon nearly two-thirds of its land-based missile power," the strongest component of its nuclear force. (About 75 percent of the Soviets' strategic capability is land based, compared to about 40 percent for the United States'.) The Soviet ICBMs carry about 70 percent of the Soviet strategic warheads, accounting for more than 80 percent of Soviet nuclear explosive power. The U.S. ICBMs account for about half of the U.S. inventory of launchers for delivering nuclear weapons. They carry about a quarter of the total number of strategic warheads, which comprise about 40 percent of the explosive power in the U.S. nuclear arsenal.

However, as Richard Burt, assistant secretary of state for European affairs, wrote in the September 1982 issue of *NATO Review,* "Today ... the United States faces the situation where its land-based missiles are vulnerable to pre-emptive attack. But this will not remain the case in the future — as technology advances, warheads are becoming more accurate. The Soviet ICBM force will not remain invulnerable forever. Thus the vulnerability of land-based missiles is a matter over which both sides should be concerned.... A primary attribute of the U.S. [START] proposal is that it will force a relative shift away from ICBMs, resulting in a less destabilizing force structure on both sides. This is in the Soviet advantage as well as our own."

Theater Nuclear Forces

President Reagan's approach to strategic nuclear issues determined in large measure his response to demands for immediate U.S-Soviet negotiations to limit theater nuclear forces (TNF) in Europe. Theater nuclear forces, which essentially refer to missiles, are those having a range of more than 1,000 kilometers but less than about 5,500 kilometers. (These weapons are referred to as longer-range IRBMs, to distinguish them from the shorter-range versions, such as the Soviet SS-22 and the American Pershing 1-A.)

The lack of a NATO intermediate-range ballistic missile (IRBM) force able to hit targets deep inside the U.S.S.R. was the focus of concern in the NATO alliance well before Reagan made public his views on the East-West military balance in Europe. By the late 1970s it had become increasingly apparent to defense experts in Europe as well as in the United States that the military scales were tipping in Moscow's favor.

The NATO countries throughout the 1970s remained at a substantial disadvantage vis-à-vis the Warsaw Pact states in conventional force strength. And in 1977 a new military development emerged that tipped the balance of strategic forces in the Warsaw Pact's favor: the Soviet Union began to deploy MIRVed SS-20 intermediate-range ballistic missiles (IRBMs) to supplement its single warhead intermediate-range SS-4s and SS-5s. Each SS-20 was armed with three highly accurate, 150-kiloton warheads. By 1983 more than two-thirds of the Soviets' estimated total of 351 SS-20 launchers were pointed toward Western Europe (the rest were in the Far East sections of the U.S.S.R.).

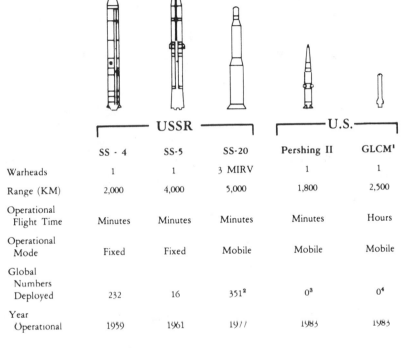

Intermediate-range Nuclear Missiles
(March 1983)

	USSR			U.S.	
	SS - 4	**SS-5**	**SS-20**	**Pershing II**	**GLCM[1]**
Warheads	1	1	3 MIRV	1	1
Range (KM)	2,000	4,000	5,000	1,800	2,500
Operational Flight Time	Minutes	Minutes	Minutes	Minutes	Hours
Operational Mode	Fixed	Fixed	Mobile	Mobile	Mobile
Global Numbers Deployed	232	16	351[2]	0[3]	0[4]
Year Operational	1959	1961	1977	1983	1983

1. *Ground-launched cruise missiles.*

2. *About 108 targeted on Asia, the rest on Europe.*

3. *108 Pershing IIs scheduled for deployment beginning December 1983.*

4. *464 GLCMs scheduled for deployment beginning 1983.*

Source: Joint Chiefs of Staff, *United States Military Posture*, fiscal 1984 (Washington, D.C.: U.S. Government Printing Office, 1983) SS-20 figures updated.

Unlike the much older, stationary SS-4s and SS-5s (which became operational in 1960-61), the SS-20s were mounted on mobile launchers, making them more difficult targets. All three types of missiles could be used on reloadable launchers, allowing them to be fired in relatively rapid succession.

The Defense Department estimated in 1983 that more than 1,300 warheads were mounted on the three types of Soviet IRBMs, which totaled 550. The Soviets were thought to have at least that number of IRBMs in reserve that could be reloaded on their launchers and fired.

Supplementing the Soviets' IRBMs were medium-range Backfire bombers carrying nuclear missiles.

NATO Two-Track Policy

To counter this Soviet threat, the NATO alliance on Dec. 12, 1979, agreed to pursue a two-track policy of modernizing its theater nuclear forces as well as encouraging negotiations to limit those weapons. NATO agreed to put into operation by December 1983 a new generation of U.S. Pershing II intermediate-range missiles as well as ground-launched cruise missiles (GLCMs). Without those weapons, NATO had no theater nuclear forces of a range comparable to the Soviets' missiles. The missile currently used by NATO, the Pershing 1-A, with a target radius of about 400 miles, could not reach the U.S.S.R. from Western Europe.

The NATO ministers also urged the start of U.S.-Soviet negotiations to limit the theater nuclear missiles. The 1979 NATO decision marked the first time a U.S. nuclear weapons program involving Europe was made dependent on prior allied consent, and the first time a decision to develop a new weapon was linked to efforts to curtail or abolish it through bilateral U.S.-Soviet arms control talks.

The fact that NATO continued to rely primarily on the U.S. nuclear deterrent at a time when Washington had lost its ICBM superiority was a principal reason for the NATO decision. The vulnerability of U.S. ICBMs had made it appear less likely to America's European allies that the United States would agree to a policy of nuclear retaliation to defend Europe if the Soviets could destroy a large portion of U.S. land-based missiles in North America. Many Europeans questioned whether the United States would risk its own survival to defend its allies.

Theater nuclear forces increasingly were viewed by the Reagan administration as an essential ingredient of the NATO defense strategy — comprising intermediate-range missiles, the U.S. ICBM force and member countries' conventional forces — that would enable the alliance to pursue a flexible military strategy.

The Pershing II was designed to achieve a 99 percent probability of destroying a Soviet command headquarters or missile silo hardened to withstand pressures of 2,000 pounds per square inch.

The range of the Pershing IIs, though classified, was thought to be about 1,100 miles and that of ground-launched cruise missiles (GLCMs) about 1,800 miles. Unlike the Soviets' MIRVed SS-20, the Pershing II carried a single "selectable" warhead, which allowed the yield to be adjusted to the magnitude of the target. However, Pershing IIs were considered by some defense specialists to be more vulnerable than GLCMs to a Soviet pre-emptive strike because of their larger size and shorter flight time, making them a greater threat to the Soviet Union.

The United States alone would control the Pershing IIs as well as pay for them. (Washington originally had offered "dual key" — joint control — of the weapons to any NATO member willing to share the cost, but the allies expressed little interest in the proposal.)

Congress in late 1982 had eliminated the Reagan administration's fiscal 1983 request of $493.3 million for production of the first 91 Pershing IIs.

Congressional leaders made it clear that they supported the TNF program, but wanted solid assurances that the missile would perform as advertised. House and Senate leaders responsible for reviewing the defense budget said they would consider a renewed request for Pershing II funds once the Army had successfully completed flight testing of the missile. The seventh successful test flight took place March 28, 1983, with 12 more test flights planned before deployment of the missile in West Germany could take place.

Bargaining and 'Decoupling'

A principal administration argument for deploying Pershing IIs and GLCMs in Europe was to prevent what was called "decoupling" of the United States from its NATO allies through Soviet pressure. With the U.S.S.R. capable of launching damaging missile strikes at Europe — while sparing the United States — and the NATO countries unable to respond with an intermediate-range weapon of their own that could match the Russians' SS-4s, SS-5s and SS-20s, Moscow might perceive that it could threaten Western Europe without fear of U.S. nuclear retaliation.

On the other hand, any attempt to create a European nuclear force independent of the United States' strategic force might convey the impression that Washington was not committed to the defense of Europe.

Enhancement of NATO's theater nuclear forces also was considered necessary to preserve a "credible" Western European military capability in both conventional and intercontinental strategic forces.

The Reagan administration looked upon the planned deployment of 572 Pershing IIs and GLCMs as a powerful bargaining lever in U.S.-Soviet arms control negotiations, particularly in light of intense Soviet objections to and apprehension about the Pershing missile. That weapon, in contrast to the slower-flying GLCMs, was viewed by the Soviets as having a first-strike potential. Moscow warned that U.S. deployment of Pershing IIs would force it to adopt an "instantaneous" retaliatory posture of launch-on-warning.

Reagan's 'Zero Option' Plan

The use of the Pershing IIs and cruise missiles as bargaining chips was a central feature of the president's Nov. 18, 1981, offer to forgo deployment of the two types of missiles if Moscow dismantled all of its Europe-targeted SS-20s, SS-4s and SS-5s. The proposal, called the "zero option," or "zero-zero," plan, was cautiously endorsed by the West European NATO allies.

Talks on Intermediate-Range Nuclear Forces — the official name of the negotiations on theater nuclear forces — began Nov. 30, 1981, in Geneva. Little progress was made during the first two rounds of negotiations on the Reagan plan.

After initially dismissing the so-called zero option proposal, Soviet leader Yuri Andropov (who took over the leadership of the Soviet Union upon President Leonid I. Brezhnev's death in November 1982), responded with an offer to trim the Soviet IRBM force targeted at Western Europe to the number of intermediate-range missiles (162) deployed by Britain and France. The Soviet Union offered to re-deploy its remaining missiles at sites about 700 miles further east (on the far side of the Ural mountains).

The Soviet proposal quickly was rejected by the NATO countries for several reasons. First, the other mobile SS-20s, those behind the Ural Mountains, could rather easily be rolled back to positions closer to Europe. And even from points beyond those mountains they would be able to reach some territory in Western Europe. Second, the older French and British missiles were no match for the SS-20s. Moreover, those weapons were considered to be independent national nuclear defenses, not part of NATO. (France in fact had withdrawn from the unified NATO organizational command structure in 1967, although it continued to coordinate its defense effort with the alliance. The French government

U.S., Soviet Intermediate-range Missiles in Europe

President Reagan has proposed to cancel or reduce NATO's scheduled deployment of 572 Pershing II and cruise missiles if the Soviet Union agrees to dismantle all or some of its approximately 600 intermediate-range nuclear missiles, including about 250 of its multi-warhead SS-20s, targeted at Western Europe. The map shows the approximate ranges of an SS-20 missile (1) launched from the European sector of the U.S.S.R. west of the Ural mountains and a Pershing II (2) and a cruise missile (3) both launched from eastern West Germany.

*France does not participate formally in the NATO military structure.

supported the 1979 NATO two-track decision, and President Francois Mitterand reaffirmed that position after he took office in 1981.)

While the European NATO governments continued officially to support Reagan's zero option plan, they let it be known that they preferred a more flexible negotiating position at the TNF talks. Although the Soviet monopoly of intermediate-range nuclear weapons was unacceptable, many European officials contended that Moscow never would accept the Reagan proposal unless it were modified. Their concern elicited a concession from the Reagan administration: the zero option proposal was not intended as a "take-it-or-leave-it" offer. Arriving in Geneva Jan. 26, 1983, for a new round of INF talks, chief U.S. negotiator Paul H. Nitze said Washington was "certainly not locked into zero option." And shortly before he left on a 12-day trip to seven European nations Jan. 30, Vice President George Bush said the United States remained "open-minded. Bring on some other proposal and let's discuss it."

Bush's trip came at an extremely sensitive period in relations between the United States and its NATO allies. Since most of the GLCMs and all of the Pershing II missiles were to be deployed in West Germany (some GLCMs also would be stationed in Belgium, Britain, Italy and the Netherlands), the position of the Bonn government was critical.

The German adherence to the December 1979 NATO decision was put to the test on March 6, 1983, when incumbent Christian Democrat Chancellor Helmut Kohl, who supported the two-track policy, won a resounding victory in the national parliamentary elections over Social Democrat Hans-Jochen Vogel, who had called for reconsideration of the missile deployment decision. Although economic and other domestic issues were equally important, the outcome was widely viewed as one of the most significant in decades in terms of NATO politics and East-West relations. Both Washington and Moscow lobbied hard to influence the outcome.

'Zero Option' Modified

Pressure in both the United States and Europe for a more flexible U.S. negotiating position increased after Kohl's victory. In a March 12, 1983, interview with *The Washington Post*, Kohl suggested that the United States propose an interim agreement to break the deadlock. Kohl, along with other West European leaders, expressed the view that the zero option, while the optimal solution, probably was not obtainable.

Reagan responded March 30, 1983, by modifying his zero-option plan. The new version was drafted after intense consultation with the European allies. The new, scaled-back proposal called for the United States and the Soviet Union to have an equal number of warheads deployed on IRBMs, "on a global basis." The latter phrase was meant to include Soviet missiles aimed at China and Japan.

The president described his proposal as an "interim" step toward an ultimate agreement by both countries to eliminate intermediate-range weapons. "When it comes to intermediate nuclear missiles in Europe, it would be better to have none than some. But if there must be some, it is better to have few than to have many," he said.

Missing from Reagan's new proposal was any reference to the number of IRBMs or warheads that would be acceptable to Washington as an interim step. However, it was reported that the United States would suggest a limit of 300 warheads for each side. Under that limit, the Soviets could have 100 triple-warhead IRBMs deployed and the United States could have 300 single-warhead missiles.

The Soviet reaction was negative. Moscow Radio said the "new ideas are not as fresh as one would think" and were the "notorious 'zero option' in a new wrapping," which did not take into account the "other types of intermediate nuclear arms or the American nuclear-capable bombers deployed in Western Europe." Soviet Foreign Minister Andrei A. Gromyko April 2 dismissed Reagan's proposal as "unacceptable" and said there was "no chance" that it could serve as the basis for an agreement on intermediate nuclear weapons. Moreover, the inclusion of Soviet Asian-targeted IRBMs was a "tall order," he said. "It is necessary to say that this and already this alone makes agreement impossible. Why should we drag Asia into this?"

Besides providing what was hoped would be a more negotiable plan for the TNF talks, Reagan's proposal was aimed at two audiences. One was Congress and the American public, where support for a nuclear "freeze" was growing, fed by considerable public concern that Reagan was not pushing hard enough for a strategic arms control agreement. The other audience was the West Europeans, especially the West Germans, who were strongly opposed to the deployment of the Pershing IIs on their territory. Reagan's plan was intended in part to defuse further demonstrations in Europe against the initial deployment of the missiles.

In Congress, where the speech generally was applauded, some critics of Reagan's arms policies expressed hope that the proposal signaled a new U.S. commitment and flexibility toward arms control negotiations.

Leaders of the NATO countries endorsed Reagan's proposal. Kohl called it a "flexible negotiation offer" and said that the Soviet Union should respond seriously to it.

In spite of the favorable response among NATO leaders to the plan, U.S. officials held out no hope that Reagan would stop or delay deployment of the Pershing IIs. Deployment of the first installment of 108 missiles was scheduled to begin in December 1983. The deployment

NATO's Nuclear Arms Strategy: . . .

Proposals that the NATO alliance should consider renouncing the first use of nuclear weapons attracted considerable attention at about the time the nuclear freeze movement was gaining momentum in the United States. In an article in the Spring 1982 issue of *Foreign Affairs*, four former high-level U.S. defense policy makers — McGeorge Bundy, national security adviser to the president from 1961-66; Robert S. McNamara, secretary of defense from 1961-68; George F. Kennan, former U.S. ambassador to the U.S.S.R. (1952); and Gerard Smith, chief U.S. negotiator to the first strategic arms limitation talks (SALT I) from 1969-72 — asserted that the end of U.S. superiority, along with the development of enormous nuclear arsenals by both the United States and the U.S.S.R., had heightened fears of a nuclear holocaust and made it more difficult to construct rational plans for using those weapons.

They suggested that the time had come for a reversal of the present "first strike" and "flexible response" defense policies in favor of "no first use" of nuclear weapons. This pledge, they maintained, would decrease the danger of conventional warfare escalating into a nuclear war, particularly in Western Europe. The former officials said it was vital that any confrontation be confined to conventional arms.

The no-first-use policy was sharply criticized by Secretary of State Alexander M. Haig Jr. in an April 6, 1982, address at Georgetown University's Center for Strategic and International Studies. A renewed emphasis on conventional arms, according to Haig, would not be realistic because it would require huge amounts of money and manpower. Moreover, the Soviets would have a greater advantage in a conventional war than in a nuclear confrontation. A no-first-use policy, a pledge made by the Soviets on numerous occasions, was "tantamount to making Europe safe for conventional aggression," Haig asserted.

Gen. Bernard W. Rogers, Supreme Allied Commander Europe, also raised objections to the no-first-use policy. Writing in the *Summer* 1982 issue of *Foreign Affairs*, Rogers said a central element in deterring Soviet aggression was Moscow's uncertainty about NATO's readiness to cross the nuclear threshold. Removing that uncertainty by a no-first-use pledge would leave Europe exposed to conventional attack.

"Another inherent danger of declared no first use is that many in Europe and the United States would see such a policy as a limitation on the American commitment to European security," Rogers wrote. "This might well create a situation in which the final guarantor of deterrence — the U.S. strategic nuclear arsenal — would be viewed as divorced from the fate of Europe."

... The Debate Over 'No-First-Use'

A policy of no first use, then, would result in "decoupling" Europe from the United States, according to the Rogers view. Therefore, to avoid the impression that a conflict limited to Europe was realistic, NATO should not relinquish the nuclear option. The possibility of using nuclear weapons should be retained as a deterrent, at least until NATO and the Warsaw Pact countries negotiated an equitable and verifiable balance of conventional forces at the on-going Mutual and Balanced Force Reduction (MBFR) talks in Vienna.

A no-first-use policy could create the false perception that the United States preferred to risk a conventional defeat in Europe rather than be the first to use nuclear weapons, warned former Secretary of State Henry A. Kissinger in May 1982. That might be construed as an invitation to the Soviets to step up actions against the West, thus increasing the risks of war rather than lessening them.

Another critic of that policy, Sen. Sam Nunn, D-Ga., a senior member of the Armed Services Committee, said that NATO's nuclear weapons made it dangerous for the Soviets to concentrate their military forces in the European theater because they then would be vulnerable to a surprise attack that could wipe out those forces.

Four West German experts also responded to the no-first-use proposal in an article in the Summer 1982 *Foreign Affairs*. The authors of the article were Karl Kaiser, director of the Research Institute of the German Society for Foreign Affairs; Georg Leber, a Social Democratic member and vice president of the West German Bundestag; Alois Mertes, a member of the Christian Democratic Party and its legislative spokesman on foreign policy; and Gen. Franz-Josef Schultze (ret.), commander in chief of Allied Forces Central Europe. They said the NATO strategy of flexible response worked to deter the Soviets by confronting them with an incalculable risk. But a policy of renouncing nuclear weapons would allow the Soviet Union to more easily calculate the West's response, thus making a conflict in Europe more likely rather than less likely. They added that any conventional conflict probably would escalate into a nuclear confrontation in any case.

Despite criticism of a no-first-use policy, many defense experts felt existing strategic doctrine should be re-examined, particularly in light of Europe's reliance on the U.S. extended nuclear deterrent at a time when America had lost its global nuclear superiority. And there was general agreement that NATO's conventional forces should be quantitatively and qualitatively improved. One result would be a shift away from primary reliance on nuclear deterrence to reliance on deterrence by conventional forces. Reducing dependence on a strategy based primarily on use of nuclear weapons, while strengthening conventional options, might lessen the risk of a nuclear confrontation.

would begin, a U.S. official said, whether or not the United States and the Soviet Union reached an interim agreement on the number of missiles to be deployed. "We believe that it is only the deployment date, the beginning of deployment, that gives the Soviet Union any incentive whatsoever to negotiate seriously in Geneva," he said. The only way for the Soviet Union to block the deployment, he said, would be to agree to Reagan's zero option plan.

On March 31 Reagan expanded on his arms control policies in a speech in Los Angeles. That speech offered no new ideas, but it was meant to show the president's commitment to a broad range of arms control efforts, including talks on limiting chemical weapons as well as the START negotiations.

The issues raised by the TNF talks and the Pershing deployment were part of a larger debate over ways to deter Soviet military threats in Europe and counter any Soviet moves that did take place. If NATO were locked in a conventional conflict with the Warsaw Pact forces, and were likely to lose, some European officials feared the Pershing IIs and GLCMs operated by Americans would be used against the Warsaw Pact nations, not the Soviet Union. In that event, they argued, Moscow might respond against the NATO allies in Europe, but not against the United States.

The problem of achieving a credible nuclear deterrent in Europe also pointed up the importance of NATO's conventional forces. In recognition of this, Reagan in June 1982 urged the Warsaw Pact and NATO countries to resurrect the moribund Mutual and Balanced Force Reduction (MBFR) negotiations in Vienna. Those talks were aimed at achieving military parity in Central Europe.

Upgrading Deterrence: The MX

The Reagan nuclear strategy was dependent upon deployment of the MX missile, viewed by U.S. defense officials as a counterweight to the array of existing Soviet missiles, as a replacement for the aging U.S. Minuteman and Titan ICBM force and as an incentive to prod Moscow to negotiate a strategic arms control agreement.

The critical aspects of the MX missile system, as it evolved during 10 years of planning, were:

● A huge, 100-ton missile carrying 10 MIRVed warheads, each more powerful and more accurate than the three on each existing Minuteman III missile.

● A "basing mode" that would permit the MX to survive a massive attack by the U.S.S.R.'s growing arsenal of extremely powerful and accurate warheads.

The MX missile took shape during the Ford administration. The final design was adopted in 1978, and two years later Congress appropriated funds to begin work on a prototype. The first test flight, scheduled for mid-1983, would make it possible for the first few MXs to be deployed in 1986.

The MX is to be armed with the new Mark 21 warhead, which has more explosive power than 300,000 tons of TNT. Because the MX also is supposed to have a more accurate guidance system than the Minuteman (allowing it to come within 100 yards of hitting its target), each of the 10 warheads on an MX missile would be able to destroy the most heavily fortified Soviet installation, such as an underground missile silo or a command post.

The Carter administration had come to the conclusion that the MX was needed to replace America's increasingly vulnerable ICBM force, composed primarily of the Minuteman III. The Minuteman, first deployed in 1967, is the newest U.S. ICBM.

Rationale for MX

The need for a powerful new missile such as the MX was based on the war-fighting theory of deterrence adhered to by the Ford, Carter and Reagan administrations. It was based on the premise that the United States had to have a powerful nuclear arsenal and the means to launch a wide variety of nuclear attacks against the Soviet Union, ranging from a "warning shot" to a massive retaliatory attack on Soviet nuclear forces if necessary.

Defense planners described what would happen in a hypothetical nuclear confrontation between the superpowers unless the United States developed the MX. The nightmarish picture went like this: the Soviets launch a few hundred MIRVed ICBMs in a pre-emptive strike and destroy 1) most of the U.S. Minuteman missile force, 2) those strategic bombers (the B-52s) not on alert and already in the air, and 3) the strategic missile-carrying submarines not at sea. (About one-third of U.S. strategic bombers are held ready to take off on five minutes' notice, and about half of America's missile submarines are at sea at any given time.) Because the U.S. SLBMs in 1983 were not accurate enough to destroy strongly protected Soviet economic and military targets, they could be aimed only at Soviet population centers. However, some U.S. defense planners contended that Moscow could shield much of its population with its large civil defense program. Moreover, the United States would have to assume that if it struck Soviet cities, Moscow would unleash its remaining missiles, including the huge single-warhead ICBMs that produce massive amounts of radioactive fallout, at American cities. In view of that possibility, according to these policy makers, Washington, with its existing array of missiles, would be reluctant to retaliate.

The danger emphasized by some politicians and defense experts was not so much that this actually would occur, but that if it were technically feasible it might be perceived throughout the world as a clear Soviet advantage. That perception could embolden the Kremlin to take greater risks to challenge U.S. global interests than Washington would take to defend them, it was argued. In other words, a U.S. threat to retaliate by destroying Soviet cities would not be credible, that is, it would not be believed by Soviet leaders and thus would not act as a deterrent.

To counter the Soviets' ICBM capability, U.S. defense planners concluded that the United States needed a weapon such as the MX that would be able to zero in on Soviet military targets and break up attacks aimed at America's ICBMs and other U.S. military installations while leaving American cities relatively unscathed.

Arms control advocates charged that this reasoning was not plausible. A one-shot attack intended to destroy U.S. land-based missiles would require the Kremlin to gamble its survival on the flawless execution of a highly complex plan, they pointed out. That would sharply deplete the U.S.S.R.'s arsenal. Moreover, they argued, either country's ability to destroy the other's missiles would only increase the risk that in a severe international crisis the other power might feel compelled to use its missiles before they were destroyed.

Deterrence Value of ICBMs

In the context of the war-fighting approach to deterrence, the ICBM leg of the strategic triad had these unique assets:

● Prompt destruction of heavily fortified targets (or "hard" targets in the Pentagon's jargon). Alone among the various strategic weapons, U.S. ICBMs combined the speed and accuracy needed to destroy Soviet command centers and missile silos on very short notice (little more than 30 minutes is needed for them to reach Soviet targets from launch sites in the United States).

● Flexibility/Accuracy. Land-based ICBMs, unlike existing submarine-launched missiles (SLBMs), theoretically could be used to conduct small attacks staged to achieve a specific political or military effect. (However, it was expected that U.S. SLBMs would rival ICBM accuracy by the end of the 1980s.) Like missile submarines, ICBM silos depend on radio broadcasts to receive their target instructions and firing orders. In this area, however, communications with submarines patroling the oceans in time of war still are considered much less reliable.

In sum, ICBMs are very reliable, readily retargeted and virtually assured of destroying their targets, in the absence of a viable anti-missile defense. They are well suited to military options that require a quick response and call for restricting damage to the intended target. However, if these attributes are to be useful in a war-fighting approach to deterrence, a U.S. ICBM force must be able to survive a Soviet first strike. Otherwise, the president would face strong pressure to put a vulnerable missile fleet on a hair-trigger. And in a case of a serious superpower confrontation, there might be pressure to initiate a pre-emptive nuclear strike.

At the very least, a missile designed for use in a measured retaliatory strike must survive long enough for U.S. decision makers to assess the gravity of the threat and be able to deliberate over their response.

How to Counter Soviet Strength?

The central issues surrounding the MX missile have been 1) whether to go ahead with production, and 2) how to deploy the heavy weapon.

MX supporters contend the MX is needed to counteract a growing threat from Soviet nuclear weapons. Opponents argue that the threat MX would pose to "hardened" Soviet military targets would elicit from Moscow a new escalation in the nuclear arms race. Thus they question whether the MX really would strengthen U.S. security.

Congress historically has been reluctant to deny a president a major strategic weapon that he said was essential. In recent years, lawmakers have backed many presidential requests for weapons that would threaten Soviet missiles. What made development of an MX system politically unpalatable was that many conservative as well as liberal members of Congress were alarmed at its huge price tag, particularly at a time of mounting deficits and a weak economy. And most members were skeptical about the adequacy of the various methods presented by Carter and Reagan for basing and protecting the missile. Their doubts were not calmed by defense experts, who themselves disagreed on the best type of basing scheme to use.

Despite the skepticism at home, Reagan in 1982-83 used the MX missile (which he renamed the "Peacekeeper") as a major bargaining chip in the U.S.-Soviet arms reduction (START) negotiations in Geneva. "Unless we demonstrate the will to rebuild our strength and restore the military balance, the Soviets, since they are so far ahead, have little incentive to negotiate with us," the president stated in his Nov. 22, 1982, arms control speech.

The debate on whether to develop the MX reflected a broader controversy over strategic defense strategy as developed by the Carter administration. By the late 1970s most U.S. national security analysts were warning that sometime between 1982 and 1985 it would be feasible for the Soviets to destroy about 90 percent of the slightly more than 1,000 stationary U.S. ICBMs with just a small portion of their missile force. According to these experts, Soviet intercontinental missiles launched from the U.S.S.R. would, by the mid-1980s, be capable of coming within 200 yards of hitting their targets in the United States.

MX Basing Mode Controversy

From the beginning, the most widely discussed issue surrounding the MX was the design of a basing method to protect the missiles from destruction by Soviet nuclear warheads.

All of the proposed MX basing plans submitted by the Carter and Reagan administrations prior to April 1983 were intended to prevent the Soviet Union from destroying U.S. ICBMs before they could be launched in a retaliatory attack.

Carter's 'Race-Track' Plan. The initial basing plan backed by the Air Force and the Ford administration, and formally adopted in 1979 by President Carter, was to hide a few hundred missiles among thousands of potential launching silos. To be sure of knocking out each missile, Moscow would have had to destroy all of the silos, the number of which could be expanded more cheaply than producing additional attacking missiles, it was argued. The theory was that Moscow might not have enough accurate warheads to demolish the MX fleet or, at worst, that it would have to use up most of its ICBMs to wipe out the MX missiles.

This theory was embodied in the so-called "race-track" basing plan approved by Carter in September 1979. Carter's design, endorsed by the Air Force (which would operate the missile), would have linked 23 launching sites by means of an oval-shaped track. Two hundred of these race tracks were to be scattered across 10,000 square miles in Utah and Nevada. Each track would contain one MX missile, which would be concealed in any one of 23 shelters along the race track. Each missile would move at random around its loop. Thus, the 200 MXs could be hidden in any one of 4,600 missile shelters. The purpose of this so-called MPS (Multiple Protective Shelters) system was to ensure that at least 100 missiles, with a total of 1,000 warheads, would survive any Soviet attack.

If the Soviets deployed more missile warheads than expected, the number of launch sites for each MX missile could be increased. If the Soviet missile force was doubled, the Carter plan called for adding an anti-missile (ABM) defense system to the MPS.

Carter's MPS plan presumed that a SALT II treaty would be in force. Thus, the plan included several features that were designed to help the Soviets verify U.S. compliance with the agreement. For instance, trap doors in the roof of all 23 shelter holes at each launch site could be removed periodically to let Soviet satellites observe that only one hole contained a missile.

Many groups and members of Congress were unhappy with the race-track plan. Traditional arms control advocates disliked the threat to future arms control agreements posed by mobile missiles (MX, under the MPS and some of the basing alternatives, would be the only U.S. land-based mobile missile; the Soviets' intermediate-range SS-20 also was mobile). Residents of Utah and Nevada feared the adverse impact that construction of the system would have on local water supplies as well as the economic and social strains caused by the tens of thousands of workers who would be needed to build the system. To non-specialists in strategic weaponry, the sheer complexity of playing a "shell game" with 100-ton nuclear missiles had more than a little bit of Alice-in-Wonderland improbability to it. And conservationists warned that the plan risked endless court fights over compliance with environmental laws. To many others — particularly lawmakers — the plan simply was too expensive.

Largely in response to these complaints, the Carter administration shelved the race-track system in May 1980, opting instead for a "linear" scheme that officials said would save land, money and manpower. Defense Secretary Harold Brown said the linear version thus would be more effective. It would use the same number of missiles and launch sites but would cost about $2 billion less and use about 20 percent less land. Manpower requirements would be reduced by 15-20 percent.

Although both the House and Senate rejected efforts to eliminate or cut the Carter administration's requests for MX development funds, doubts persisted in Congress about the basing system.

'Linear' Alternative Scrapped. With Ronald Reagan in office, the linear plan officially was scrapped Oct. 2, 1981. Instead, the president announced that the first few dozen missiles would be put in 20-40 existing missile silos that would be "superhardened" with additional concrete armor six-to-eight feet thick to ward off nuclear attack for a few years. At the same time, he said the administration would select a permanent system based on one of three long-term basing methods: large airplanes that could cruise for days and launch an MX in midair; silos thousands of feet underground, too deep to be destroyed by attacking missiles; or silos defended by anti-ballistic missile defenses.

The Reagan administration's technical arguments against Carter's mobile basing proposals was that an untrammeled expansion of the Soviet missile force could simply overwhelm the system. With enough warheads, Moscow could fire at all 4,600 planned launch sites, thus ensuring the destruction of all 200 MXs. "There is no way the United States can build [launch] shelters faster than the Soviet Union can build missiles," said Defense Secretary Weinberger at an Armed Services Committee hearing Oct. 5, 1981. That criticism also had been made by a blue ribbon panel established by Weinberger, and chaired by Nobel physics laureate Charles Townes, to review methods of basing the MX.

The Pentagon released an executive summary of the Townes panel report March 23, 1982. The full report, which had been submitted to the Pentagon in July 1981, was classified. "Although Multiple Protective Shelters can extract a substantial price [from an attacker]," the summary said, "the Soviet Union can readily compete in a U.S. shelter versus Soviet ICBM warhead race." But the panel also concluded that there was "no practical mode" of basing missiles on the ground that would guarantee survival from an enemy attack. It said the most promising technique for protecting U.S. missiles against destruction would be a fleet of large airplanes that could patrol for several days at a time and launch MXs in midair.

The Reagan administration's interim basing plan encountered considerable skepticism in Congress, which had been told frequently that existing silos could not be hardened against increasingly accurate Soviet warheads. The administration's basing plan "only places more lucrative targets in already vulnerable fixed silos," said Senate Armed Services

Committee Chairman John Tower, R-Texas.

In passing the fiscal 1982 appropriations bill for the Defense Department, Congress barred the use of any funds to superharden the existing Titan and Minuteman silos and ordered the administration to select a long-term MX basing mode by July 1983. Congress also denied funding for the air-launched MX missile option favored in the Townes report. Some defense-oriented members pressured the administration, as an alternative, to combine mobility — basically, Carter's MX shuttle system — with an anti-missile defense.

Despite previous congressional skepticism about using "hardened" existing silos for the MX, a top-level presidential commission recommended doing just that in a report made public April 11, 1983. *(Details, p. 92)*

Reagan's 'Dense Pack' Scheme. The Pentagon dropped the suggested airborne basing proposal in June 1982. The long-term plan initially selected by the Reagan administration, and formally announced by the president Nov. 22, 1982, envisioned clustering the missiles in a "dense pack" network. The plan, officially labeled Closely Spaced Basing, called for building a launch site for each of 100 MXs (100 fewer than Carter envisioned) 1,800 feet apart in a column 14 miles long at Warren Air Force Base near Cheyenne, Wyo.

In contrast to the race-track and linear designs, the dense pack configuration presented Moscow with only a small number of concentrated targets, but it relied on the self-defeating effects of the Soviet ICBMs themselves to protect the U.S. missiles. According to the theory behind the dense pack idea, the MXs would be close enough to each other so that the blast effect created by the first few attacking missiles to hit the MXs would destroy or disable all the other incoming Soviet missiles. (Existing Minuteman silos are three to five miles apart.) At the same time, the MXs would be far enough apart so that any Soviet warhead could destroy only one MX missile. The lethal effect of an exploding nuclear warhead on nearby warheads is called "fratricide."

Existing Minuteman silos reportedly can withstand explosions of up to 2,000 pounds of pressure per square inch. Under dense pack, the MX missiles were to be placed in very strong silos having resistance to 5,000 pounds of pressure per square inch from a warhead exploded next to it in the ground, and up to 20 times that much pressure from a warhead exploding overhead. Proponents of this basing mode argued that if an array of 100 such silos were attacked simultaneously by Soviet warheads, each with an explosive force equal to one million tons of TNT (one megaton), most of the U.S. missiles would survive and would be usable for a counterattack against the Soviet Union. The Soviet warheads aimed at the surviving MXs would be neutralized by the first Soviet warheads to explode. Either they would malfunction because of the intense radiation or they would be blown off course by the blast from the explosions.

These radiation and blast effects would fade rather quickly. But within seconds, the mushroom clouds of debris thrown up by the first explosions would deflect any later warheads that flew through them. Before the dust cloud dissipated enough to allow a second Soviet attack, the surviving MXs could be launched. In the first few minutes of flight, the MXs would be protected by heavy shields and would be traveling slowly enough to escape damage from the impact of the debris, dense pack planners reasoned.

Skepticism in Congress. Compared to Carter's race-track plan, dense pack had some political advantages. An entire force of MXs could be deployed in a 12-square-mile area. Since it could be located at any of several military bases, it would encounter less local resistance than either of Carter's proposals. Although few states wanted a prime Soviet missile target in their backyard, acceptance, if not enthusiastic support, came from Wyoming's Democratic Gov. Ed Herschler and the state's entire congressional delegation, all Republicans: Sens. Malcolm Wallop and Alan K. Simpson and Rep. Dick Cheney.

In its simplest form, dense pack also was touted as less expensive than any of the other basing methods considered. In mid-1982 the Pentagon estimated that it would cost $23.6 billion in fiscal 1982 dollars to base 100 missiles in a series of 100 shelters. The official estimate for Carter's MPS program was $33.8 billion in fiscal 1980 dollars. Some estimates of the cost of an airborne launching method ran to nearly triple that figure.

Despite concentrated lobbying by the Reagan administration, the dense pack scheme failed to sway members of Congress, whose principal objections to the program were its cost, its impact on the arms race and uncertainty about whether it would work as planned.

Some defense specialists, including Sen. Sam Nunn, D-Ga., argued that dense pack might run afoul of the limitations agreed to in SALT II. The unratified treaty, which both U.S. and Soviet leaders have promised to adhere to, prohibited enlarging the size of any existing missile silo by more than 32 percent. Defense officials conceded that Minuteman silos would have to be enlarged by more than that extent if they were to be superhardened and still accommodate the considerably larger MXs. However, they maintained the change still would be compatible with the treaty, since the actual launchers were movable, self-contained canisters that would hold the MXs and the associated launching equipment, not the armored silos that would house those launchers.

The silos of the much larger Titan missiles being retired would not have to be enlarged in order to be superhardened for the MX. However, because the Titan silos were constructed farther from Soviet targets than the Minuteman silos, MXs housed at those sites would have to carry a reduced number of warheads in order to reach the Soviet Union.

The Carter administration had argued that its MX shuttle plan did not violate the SALT ban on new, fixed launchers. But that case was somewhat easier to make than was Reagan's scheme because each missile under the Carter plan would have been shuttled at random on a regular basis among several launch sites, and the holes would have been much less heavily armored than existing missile silos.

Another potential problem was that construction of an anti-ballistic missile (ABM) defense for dense pack anywhere except at Grand Forks, N.D., would be inconsistent with the 1972 U.S.-Soviet treaty governing ABM systems. That pact, a part of the SALT I agreement, allowed deployment of up to 100 anti-missile missiles only at Grand Forks, where an earlier ABM system had been under construction around a Minuteman base.

MX Funding Blocked. On Dec. 7, 1982, by a vote of 245-176, the House deleted from the fiscal 1983 defense budget $988 million requested to procure the first five MXs.

In dropping the funds, the House rejected repeated administration warnings that a vote against MX would undermine the U.S. bargaining position in the arms reduction talks with the U.S.S.R. Unless the United States were committed to deployment of the MX, Moscow would have no incentive to agree to reductions in its ICBM force. "We must move forward with the MX to have any hope of achieving meaningful progress at the arms negotiations in Geneva," Reagan said in a letter to all House members the day before the MX vote.

During the debate on the measure, some MX opponents denounced Reagan's logic. "The history of the arms race shows that weapons which are intended to force the other side to the negotiating table simply add more momentum to the arms race," said Rep. Mike

Lowry, D-Wash. (After Reagan announced the dense pack plan, the Soviets responded that deployment of MX would lead to production of a "not inferior" weapon of their own.)

House Defense Appropriations Subcommittee Chairman Joseph P. Addabbo, D-N.Y., who sponsored the amendment to cut the MX funds, argued that production of the weapon was not yet necessary. To whatever extent the bargaining chip argument for MX was valid, he said, continued development of the missile would provide U.S. negotiators with adequate leverage.

Congressional critics also were disturbed about the novel and untested character of the dense pack theory. It was attacked by some members as violating the common-sense rule against putting all of one's eggs in a single basket.

Les AuCoin, D-Ore., likened it to the consequences of the decision by military chiefs in Hawaii before the Japanese attack on Pearl Harbor to cluster U.S. planes on the runways.

After the House rejected the MX funds, the Senate voted to restore them, but with the proviso that the money not be spent until Congress approved an MX basing method by concurrent resolution. In other words, either house could reject a basing method by majority vote. The amendment, offered by Henry M. Jackson, D-Wash., required the administration to report on dense pack and its alternatives after March 1, 1983. The final version of the defense procurement bill, which incorporated the Jackson amendment, contained $2.5 billion to continue research and development on the MX missile and its basing system. Of that amount, $1.7 billion was for research and development of the missile itself.

In its fiscal 1984 defense budget, the administration requested $2.8 billion to procure 27 MX missiles, $3.38 billion to continue development of the weapon and $390 million in related military construction.

1983 Presidential Commission Report

On Jan. 3, 1983, in accordance with a congressional directive, the president named a panel of 11 defense experts to advise him on the MX missile basing dilemma. The panel, formally named the Presidential Commission on Strategic Forces, was chaired by retired Air Force Gen. Brent Scowcroft, who had been national security adviser to President Ford. Among the other members were Harold Brown, Carter's defense secretary, and former Secretary of State Alexander M. Haig Jr. The panel released its report April 11, 1983.

Concluding that the MX was necessary, at least for the 1980s, the commission opted for what had been Reagan's "interim" basing mode plan: deploying the missiles in existing ICBM silos. At the same time, as part of what it stressed was an "inseparable package," the panel recommended a major effort to develop smaller, single warhead, mobile ICBMs by the 1990s. "In the meantime, however, deployment of MX is essential in order to remove the Soviet advantage in ICBM capability and to help deter the threat of conventional or limited nuclear attacks on the [NATO] alliance," the report concluded. The commission cited four principal reasons for going ahead with deploying 100 MXs (the number Reagan had sought).

Arguments for the MX. Many of the commission's arguments in favor of MX production were similar to those previously advanced by the Reagan administration.

● Impact on the START negotiations. Past experience indicated that "arms control negotiations — in particular the Soviets' willingness to enter agreements that will enhance stability — are heavily influenced by ongoing programs," the panel said. "It is illusory to believe that we could obtain a satisfactory agreement with the Soviets limiting ICBM deployments if we unilaterally terminated the only new U.S. ICBM program that could lead to deployment in this decade. Such a termination would effectively communicate to the Soviets that we were unable to neutralize their advantage in multiple-warhead ICBMs. Abandoning the MX at this time in search of a substitute would jeopardize, not enhance, the likelihood of reaching a stabilizing and equitable agreement."

● Impact on Soviet perceptions. "Effective deterrence is in no small measure a question of the Soviets' perception of our national will and cohesion," the panel stated. "Cancelling the MX, when it is ready for flight testing, when over $5 billion have already been spent on it, and when its importance has been stressed by the last four presidents, does not communicate to the Soviets that we have the will essential to effective deterrence. Quite the opposite."

● Impact on the strategic balance. "The serious imbalance between the Soviets' massive ability to destroy hardened land-based military targets with their ballistic missile force and our lack of such a capability must be redressed promptly," the report warned. The ability to respond to a range of Soviet threats, especially those directed at Europe, was essential. The MX would give the United States a "credible capability for controlled, prompt, limited attack on hard targets" to counter the Soviets' existing "massive ability to destroy hardened land-based military targets." According to the panel, such capability would make it harder for Moscow to calculate the U.S. response and, therefore, would deter Soviet "risk-taking at any level of confrontation with the West."

● Need to retain and modernize the ICBM force. Noting that the existing ICBM fleet was "aging significantly," the panel said the MX, with its greater throw weight, would be better able than the Minuteman to get through Soviet missile defenses by carrying decoys and other penetration devices. However, because the 100 MXs would replace Titans and Minuteman IIIs with comparable total throw weight, their deployment would not threaten stability, the commission argued.

Vulnerability Issue Downgraded. The panel dismissed Carter's mobile basing plan because of "significant" local political opposition and recommended against Reagan's dense pack alternative because it required newly developed and untested techniques for hardening the silos. Moreover, the anti-missile system required to defend dense pack's closely spaced missiles would violate the 1972 ABM treaty, the commission maintained.

At the same time, the commission sought to downgrade the widespread concern, particularly in Congress, that existing Minuteman silos were too vulnerable to be used for the MX. That concern had been evident in Congress' prohibition on the use of those silos as envisaged in Reagan's interim basing plan.

Although the panel acknowledged that "reasonable survivability of fixed targets, such as ICBM silos, may not outlast this century," it implicitly called into question the so-called window of vulnerability emphasized in the early days of the Reagan administration. In so doing, the commission reaffirmed the longstanding commitment to the strategic triad of forces by noting that the Soviets would have to count on the survivability of some U.S. bombers and submarines if they launched a massive attack on American land-based ICBMs. And Moscow also would have to take into consideration the possibility that MXs would be available for use "in any circumstances other than that of a massive surprise attack on the United States."

Over the longer term, however, the panel came down solidly in favor of developing a small, single-warhead, mobile missile, which it saw as the weapon of the future that might bring some stability to the nuclear balance if Moscow could be induced to shift its missile force from "unstable" MIRVs to single-warhead weapons.

The commission had openly presented its recommendations as a compromise between proponents of the MX and supporters of the small, single-warhead missile. "For the last decade," the commission's report stated, "each successive administration has made proposals for arms control of strategic offensive systems that have become embroiled in political controversy. . . ." Thus neither an arms control treaty nor modernization of the U.S. missile force had been possible.

"A more stable structure of ICBM deployments would exist if both sides moved toward more survivable methods of basing than is possible when there is primary dependence on large launchers and missiles," the report said. A smaller missile would be more invulnerable than the large, stationary, hard-to-conceal MX (or similar Soviet weapon); and a single-warhead missile would present a less attractive target by denying an attacker "the opportunity to destroy more than one warhead with one attacking warhead." In other words, the aim was to have a situation in which both Washington and Moscow had fewer warheads, but more targets than the other would be able to knock out.

Deterrence and Symmetry. In concluding that silo-based MX missiles would be as vulnerable to Soviet missiles as the existing Minuteman, the president's advisory commission abandoned the argument for MX that it would be a more "survivable" successor to Minuteman. Instead, deployment of the MX was justified on the basis of its military potency and political symbolism: as a counterweight to the Soviets' vast array of ICBMs even more powerful than MX. But by divorcing the MX from the quest for survivability, the commission opened up for future debate what long had been a key issue among defense and arms control specialists: whether deterrence required a rough symmetry in the U.S. and Soviet ICBM forces, that is, whether the United States needed missiles that were militarily and symbolically equivalent to the Soviets'.

If either side's strategic forces could be made more secure "by arms control agreements which lead both sides toward more survivable modes of basing than is possible with large launchers and missiles, the increase in stability would be further enhanced," the panel predicted. U.S. initiatives in that direction might prod the Soviets to do likewise.

But commission member Harold Brown listed some of the problems involved in trying to get the Soviet Union to agree to the arms stabilizing proposals presented by the commission, particularly the recommendation to alter Reagan's START proposal. Reagan wanted to

95

reduce the number of missiles, as well as warheads, on both sides. It was unlikely that the Soviets would easily give up their advantage in large, fixed ICBMs, Brown pointed out.

"Unless the United States can negotiate severe limits on the level of ICBM warheads, the number of single warhead missiles needed for a force of reasonable capability and survivability could make the system's costs, and the amount of land required, prohibitively great," Brown said.

The panel recommended that full-scale development of a 15-ton missile begin by 1986, with deployment by the 1990s. The cost of the new missile, as well as deployment of 100 MXs in existing silos, was estimated by the commission at $19.9 billion, compared to $27.9 billion for Reagan's dense pack plan.

"We should keep in mind, however, that having several different modes of deployment may serve our objective of stability," the report said. "The objective for the United States should be to have an overall program that will so confound, complicate and frustrate the efforts of Soviet strategic war planners that, even in moments of stress, they could not believe they could attack our ICBM forces effectively."

Is MX Really Needed?

Scowcroft, the commission's chairman, said the report was a "consensus" approach that had "the best chance" of success on Capitol Hill. Nevertheless, the report's recommendation for a return to a basing plan that had been attacked in Congress as vulnerable to Soviet attack, and its emphasis on a new generation of missiles, might "confound, complicate and frustrate" efforts to go ahead with MX production and deployment, conceded Scowcroft. However, Thomas C. Reed, vice chairman of the panel and secretary of the Air Force under President Ford, said Congress had been closely involved in the panel's deliberations in the hope of building solid support for the recommendations.

"It's a realistic package, but it's negotiable," said Sen. Jackson, who had offered the amendment to establish the panel. "I see the House and Senate going for the MX, but I don't think 100 missiles is the final number." Other members of Congress indicated that they would support a bipartisan agreement. "This [the commission report] is a straight-out political compromise," said Rep. Les Aspin, D-Wis., a member of the Armed Services Committee. "There's no good way to base the MX, so you might as well stick 'em into the old Minuteman holes as a short-term solution. It's a pretty good idea. It's time we settled the damn issue."

However, a few moderate members, including Sens. J. James Exon, D-Neb., and Mark Andrews, R-N.D., rejected support for any MX deployment scheme that did not promise to be invulnerable to Soviet attack.

And liberal members remained adamantly opposed to deployment of powerful, accurate missiles. In their view, deterrence resulted from the sheer destructive power of each superpower's nuclear arsenal and not from either side's detailed calculations of how particular nuclear war scenarios might be played out. From this perspective, the alleged advantages of Soviet ICBMs were inconsequential, given the thousands of U.S. warheads on bombers and missile submarines that would survive a Soviet attack on U.S. ICBMs. Efforts to copy the Soviet ICBM force thus would be a futile extravagance at best and likely would provoke further escalation of the arms race, as Moscow developed new weapons to offset the MX.

Liberals believed deployment of a U.S. "hard target kill" MX ICBM might encourage U.S. decision makers dealing with an international crisis to contemplate nuclear war in the hope that it would remain limited.

The commission's conclusions were endorsed by President Reagan April 19, and Congress had until mid-June to act under a deadline established by Congress in 1982.

Arguments for Smaller Missiles. Some of the issues raised by the commission had been discussed well before the panel reached its conclusions.

While the 1,049 existing land-based Minuteman and Titan missiles still posed a substantial threat to the U.S.S.R., the general policy of relying on the deterrent capabilities of giant ICBMs had by the early 1980s lost some of its credibility, particularly as an option in defending America's allies.

In an article in the March 13, 1983 *New York Times Magazine*, Adm. Stansfield Turner, director of the Central Intelligence Agency from 1977 to 1981, argued that rather than focusing on the power and number of ICBMs, defense planners should be emphasizing mobility and concealment, a conclusion similar to that reached by the MX commission. These are the defense features essential to the survivability of the U.S. deterrent, he wrote. Submarines, small cruise missiles and new radar-evading bombers were very mobile and difficult to detect, he emphasized, while large, land-based ICBMs were relatively immobile and almost impossible to hide and defend. Like ICBMs, cruise missiles and bombers were capable of striking hardened targets, and submarines would be able to do so in several years, he added.

Turner also claimed that ICBMs such as the MX were destabilizing to national security. Since they could reach their targets in minutes after launch, such weapons could be perceived by the Soviets as much more of an offensive threat than the relatively slow-flying cruise missiles and B-52 bombers. Moreover, without the large ICBMs, Washington and Moscow would not have to make split-second decisions on whether to launch their missiles in a first strike if they believed an enemy attack was imminent. In other words, the time allowed the Soviets to decide on their response to the launching of a MX missile would force them to react hastily, rather than to negotiate, said Turner.

Turner's concern was shared by Sen. John H. Chafee, R-R.I., a member of the Select Intelligence Committee, who also stressed the difficulty for both sides of having to track and verify small, mobile missiles. But in contrast to the Reagan commission's conclusion, Chafee said deployment of small, mobile missiles would add "a destabilizing element" to the arms race.

Sen. Malcolm Wallop, R-Wyo., previously had questioned the viability of so large a weapon as the MX and the basing structure needed to accommodate it, although he still felt it was necessary to deploy a few MXs as part of a counterforce strategy. Writing in the Feb. 6, 1983 *Washing Post*, Wallop anticipated much of the commission's thinking about the need to introduce mobile missiles:

> MX is the brainchild of wrong-headed thinking about nuclear war. It is born of the utopian thought that we can deter the Soviets by adding megatonage to our arsenal without figuring out what we want to do with it. The MX is too big and has too many warheads, and it probably has to be based in stationary silos that cannot be hidden or fully protected. . . . Since 1978, we have witnessed a series of attempts to do the impossible: to find a means by which our valuable, relatively immobile MX missile could survive in *known* locations. . . . We must finally recognize that the flaws of dense pack, and of every other deployment scheme for land-based missiles, exist because increasing Soviet missile accuracy has narrowed our strategic options. Since nothing fixed and undefended can resist modern attacks, land-based missiles either must be launched on warning or must be made mobile. Launch on warning is too dangerous, too prone to error. So we must go mobile.

The possibility of substituting a smaller, more easily movable missile for the large MX also was discussed by Richard D. DeLauer, under secretary of defense for research and engineering, in testimony March 2, 1983, before the House Armed Services Research and Development Subcommittee. DeLauer said it could be just as accurate as the MX. But he also warned that the missile could not be deployed until the 1990s. In the meantime, some MXs would be needed.

Bombers and Cruise Missiles

MX was not the only controversial weapon in the U.S. strategic nuclear arsenal. The future of the U.S. long-range bomber force was the subject of an equally heated and even more lengthy debate that began in the mid-1970s. The question was not so much whether a long-range missile-carrying, penetrating bomber was needed but, rather, what kind of plane would serve U.S. defense objectives in the 1990s and beyond.

While ICBMs provided a quick strike capability against hardened enemy targets, and SLBMs were considered invulnerable to attack, the manned bomber had the advantage of greater flexibility. And like the missiles, it could penetrate the most heavily protected military targets. It also was highly survivable once air-borne and beyond the reaches of enemy defenses. Bombers were flexible because they were manned by crews that could make changes in target directions, choose new routes and make decisions beyond the capability of computerized missiles.

Bombers on alert could be launched for survival, then directed to their target, recalled, diverted or dispersed as the situation developed and the president and his national security advisers directed. And bombers provided the best strategic force capable of attacking mobile enemy targets. However, ground-, sea-and air-launched cruise missiles increasingly are expected to supplement this capability.

While few defense planners or members of Congress questioned the need to retain a strategic bomber fleet, the B-1 — pushed by the Reagan administration as a replacement for the aging, nuclear weapons-carrying B-52s — encountered vigorous opposition because of its high cost and the possibility that development of a new bomber in the 1990s would make it outdated. Assessments of the B-1's usefulness were closely linked to development of the so-called "stealth" radar-evading plane and to the deployment of improved cruise missiles (the United States in 1983 had a commanding technological lead in cruise missile development) and Washington's assessment of future Soviet air defense capabilities.

After years of doing battle over production of the controversial B-1, Congress in 1982 went along with President Reagan's request to procure the first 100 planes. But doubts remained about the wisdom of that decision.

B-1 Planning: A Delayed Takeoff

The B-52 was engineered to penetrate Soviet airspace at very high altitudes. But the development of accurate Soviet anti-aircraft missiles forced the Air Force to re-evaluate its tactics. Throughout the 1960s, Strategic Air Command (SAC) crews were trained to fly the big bombers over Soviet territory only a few hundred feet above ground, where they would be nearly immune to detection by the then-existing Soviet radars.

The B-1 Mission. On the drawing boards since the late 1960s, the medium-sized, needle-nosed B-1 was designed for the mission the B-52 had been adapted for: to fly fast and at very low altitudes so it could elude radar detection. But the B-1 would have these advantages:

● In less than the seven minutes warning that might be available, the plane can sprint far enough from its airfield to survive the nuclear blast of Soviet submarine-launched missiles.

● The B-1 will be even harder to detect than the B-52 since it can fly lower (200 feet according to one estimate) and should give its crew a smoother, less fatiguing ride in dense, turbulent air close to the ground.

● By comparison to the slab-sided B-52, the streamlined B-1 presents a much less prominent target for Soviet radar. By one estimate, its "radar cross-section" is one-30th that of the older plane.

● In contrast to the B-52's speed of less than 600 mph, the B-1 can fold its wings back close to the fuselage and dash at supersonic speeds for short distances, further complicating an effective Soviet air defense.

B-1 and the Budget Crunch. Despite these advantages, the B-1 from the outset faced numerous problems. With the end of the Vietnam War, the B-1 became a surrogate target for critics of defense spending. They ridiculed the plane as an anachronism in the missile age — a monument to the generals' nostalgia.

But beyond the symbolism, questions about the plane's cost and technical performance engaged the attention of members of Congress who had no affinity for the Pentagon's ideological critics. In 1976, for example, the Air Force agreed to reduce the plane's top speed — originally set at twice the speed of sound — so that the engine could be simplified to cut costs. Congress was awash in conflicting cost estimates, but there

Intercontinental and Medium-range Bombers
(March 1983)

United States:

- 241 long-range B-52s: of these, 151 are B-52Gs, 16 equipped with air-launched cruise missiles (ALCMs), the others with short-range attack missiles (SCRAMs) and bombs. Unrefueled combat range: 8,000 kilometers (km). Maximum speed: 589 knots (kts). Each plane carries 4 bombs larger than 1 megaton (mt) each and up to 20 SCRAMs of 170 kilotons (kt) each. By 1990 every B-52G is to be equipped with 20 ALCMs. 90 B-52Hs, the latest model, serving as penetrating bombers and cruise missile carriers.

- 56 medium-range FB-111s; each carries up to 6 short-range SCRAM missiles.

- 100 long-range B-1Bs currently under production.Unrefueled combat range: 7,500 km. Maximum speed: 796 kts. Can carry ALCMs or bombs. First B-1Bs scheduled to be deployed in fiscal 1985, the rest by fiscal 1988.

- Under development: advanced technology bomber (ATB, or "stealth") currently scheduled for deployment in 1990s.

Soviet Union:[1]

- 100 TU-95 Bear, 45 Bison and 200 Backfire-B bombers. The Bear is the primary intercontinental bomber. Unrefueled combat range: 8,300 km. Maximum speed: 500 kts. Can carry bombs or air-to-surface missiles. According to the USSR, Backfire-B bombers are intended for combat in Europe and Asia, but also are capable of intercontinental missions. Unrefueled combat range: 5,500 km. Maximum speed: 1,100 kts.

- More than 600 Badger and Blinder medium-range bombers.

- Blackjack-A long-range bomber under development. This is a multiple-role aircraft, similar to the B-1B. Unrefueled combat range 7,300 km. Maximum speed: 1,200 kts. Expected to be operational by 1986-87.

[1] *Soviet figures are U.S. government estimates.*

Source: Secretary of Defense, *Annual Report to the Congress*, fiscal 1984 (Washington, D.C.: U.S. Government Printing Office, 1983); Joint Chiefs of Staff, *United States Military Posture*, fiscal 1984 (Washington, D.C.: Government Printing Office, 1983); Department of Defense, *Soviet Military Power* (Washington, D.C.: U.S. Government Printing Office, March 1983); *Jane's Weapon Systems, 1982-83*, ed. Ronald T. Pretty (London: Jane's Publishing Co. Ltd., 1982)

was general agreement that the cost of the planned fleet of 244 planes would total more than $20 billion. According to one widely cited calculation at the time, the price tag had risen from $41 million a plane in 1970 to $100 million six years later.

With the contract for the first three production copies of the B-1 scheduled to be signed in late 1976, opponents devised a plan to circumvent Congress' traditional reluctance to challenge the White House on a major weapons decision. By a vote of 44-37, the Senate had approved an amendment to the fiscal 1977 defense authorization bill that blocked the production contract until February 1977, thus allowing the winner of the 1976 presidential election to review the decision. The House had rejected a similar provision, and the amendment was dropped in the House-Senate conference on that bill. However, the Senate Appropriations Committee added the same provisions to the defense appropriations bill, and it then was enacted into law.

Carter Opts for Cruise Missile

In his 1976 presidential campaign, Carter had cited the B-1 as an example of an unnecessary weapon that should not be built. But his decision was not announced until six months after his inauguration.

On June 30, 1977, the president announced that instead of the B-1 he would modernize the U.S. bomber force by equipping B-52s with thousands of air-launched cruise missiles (ALCMs) — small robot jet-powered planes that can carry a nuclear warhead thousands of miles to within a few hundred feet of a target. The missiles could be launched from planes flying beyond the reach of Soviet air defenses and could be loaded with conventional or nuclear warheads. Unlike ballistic missiles, which follow a trajectory similar to an artillery shell, cruise missiles are able to maneuver and hug the terrain like a manned aircraft.

Carter Defense Secretary Brown insisted the decision favoring cruise missiles over the B-1 was based on a technical judgment that cruise missiles were more likely than B-1s to penetrate Soviet defenses. Carter planned to swamp Soviet defenses with thousands of ALCMs, which would be much harder to detect than the B-1. An ALCM according to one published estimate had about the same radar cross-section as a sea gull — much smaller than the B-1.

Critics warned that the slow-flying drones would be easy targets for an improved Soviet air defense. In particular, they warned that Soviet nuclear missiles, command headquarters and other small military targets

Submarine-launched Ballistic Missiles
(March 1983)

United States: 33 submarines; 544 SLBMs; 4,750 warheads

● 496 Poseidon C-3 and Trident I C-4 SLBMs on 31 Poseidon submarines. Each submarine carries 16 Poseidon missiles, except 12 that are modified to carry the more accurate Trident I SLBM. Poseidon SLBMs: range: 4,630 kilometers (km.); each carries 10-14 warheads of 40 kilotons (kt); to be retired in 1990s. Trident I SLBMs: range: 7,400 km.; each carries 8 warheads of 100 kt each.

● Trident II D-5 SLBMs, to be deployed on Trident (*Ohio*-class) submarines. Two Trident submarines currently deployed, each able to carry 24 Trident II missiles. Trident II missiles to be procured at the rate of 72 per year and deployed on all new Trident submarines, starting with the 9th, and retrofitted into the first 8; range: more than 7,400 km.; each carries 6-7 warheads of 330 kt each; scheduled for deployment about 1989.

Soviet Union:[1] 70 submarines; 950 SLBMs; 2,570 warheads

● 18 SSN-5s on 6 submarines; range: 1,400 km.; each SSN-5 carries 1 warhead in 1 megaton (mt) range.

● 352 SSN-6s on 22 submarines; range: 3,000 km.; each SSN-6 carries 1 warhead of about 1 mt. A new model carries 2-3 warheads of unspecified yield.

● 292 SSN-8s on 24 submarines; range: 8,000-9,000 km.; each carries 1 warhead of 1-2 mt.

● 28 SSN-17s on 2 submarines; range: 3,900 km.; each carries 1 warhead of unspecified yield.

● 240 SSN-18s on 15 submarines; range: 6,500-8,000 km. Three types, carrying 1, 3 or 7 warheads. Comparable to Trident II.

● 20 SSN-20s on 1 *Typhoon*-class submarine (larger than Trident), with a second launched; range: 8,300 km.; each carries 6-9 warheads comparable to Trident II.

[1] *Soviet figures for SLBMs are U.S. Government estimates.*

Source: Secretary of Defense, *Annual Report to the Congress*, fiscal 1984 (Washington, D.C.: U.S. Government Printing Office, 1983); Joint Chiefs of Staff, *United States Military Posture*, fiscal 1984 (Washington, D.C.: Government Printing Office, 1983); Department of Defense, *Soviet Military Power* (Washington, D.C.: U.S. Government Printing Office, March 1983); *Jane's Weapon Systems, 1982-83*, ed. Ronald T. Pretty (London: Jane's Publishing Co. Ltd., 1982)

easily could be protected against the undefended 600-mph ALCMs by anti-aircraft guns and missiles.

The Senate accepted Carter's decision by a margin of three to two. But in September 1977 the House voted to drop $1.4 billion in B-1 funds from the defense appropriations bill by a margin of only three votes (202-199), signaling trouble ahead.

Carter also requested the deletion of funds previously appropriated for B-1 production as part of a fiscal 1977 funding bill. But before the House took up that measure, portions of the tentatively agreed upon U.S.-Soviet strategic arms treaty (SALT II) were leaked to the press, including a provision to limit the range of ALCMs to 1,500 miles. Scenting political blood, B-1 proponents moved to keep the plane alive by rejecting the funding rescission sought by Carter. They said a 1,500-mile-range ALCM could not reach some important Soviet targets unless the planes launching them came well within the reach of Soviet jet fighters.

It took two tries in the House, but the rescission finally was approved in February 1978, after a bare-knuckled lobbying campaign of rare intensity for the Carter White House. (The supplemental contained several politically attractive programs that benefited hundreds of congressional districts.)

The 'Strategic Bathtub'

In the summer of 1979, Senate hearings on the proposed SALT II treaty generated a powerful wave of support for a more rapid defense buildup. And B-1 proponents had just the surfboard to ride it: the "strategic bathtub."

The concept was conceived in late 1979 and early 1980 by Gen. Richard H. Ellis, commander of the Strategic Air Command (SAC), as a way of highlighting Moscow's growing advantage in the relative power of U.S. and Soviet nuclear forces capable of destroying armored military targets, such as missile silos or command posts. A secret but widely discussed SAC study featured a graph representing projected changes in the relative capability of each superpower's forces. As new, accurate Soviet missiles entered service in the late 1970s, the curve dropped sharply to indicate a Soviet advantage. In the early 1980s, with air-launched cruise missiles projected to enter the U.S. arsenal, the curve leveled off. Not until the late 1980s, when the MX missile was due to enter service, did the line curve rise back to its original level. The overall shape of the line resembled that of an old-fashioned bathtub.

Only a new bomber would quickly overcome the problem of the "strategic bathtub," said Gen. Ellis, who favored enlarging the F-111 jet fighters already in service. It would cost only about half as much as the B-1, Ellis said. More importantly, the plane could enter service more than a year earlier than the B-1, he added. Ellis also cited a long-term reason for opposing resumption of B-1 production. By 1990, he told congressional committees, the B-1 would not be able to penetrate Soviet air defenses. The still-secret stealth plane could, but he feared that the cost of a B-1 program would slow development of the stealth bomber.

The House Armed Services Committee, however, seized the "bathtub" argument as a reason for resuming work on the B-1. It added to the fiscal 1981 defense authorization bill $600 million to prepare for production of a simplified version of the B-1 to serve as an air launcher for ALCMs. The House backed the move on May 14, 1980, by a margin of nearly three to one.

When the bill reached the Senate floor, several members offered an amendment earmarking $91 million to develop a bomber that could be ready by 1987 to carry out several roles: that of penetrating strategic bomber; missile launcher; and conventional heavy bomber. The Pentagon was to choose from among the B-1, the F-111 and an "advanced technology aircraft" on the basis of their relative cost and military effectiveness in those roles.

The 'Stealth' Funding Dilemma

What only a handful of senators knew was that the third option listed in the amendment was the so-called stealth plane that was supposed to be so much harder for Soviet radar to detect than the B-1. The stealth would:

● Provide a much smaller radar image than the B-1 since it would be shaped with fewer corners and because the big compressor fan for each jet engine would be concealed behind a curving air intake duct.

● The plane's skin would use materials that absorb some radar energy rather than reflect it back to the radar antenna.

The Air Force clearly was committed to developing a stealth bomber for the 1990s. The dilemma for Congress and the administration was whether to produce some expensive B-1s to replace the B-52s in the interim before stealth was in service. On May 21, 1981, the Air Force recommended to Weinberger that the Pentagon buy both 100 modified B-1s

($20.5 billion in fiscal 1982 dollars), which would enter service in 1986-87, and 110 stealth planes (estimated to cost $30 billion).

Throughout 1981 congressional critics of the B-1 sparred with the Pentagon over three issues: 1) whether cost estimates for a fleet of 100 B-1Bs (the latest version of the plane) had been understated (the Pentagon put the price of each plane at $200 million, but other estimates ran as high as $285 million); 2) whether the plane would be any more effective than the existing B-52s against Soviet air defenses; and 3) whether a stealth-type bomber could be in service about as soon as the B-1.

The critics cited secret data of the Central Intelligence Agency that maintained "there would be practically no difference" between the existing B-52 and the B-1 in terms of their ability to penetrate Soviet air defenses in the 1980s. Senior Air Force and Pentagon officials responded by insisting that the CIA analysis did not take into account changes made in the original B-1 design that made the plane much harder for Soviet radar to detect. For instance, the air intakes for the B-1's jet would be reshaped to make the new version 10 times harder for enemy radar to detect and 100 times harder to detect than the B-52.

Air Force and Pentagon officials also tried to knock down the argument that the stealth bomber could be in service almost as quickly as the B-1. They insisted it would require a crash program to field the stealth plane that quickly, risking cost overruns and perhaps forcing some technical decisions to be made prematurely that would have to be revised later at great cost. A central argument for buying an interim bomber was that the stealth plane was too big a technical gamble to count on having it ready to replace the B-52s by the end of the 1980s.

Moreover, DOD officials argued that if both planes were built, the Soviets would have to deploy a very expensive new defense system, which, though eventually able to stop the B-1, would be ineffective against the stealth.

Nevertheless, some members said the B-1's cost would threaten adequate funding for stealth. "There simply is not enough money to build both," said Joseph P. Addabbo, D-N.Y., chairman of the House Defense Appropriations Subcommittee and a longtime opponent of building the B-1.

B-52s and Cruise Missiles. Meanwhile, in December 1982, 15 B-52s became the first to be armed with cruise missiles. In April 1983 the administration said it would continue to buy ALCM-Bs while developing a new, more maneuverable cruise missile, reportedly having the stealth technology and a longer range than the existing model. The present air-launched cruise missile has a range of about 1,500 miles.

The growing importance of cruise missiles in the U.S. arsenal had significant implications for future arms control agreements. Small, concealable and quickly reloadable, the missiles could be a nightmare for surveillance and arms control verification procedures.

Reagan and the Nuclear 'Freeze'

Although many Americans voted for Reagan in 1980 because they supported his "get tough approach" to the Soviet Union, the president's uncompromising position on high defense spending and commitment to a massive military buildup had, by 1982, given rise to widespread anxiety about the direction of U.S. military policies. That concern was fed by the increasingly bitter tone in U.S.-Soviet relations, Reagan's initial reluctance to give priority attention to arms control and the White House's rhetoric about nuclear war, particularly the feasibility of fighting and winning a limited nuclear exchange.

Criticism of the Reagan administration's hard-line approach to arms control negotiations with the U.S.S.R. found expression in the so-called nuclear freeze movement that took hold in many parts of the country in the spring of 1982. Widespread doubt about the sincerity of the president's commitment to an arms control agreement, more than the merits of any specific U.S. policy, led to a campaign to place a freeze on the production and deployment of strategic nuclear weapons. In June 1982 more than 500,000 people rallied in New York City's Central Park to protest the arms race. Referenda calling for a nuclear freeze were adopted by voters in eight states, and similar initiatives were ratified by 11 state legislatures, more than 400 town meetings and 195 city councils in 1982.

Supporters of the freeze hoped at the very least to slow down development of some nuclear arms programs; they also sought to prod Reagan to move faster toward strategic arms reductions talks (START) with the Soviet Union.

Freeze backers contended that Reagan publicly addressed the issue of arms control only after being confronted with severe political pressure both at home and in Western Europe to moderate his anti-Soviet rhetoric and demonstrate serious movement on concrete arms reduction proposals.

Reagan had contributed to the anti-nuclear, and anti-American, movement in Europe by remarking to a group of newspaper editors in October 1981 that he "could see where you could have the exchange of tactical weapons against troops in the field [in Europe] without it bringing either one of the major powers to pushing the button." That statement was widely interpreted in Europe as a reflection of U.S. indifference to its allies' fate in the event of nuclear war.

The president temporarily regained the political initiative on the arms control issue in November 1981 when he unveiled his "zero option" proposal to bar deployment of all U.S. and Soviet medium-range missiles in Europe. This was followed by his offer of May 1982 to begin strategic arms reduction talks (START) with Moscow. Although these belated initiatives may have defused more widespread criticism at the time, the freeze movement had gained too much momentum to be stopped by the START negotiations.

The political beneficiaries of public dissatisfaction with Reagan's approach to arms control were the critics of the administration's basic premise that deterrence depended on a broad range of U.S. nuclear weapons systems that could be used to wage both limited and massive nuclear strikes. They sought to make the dangers of nuclear war, rather than Reagan's concentration on the size of the Soviet arms buildup and military threat, the focus of the nuclear arms debate.

Congressional Action and Reaction

Both in 1982 and 1983 freeze advocates in Congress rallied behind resolutions calling for "a mutual [and] verifiable" freeze to be followed by arms reductions.

The White House strongly opposed all freeze resolutions on the ground that they would prepetuate a nuclear balance favoring the U.S.S.R. The 1982 version (H J Res 521) was sponsored by House Foreign Affairs Committee Chairman Clement J. Zablocki, D-Wis. (A joint resolution, which has the force of law, requires passage by both chambers and the president's signature.)

To counter sizable congressional support for H J Res 521, the Reagan administration in 1982 lobbied vigorously to secure passage of a competing measure more attuned to its position. The substitute, sponsored by Rep. William S. Broomfield, R-Mich., called for a freeze at "equal and substantially reduced levels" of nuclear arms. The administration succeeded in deflating support for the Zablocki version when the House Aug. 5 voted 204-202 to substitute the Broomfield language. The resolution, somewhat inocuous by this time, then was passed, 273-125.

By all accounts, the administration's most effective argument in winning the last few votes for the substitute was that an immediate across-the-board freeze would jeopardize arms reduction talks under way in Geneva at the time. From that perspective, the administration's two-vote victory was an endorsement of its position, though not a very enthusiastic one.

Reagan supporters underscored the president's commitment to substantial arms reductions, as outlined in his START proposal. "I think everyone here is for a nuclear freeze," Rep. William L. Dickinson, R-Ala., told the House late in the 1982 debate. "They are for an end to the arms race. The only question is, on what terms?"

Zablocki's freeze language would end the arms race on the wrong terms, Dickinson warned, "lock[ing] ourselves into a position of inferiority vis-à-vis the Soviet Union."

But skepticism about the administration's commitment to arms control persuaded a number of members to vote for the Zablocki amendment. Les Aspin, D-Wis., who favored resuscitation of the SALT II treaty in preference to the freeze, was one of several members who explained his support of the Zablocki language as an effort to nudge the administration toward faster progress in arms control talks with Moscow.

The Republican-controlled Senate did not act on the 1982 measure.

A new version of the Zablocki resolution was introduced early in the 98th Congress. The House Foreign Affairs Committee on March 8, 1983, approved a freeze resolution (H J Res 13) calling on the United States and the Soviet Union to pursue a mutual and verifiable freeze and to include negotiations on intermediate-range weapons in the START process. The measure, drafted by Rep. Stephen J. Solarz, D-N.Y., did not endorse an "immediate" freeze but said one should be "negotiated."

As the committee was voting, about 4,000 freeze advocates from 43 states rallied outside the Capitol on behalf of the National Nuclear Freeze Campaign, while a smaller group organized by the National Coalition for Peace Through Strength gathered to protest a freeze.

Taking note of these events, Reagan repeated his opposition in a speech to the National Association of Evangelicals, delivered the day of the committee's vote. Warning that "simple-minded appeasement or wishful thinking about our adversaries is folly," the president added, "a freeze would reward the Soviet Union for its enormous and unparalleled military buildup."

The president's warning that an immediate freeze would lock in Soviet military advantages appeared to have some impact. The resolution came within a hair of being amended by the House March 16 to endorse Reagan's arms control approach. Nonetheless, the House, during 42 hours of debate, turned back several weakening amendments. The resolution was finally passed May 4 by a hefty margin of 278-149, but only after an amendment was adopted that could require suspension of a freeze agreement if it were not followed by mutual arms reductions within a specified period of time. Senate passage was extremely unlikely, and a presidential veto would be certain in any case.

Mandate for Arms Freeze?

Much of the congressional support for arms control and the nuclear freeze came from liberal and moderate members who favored substantial cuts in defense spending. They held that deterrence depended on the broad strokes, not the details. Each superpower, they argued, was deterred from using its nuclear arms by the simple fact that it would be devastated by the other's nuclear weapons. From that perspective, technical differences between the U.S. and Soviet nuclear arsenals became almost meaningless, within very broad limits.

Said Matthew F. McHugh, D-N.Y., during a seven-hour House colloquy on the 1982 nuclear freeze resolution: "We have become victims of the tyranny of numbers, not recognizing that at some point, the difference between 300 megatons and 3,000 megatons is largely irrelevant." A continued U.S. buildup to offset some imagined Soviet advantage, according to this argument, would simply elicit a corresponding increase in the Soviet arsenal.

A key theme among many freeze proponents was that Congress was obliged to accept the original freeze concept because of its extraordinary grass-roots support. "We are not here as leaders; we are here as followers," Norman E. D'Amours, D-N.H., told his colleagues, citing 50 towns in his state that had voted "overwhelmingly" in favor of the freeze in 1982.

"The public may not follow in detail all the ins and outs of debates about counterforce weapons and instability in the arms race," said Tom Harkin, D-Iowa. "But people do have a gut level understanding of what the issues are all about. They understand ... that the nuclear race is growing more and more irrational and dangerous."

Proponents of a freeze rejected the administration's argument that deterrence was made more credible by new weapons, such as the MX ICBM and Pershing II intermediate-range missile. Since any nuclear conflict was likely to escalate out of control, they argued, those weapons were extravagant at best. It would make more sense to freeze immediately, said Rep. Solarz, rather than spend "billions of dollars . . . in an effort to achieve absolute nuclear equality with the Soviet Union, when we probably will not be able to achieve exact equality and would not be significantly better off if we could."

Fear of Nuclear Conflagration. The driving force in Congress behind the freeze was concern that escalation of the arms race not only would be costly but also would increase the risk of a nuclear holocaust. By this reasoning, a freeze on U.S. and Soviet nuclear arsenals at their existing levels was imperative as a means of dampening U.S.-Soviet tensions caused by production of ever more sophisticated arms as well as research and development of new generations of war-fighting weaponry. The danger presented by new weapons was due to the combination of greater and greater speed and accuracy, enabling either superpower to destroy the other's weapons and command posts in a surprise attack.

"If we produce and deploy these dangerous new weapons," said Jonathan B. Bingham, D-N.Y. (1965-83), "you know the Soviets are not going to stand still. They are bound to respond with new and more dangerous systems of their own." The United States, in turn, would view the new Soviet arms as "intolerable threats," he said. "As weapons accuracy increases and as warning times shorten," Bingham warned, "both nations may be forced to adopt a launch-on-warning strategy," which would call for firing their missiles at the first sign of an enemy attack. Since missiles could not be recalled once launched, this would greatly increase the risk of nuclear war by accident.

"If we continue to play this game of we have to have a little more so they have to have a little more so we have to have a little more," declared Charles E. Schumer, D-N.Y., "we are sealing our own fate. 'Enough,' is what the people are saying. Forget the numbers, forget the throw weights, forget the abstract concepts. This is different."

Nuclear Stability or Soviet 'Advantage.' In presenting the anti-freeze position during the 1982 House debate, Minority Leader Robert H. Michel, R-Ill., rejected the whole image of an arms race as an accurate description of the U.S.-Soviet nuclear relationship. "The United States is not in a nuclear arms race," he said. "We are instead in a desperate, dangerous and deadly nuclear arms predicament brought about by 10 years of a Soviet nuclear arms buildup unanswered by the United States."

Broomfield added that Soviet advantages in two areas were especially perilous: the U.S.S.R.'s much more powerful force of multi-warhead ICBMs, and its monopoly of medium-range missiles based in Europe.

In the political atmosphere generated by the freeze campaign, Broomfield's allies were careful not to dwell on what would happen if Moscow took up Reagan's implicit dare to compete in an arms race. They proceeded instead from the premise that a demonstrated U.S. willingness to match any new Soviet weapons system would convince the U.S.S.R. to accept arms parity at much lower levels. If that assumption were made, Broomfield argued, "the single, clearest, easiest-to-understand difference between the two measures before us [is that] our substitute is for less; their resolution is for more."

An immediate freeze, on the other hand, would eliminate any Soviet incentive to reduce its existing arsenal, particularly in those areas where the Soviets enjoyed an advantage, administration supporters warned. And a freeze would have a direct and adverse impact on the U.S.-Soviet arms talks. "Is the Soviet Union likely to sit down and negotiate seriously in Geneva with an administration whose position has been repudiated by Congress?" Broomfield asked. "Do we want the Soviets to think they should hold out for a better deal from the U.S. Congress?"

Alternatives to a Nuclear Freeze

Several defense specialists from the center of the political spectrum sought a position between the administration and defense conservatives, on the one hand, and the freeze proponents, on the other. Among this group were several former Carter administration officials as well as moderate Republicans. Members of this group typically shared with the last several administrations the orthodox belief in "deterrence by detail." The freeze, they warned, would undermine U.S. bargaining leverage that might induce Moscow to accept significant mutual weapons reductions.

In general, the centrists viewed the existing U.S.-Soviet balance as much more acceptable than did the administration, and they did not share the Reagan Defense Department's evident suspicion of the arms control process.

However, barring agreed-upon weapons reductions, many members of this group supported the new generations of nuclear arms — the MX, the Pershing II and GLCMs — to offset corresponding Soviet weaponry.

Return to SALT II. Among the specific proposals that emerged from this group were suggestions to resurrect the SALT II treaty. Senate Foreign Relations Committee members John Glenn, D-Ohio, and Joseph R. Biden Jr., D-Del., were among those pushing for Senate approval. "We have already negotiated something better [than the freeze], and the Soviets have agreed to it," Biden told the Senate April 21, 1982. SALT II proponents emphasized that the pact would require Moscow to scrap about 250 of its existing strategic weapons launchers.

The relationship of the size of the U.S. and Soviet nuclear arsenals to the substance of the arms control negotiations was implicit in an article written by Gen. Maxwell D. Taylor, who served as chairman of the Joint Chiefs of Staff from 1962 to 1964. Criticizing what he called "the numbers fallacy" in calculating the strategic balance, Taylor wrote in the March 6, 1982 *Washington Post*: "Obviously, it is not numbers of weapons per se that will restrain Moscow. It is [the weapons'] destruction potential, which depends in large measure on their reliability in getting to target and their survivability in a combat environment. Thus, sufficient destruction potential, not numbers alone, should be the measure of adequacy for our forces, one based not upon what the Soviets have but on what our security is likely to require."

Mutual Guaranteed 'Build-down.' In an article appearing side-by-side with Taylor's, former Sen. Edmund S. Muskie, (D-Maine, 1959-80), who served as Carter's secretary of state in 1980, endorsed another approach to arms control negotiations: a "mutual guaranteed build-down of nuclear forces." Under that plan, also backed by Sens. William S. Cohen, R-Maine, and Sam Nunn, D-Ga., and by Rep. William L. Dickinson, R-Ala., the United States and Soviet Union would agree to eliminate from their deployed forces two nuclear warheads for each newly deployed warhead.

According to Muskie, a "build-down" would require that force modernization be accompanied by greater force reduction. As a result, Muskie wrote, "the American and Soviet military establishments . . . would be both liberated and constrained. They would have broad flexibility to choose which new systems to deploy, but they would have to decide whether modernization was worth the price. Presumably, as forces began to shrink, the military incentives would favor emphasizing the most survivable weapons, thereby promoting strategic stability."

The "build-down" approach was incorporated in an amendment to the 1983 freeze resolution offered by Elliott H. Levitas, D-Ga., and John

Edward Porter, R-Ill. It would have allowed members to vote for a reduction in nuclear arsenals while implicitly endorsing Reagan's decision to deploy the B-1 bomber and the MX. But their proposal was rejected by a 229-190 vote.

President Reagan endorsed the build-down approach in letters sent to a bipartisan group of senators and representatives in early May 1983. The president generally supported the approach recommended by his blue-ribbon panel on strategic forces. Congressional advocates of the build down had warned that their support for MX would depend on Reagan's endorsement of the Scowcroft commission's recommendations. *(Commission report, p. 92)*

In addition to endorsing the panel's goal of strategic nuclear stability through a build down, Reagan agreed to the following points:

● Revision of his proposal for reducing U.S. and Soviet strategic missiles. The purpose was to encourage both superpowers to rely on small, single-warhead ICBMs.

● Tying the number of MXs ultimately deployed to the outcome of arms control efforts and stating that the United States would not seek the ability to launch a surprise attack that would wipe out the Soviet force.

● Development of a small, single-warhead ICBM, as a complement to MX, as a matter of "high priority."

Reagan's endorsement of the Scowcroft commission's recommendations led the way toward deployment of the MX. The House May 24 and the Senate May 25 approved legislation that permitted funds to be used for MX flight testing and for housing the missile in reinforced Minuteman silos. During the MX debate, several members from each chamber warned the White House that their support for MX when the annual defense funding bills came before Congress would depend on the administration's good faith in pursuing arms control efforts.

The president followed up his assurances by announcing modifications in the U.S. position at the START talks. In a June 8 statement, Reagan said the United States would retain the proposed ceiling of 5,000 on the number of missile warheads, but would raise the ceiling on the number of missiles themselves, thus requiring a less radical reduction in the existing Soviet missile force. The new proposal brought the U.S. position more in line with the commission's recommendation that U.S. policy encourage a gradual shift in both arsenals away from large MIRVed warheads to smaller, single-warhead missiles.

TNF proposals, as well as his continuing emphasis on the need to beef up U.S. strategic defenses — all were part of the broader, ongoing discussion over how much is "enough"; whether the U.S. strategic triad of land-, air- and sea-based weapons should be retained, or modified; whether deterrence requires a rough symmetry in the U.S. and Soviet ICBM forces; and how much weight should be given to a weapon's sheer destructive potency and political symbolism.

Beyond sheer numbers of missiles, warheads and launchers, a host of other variables and qualitative factors must be figured into any calculation of the strategic balance in order to determine what is "equitable," sufficient and stable. Any acceptable arms control agreement must be based on an assessment of the survivability of each side's strategic forces and the ability of each side's weapons to reach a target through the other's defenses.

But accurate predictions about future weapons developments and the other side's intentions and perceptions are extremely difficult, if not impossible, to make. Moreover, defense experts themselves differ about the types of weapons to include in an arms control agreement and the kinds of limits to place on them. Technological advances by both nations, such as the development of modernized ICBMs, hard-to-detect cruise missiles and SLBMs, radar-evading supersonic aircraft and futuristic anti-missile weapons in space, have raised the alarming prospect that one side might resort to a dangerous policy of "launch on warning" to foil a perceived advantage by the other.

Perhaps more serious for the future of the nuclear balance and for the prospects of arms control was the state of U.S.-Soviet relations. To many observers there appeared to be a gradual return to the "Cold War" climate of East-West confrontation and a growing paranoia, accompanied by strident denunciations, on both sides. Reagan's reference to the U.S.S.R. as an "evil empire" in a March 8, 1983, speech, and the Soviets' consistently negative reaction to U.S. arms control proposals provided evidence of increasing mutual suspicion. Many Americans, listening to their president warn of the Soviet military buildup, remained deeply apprehensive about rising Soviet power and skeptical about Soviet intentions.

Chapter 3

THE ROLE OF CONVENTIONAL ARMS

A fundamental question of defense policy that has vexed the Reagan administration and all its predecessors since the beginning of the atomic age is: Why build up large conventional armies to fight a non-nuclear war when either superpower can destroy an entire city with just one of its thousands of nuclear warheads?

A few American defense policy observers doubt that the balance of U.S. and Soviet conventional forces really matters in an age of intercontinental nuclear missiles. Some argue that the resources and money now being committed to U.S. conventional forces at home and abroad ultimately will be needed to develop anti-ballistic missile systems and civil defense programs that can defend the United States against nuclear attack.

Others, with greater charity toward U.S. allies, maintain that it is the nuclear deterrent, not conventional weaponry, that keeps Western Europe free from Soviet domination.

Though perhaps unfamiliar with the complexities of strategic military doctrine, many members of Congress long have suspected that some conventional force commitments are futile in the nuclear age. Contributing to this view is the belief that any U.S.-Soviet war would be over in the 30 minutes it would take each country's ICBMs to obliterate the other. No recent congressional debate provides a gauge of how widespread such sentiment is in Congress. But in 1978 one of the senior defense "hawks" in the House invoked this argument to oppose construction of another nuclear-powered aircraft carrier. "A war with the Soviet Union would be bang, bang, bang," George Mahon, D-Texas (1935-79), told the House, "and what is left would be very little."

According to this view, the weapon of today and tomorrow is the intercontinental missile with multiple nuclear warheads. Neither the

American B-52 bombers nor the U.S. fleet of aircraft carriers would play more than a marginal role in any conflict with the Soviet Union.

Yet the U.S. defense effort has continued to be oriented toward conventional warfare. Although strategic weapons such as the proposed MX intercontinental missile are widely publicized, the share of the budget devoted to nuclear forces amounted to only 10.26 percent of President Ronald Reagan's fiscal 1984 defense budget request.

Conventional forces remain an important consideration in defense strategy because nuclear arms no longer constitute a feasible instrument of war. "The threat of massive [nuclear] retaliation was fully credible as long as the Soviet Union could not respond in kind," Secretary of State Alexander M. Haig Jr. said in an April 1982 speech at the Georgetown University Center for Strategic and International Studies. "As the Soviet Union's nuclear arsenal grew, however, this threat began to lose credibility."

The Joint Chiefs of Staff echoed this point in their 1983 military posture statement. The burden of deterrence gradually has shifted to conventional forces. To deter Moscow from using its own vast land, air and naval forces in Europe or the Middle East, the United States and its allies would have to field a conventional force strong enough to hold its own against a massive Soviet attack.

Some strategists, however, viewed conventional military forces as playing a much broader role than simply deterring overt Soviet aggression. As Haig put it in his Georgetown speech, the military balance casts "a shadow over every significant geopolitical decision. It affects on a day-to-day basis the conduct of American diplomacy. It influences the management of international crises and the terms on which they are resolved." With its preponderance of conventional forces, Moscow, according to this view, might be emboldened to step up attacks on U.S. interests around the world, Washington might become increasingly hesitant in defending those interests, and third countries might be more inclined to be accommodating to the Russians.

Perceptions of the Security Threat

The 1973 Middle East War and Moscow's involvement in Angola and other African countries in the mid-1970s made official Washington increasingly suspicious of Soviet global intentions. With it came a perception that U.S. interests were being jeopardized. But in the early post-Vietnam years, Congress and the American public became aroused only gradually. At that time, many U.S. leaders, including members of Congress, had held out the hope of a "peace dividend" — in the form of more individual benefits or lower taxes — after the Vietnam War ended.

Congressional hesitancy to commit American arms and military personnel to overseas trouble spots eventually was superseded by expressions of willingness to actively protect U.S. interests and commit more funds to defense.

Shocks to the Carter Administration

When Jimmy Carter entered office, his initial defense concerns in the area of conventional arms policy included the strengthening of U.S. forces in Europe and maintenance of the military balance in South Korea. However, Carter also promised to withdraw U.S. ground forces from South Korea and restrain the growth in the defense budget. Administration assessments of Soviet military power, while sobering, were less alarming in tone than those that had been made by President Ford.

Over the next two years, the president appeared to be relatively sanguine about U.S. national security issues, particularly conventional capabilities. As late as 1978 the Carter administration still was standing by a rather vague campaign pledge to cut the growth in defense spending by $5 billion to $7 billion. And the president succeeded in getting Congress to drop $2 billion appropriated for another nuclear-powered aircraft carrier. The president was sheltered somewhat from hard-line attacks on his defense policies as Moscow temporarily toned down its rhetoric and relaxed some of the policies that had conjured up the image of Soviet imperialism on the march.

By 1979, however, the Defense Department was getting more attention and more money. The additional funding was explained in terms of Carter's 1977 pledge to NATO to increase defense spending in real terms (after taking the cost of inflation into account) by 3 percent annually. The president sought to allocate the largest part of his fiscal 1980 defense request — some $50 billion — to conventional combat forces, with a strong emphasis on tanks, planes and artillery designed to offset Russia's larger forces in Europe. The request also reflected plans to augment supplies of arms and equipment stored in Europe that could be used by U.S. Army reinforcements in the event of an international crisis. Yet the key turning point in U.S. perceptions of the need to enhance conventional force strength would come later that year.

Closing the Post-Vietnam Book. By the end of 1979 — nearly seven years after the last U.S. combat troops had left Vietnam — a senior official in the Carter White House could tell reporters that the post-Vietnam syndrome finally was at an end. There no longer was serious talk of disengaging from overseas commitments or cutting defense spending.

World events that year had forced the administration to focus on security needs. An early goal of the Carter administration, that of reaching an agreement with Moscow on demilitarizing the Indian Ocean, was abandoned at about the time of the Iranian revolution in February. And in November, after Iranian militants seized the U.S. Embassy in Tehran, large U.S. naval forces were transferred to the Arabian Sea/Indian Ocean area. Soon after the Soviet occupation of Afghanistan in late December, administration officials announced that such deployments would continue essentially on a permanent basis.

Also during this period, Carter's pledge to withdraw U.S. ground troops from South Korea was shelved.

Response to Setbacks Abroad. With the events of that turbulent year in mind, Carter requested an $11 billion increase in defense spending for fiscal 1981. That request included $10 billion to organize and equip a sizable U.S. force that could be moved into the Persian Gulf or other trouble spot at the request of local governments. This later was designated the Rapid Deployment Force.

For the first time in 13 years Congress in 1980 actually increased appropriations for defense above the amount recommended by the executive branch. The $159.7 billion funding bill featured additions for military hardware, including an 18 percent increase for Navy fighter planes and a 17 percent increase for warships.

The Reagan Perspective

Not content with Carter's spending projections for defense, some of President-elect Reagan's conservative advisers in 1980 and 1981 called for much larger defense budgets to pay for a crash program of new nuclear weapons and expanded conventional forces. One group, represented by Sen. John Tower, R-Texas, chairman of the Senate Armed Services Committee, and other senior Republicans, argued that the Soviet's conventional forces posed a much more immediate threat to the United States than did the emerging nuclear imbalance.

During the presidential campaign, Reagan promised a U.S. defense buildup to provide a "margin of safety" with which Soviet threats could

Nonnuclear Weapons Production, 1974-82

Category	U.S. and Other NATO	U.S.S.R. and Other Warsaw Pact	Ratio of Warsaw Pact to NATO Forces
Tanks	9,000	20,800	2.3:1
Other Armored Vehicles	15,100	45,750	3.0:1
Artillery/ Rocket Launchers	1,650	14,650	8.9:1
Tactical Combat Aircraft	5,700	6,900	1.2:1
Major Surface Warships	151	95	0.6:1
Attack Submarines	60	61	1.0:1

Source: Department of Defense

be offset. But he provided almost no details of what his new defense program would entail.

Nature of the Threat. While Reagan's specific military priorities remained unclear well into his first year in office, the case for U.S. military expansion generally was made during and after his election campaign, particularly in relation to the perceived Soviet threat. Reagan and his advisers stressed that Soviet forces were better equipped than ever to launch a blitzkrieg-type attack, without the prolonged, visible preparations that would provide advance warning to the West. U.S. intelligence agencies maintained in 1982 that Soviet military forces and stockpiles had grown to such an extent that it would be possible for them to sustain a nonnuclear offensive for a considerable period.

Moscow retained its longstanding numerical advantage in conventional weapons, particularly armored ground forces. According to Defense Department data for the period 1974-82, Soviet weapons production outstripped that of the United States by substantial ratios: 2.3-to-1 for tanks, 3-to-1 for other armored vehicles and 8.9-to-1 for artillery and rocket launchers.

Meanwhile, the technological advantage on which U.S. forces had relied through the mid-1970s to equalize Moscow's numerical advantage in conventional forces had steadily eroded. Moreover, U.S. officials warned that the development of new weapons and equipment were broadening the threat represented by Soviet forces. This was especially the case with the U.S.S.R.'s navy, which was being equipped to allow it to maintain a powerful fleet at sea for extended periods.

Against this backdrop, Reagan officials maintained that the U.S. buildup was modest. "The pace of modernization ... [is] slower than would be desirable," said Secretary of Defense Caspar W. Weinberger in his fiscal 1983 annual report. "Nor can we increase the level of defense forces as much as might be prudent."

Conventional Buildup. After taking office, Reagan concentrated initially on modernizing existing equipment and improving the combat-readiness of U.S. forces in the field. But in fiscal 1982 and subsequent years, the administration's focus in conventional weaponry was on expansion of the Navy, which Reagan pledged to enlarge from roughly 450 to 600 ships. The procurement of two new *Nimitz*-class, 1,000-foot-long nuclear-powered aircraft carriers in fiscal 1983 was the most ambitious — and expensive — part of this program. *(Navy buildup, p. 139)*

For the other services, Reagan asked for additional funds for warplanes, missiles, communications equipment, tanks and other armored vehicles. The Pentagon planned no expansion of its force of 16 active and eight Army Reserve divisions until 1986 or 1987, when two more reserve divisions were to be organized, although small units were added to the existing divisions in 1982.

Air Force combat units were to be expanded from 36 fighter wings (24 active and 12 reserve) to 40 wings by fiscal 1986 (26 active and 14 reserve). (A wing contains three squadrons of 24 planes each.) There also was an acceleration of Carter's 1979 program to deliver ground units to overseas trouble spots by means of the RDF.

The Pentagon in 1983 expected to augment and upgrade its non-strategic nuclear weapons — nuclear artillery, short-range missiles, bombs and sea-based weapons — which might be employed on the battlefield or in ship-to-ship combat.

In nearly every case, the initial Reagan plan accelerated purchases of arms or equipment to which the Carter administration already had committed itself.

Defense Debate in Congress

Congressional critics of the Reagan defense program charged that it lacked any strategic rationale. They sought to cut back Reagan's five-year, $1.6 trillion military spending plan. Generally, however, they did not challenge specific items of the program in Reagan's first year. This may have been because members of Congress were encouraged by a variety of circumstances to concentrate more on the budgetary than on the strategic aspects of defense policy. In 1982 and 1983, however, the president did face a broad range of real or potential congressional challenges to his plans for a conventional military buildup.

Military Policies and Budget Cuts. Some members insisted upon linking defense cuts to changes in specific military strategies.

Congressional defense specialists, including some who were deeply committed to the basic thrust of Reagan's military expansion, in 1982 probed the administration's intentions on such questions as the shape of U.S. military plans for the Middle East. They questioned whether Soviet threats in the Persian Gulf region could be deterred by U.S. threats to retaliate against Soviet interests elsewhere. Should U.S. war plans for the Persian Gulf, for example, focus on repelling a Soviet invasion or foiling a local threat to the flow of oil? What was the mission of the Navy's carrier fleet? How quickly should stockpiles of ammunition and supplies be expanded to allow for a long conventional war?

These defense-oriented lawmakers, including Sens. Tower, Sam Nunn, D-Ga., and Gary Hart, D-Colo., had an impact on Reagan's military policies far beyond the scope of their specific criticisms and recommendations. Their personal authority and prestige often influenced other members who were less familiar with the mundane aspects of defense policy but suspicious of certain longstanding and fundamental premises of U.S. conventional war policy.

One of those premises was that the balance of U.S.-Soviet

conventional forces remained of real consequence in an age of nuclear missiles, a point emphasized in Weinberger's fiscal 1984 report to Congress. Another was that military alliances with NATO and Japan served U.S. interests despite allied opposition to other aspects of U.S. foreign policy and despite those countries' more limited financial commitments to national defense.

European Alliance Issues. Longstanding U.S. defense policies dealing with Europe, particularly the stationing of more than 300,000 American soldiers and airmen in Western Europe, was the component of U.S. conventional military strategy that generally faced the broadest political challenge.

In 1982 Rep. John J. Rhodes, R-Ariz. (1953-83), challenged the traditional U.S. commitment to Europe, which, he said, was based on the continent's pre-World War I position in the world. In terms of pure economic and military power, he argued, it had been vital to bar any outside nation's hegemony over Europe because of the European states' control of colonies around the world and their industrial and technological power.

By the mid-20th century, by comparison, Europe's power was "infinitesimal," Rhodes insisted. "Its colonial system is gone, and while its scientific and technological capabilities are indeed formidable, they are not in the dominant position which they occupied in the early part of the century."

Senate Armed Services Committee member Carl Levin, D-Mich., propounded a less radical critique. He supported a conventional defense of Europe, but alleged that the Pentagon routinely bad-mouthed NATO's defense strengths to justify inflated budget requests. The Pentagon replied that it did not exaggerate the Warsaw Pact's advantages over NATO.

'Military Reform' Movement. A much-publicized congressional "military reform" movement, conceived in 1981 by Sen. Hart and Rep. G. William Whitehurst, R-Va., was galvanized by a suspicion that the Defense Department often subordinated strategic policy judgments to bureaucratic interests.

As of 1983, some 80 members of both houses were organized loosely in a Military Reform Caucus. Co-chaired by Sen. Hart and Rep. James A. Courter, R-N.J., the caucus included, among others, Senate Armed Services Committee members Nunn and William S. Cohen, R-Maine.

Caucus members generally believed the existing conventional war strategy was unworkable, and sought to overcome what they regarded as Pentagon decision making skewed by such factors as the career interests of defense officials and the agenda of defense contractors. Yet the caucus deliberately did not draw up alternative policies. It functioned rather as a clearinghouse to help members explore ideas that challenged conventional wisdom, rather than as a lobby for specific changes in U.S. defense programs.

Most of the military reformers' doubts about strategy focused on the question of how future battles would be fought, rather than on the narrower question of where U.S. forces should be ready to fight. And they generally were concerned that the Pentagon was bent on procuring sophisticated new weapons that they perceived to be of dubious combat value. However, broader programs of the Reagan administration — naval expansion, strategies to counter Soviet adventurism, readiness and procurement procedures — also were probed.

Armed Services Committees. By contrast to the military reform movement, the Senate and House Armed Services committees generally were sympathetic to the administration's concerns. They shared the view that the 1980s promised to be a dangerous decade. Sen. Tower, who became chairman of Senate Armed Services when Republicans took control of the Senate in 1981, warned that the United States and its allies were threatened by "more powerful opposing forces — political, military, and economic" as well as "unfavorable trends in the East-West military balance."

Both committees were in agreement that the Reagan defense buildup was both affordable and essential. Expounding on this theme in 1982, the House committee said defense spending increases similar to those projected by the administration's five-year plan were "necessary to maintain the military forces required to protect United States interests throughout the world and ensure that the United States would not end up second best if it should become involved in armed conflict."

U.S. Defense Commitments

While the list of what areas of the world are "vital" to U.S. national security has changed through the years — South Vietnam, for example, was in that category until 1975 — there has been little alteration since World War II in basic U.S. foreign defense commitments. Most important are the NATO countries of Western Europe and Japan.

125

Spain Enters NATO

The Senate on March 16, 1982, approved a protocol (Treaty Doc. 97-22) authorizing the entry of Spain into NATO.

Spain officially became the 16th member of the NATO alliance on May 30 that year, after all other members ratified the treaty. Spain became the first new member since West Germany joined in 1955.

Spain formally requested membership in NATO in November 1981, and the NATO foreign ministers signed the treaty Dec. 10.

The United States maintained two active Air Force bases in Spain — at Torregon and Zaragoza. The two countries ratified a military and economic cooperation treaty in 1976.

However, as the time required for communications and travel has decreased with the advent of new technology, additional regions of the world have been designated by Washington as vital U.S. security concerns.

The Major Allies

The need to shield NATO's European members and Japan from Soviet political and military pressure has been a basic tenet of U.S. foreign and defense policy of every U.S. administration since World War II. Because of the Korean peninsula's proximity to Japan, that also implied a need to protect the security of South Korea.

NATO. When various members of Congress in March 1982 suggested a token withdrawal of U.S. forces to encourage other NATO members to spend more on defense, Reagan administration officials appeared to be at a loss to clearly enunciate precisely what was entailed by the U.S. commitment to Western Europe.

"I don't believe we could exist in the world with a Europe that was overrun by the Soviets," Weinberger told the Senate Appropriations Defense Subcommittee, whose chairman, Ted Stevens, R-Alaska, had criticized the cost to the United States of deploying more than 300,000 U.S. troops in Europe. "We have an enormous national interest in NATO as well as an interest that derives from a long history of shared traditions and friendships and similar values," he said.

The Defense Department has listed three major tasks that would confront NATO members should a war with the communist bloc ever break out: 1) fending off the Warsaw Pact's massive ground forces in Central Europe; 2) protecting the trans-Atlantic sea lanes across which hundreds of ships would have to carry supplies and additional U.S. troops; and 3) holding the alliance's northern and southern flanks — Norway and Greece and Turkey — to block Soviet end-runs around NATO's central front.

Japan, South Korea. Japan in 1983 faced growing Soviet air and naval strength centered at Vladivostok and Petropavlosk, in the eastern extremities of the U.S.S.R. And large, heavily armed ground forces of North Korea, whose government was committed to reunification of Korea, presented a continuing threat to the Republic of South Korea. In case of war in that area, both South Korea and Japan as well as Alaska and Hawaii would depend for supplies and reinforcements on sea lanes across the northern Pacific.

Israel. Another important country in the network of U.S. foreign commitments was Israel. The longstanding U.S. pledge to ensure the security of that country was based on emotional and cultural ties, rather than on the strategic importance of that country to the United States. In fact, Israel is so small that, in the event of war in the Middle East, U.S. forces would have to be able to move in quickly if they were to do any good.

Other Strategic Interests

The United States also has other overseas interests that, while definitely political and military in nature, in recent years have taken on critical economic importance.

Persian Gulf. A relatively new "vital" U.S. interest, dramatically underscored by the 1973 oil embargo, was access to the petroleum of the Persian Gulf nations.

Accounting for 30 percent of U.S. petroleum consumption in 1981, Persian Gulf oil became somewhat less critical to the United States than to Europe, which received 60 percent of its oil from that region, and to Japan, which depended on the gulf for 70 percent of its oil supplies. But because of domestic political and economic constraints in Europe and Japan, and the limited reach of those countries' armed forces, the United States had assumed the primary defense of U.S. and allied interests in

Southwest Asia. *(Details, see Rapid Deployment Force, p. 179)*

Seizure of gulf oil fields by Soviet forces, or their proxies, would be so catastrophic to the West that the Carter administration had developed contingency plans in case the Soviets ever attempted to move into that territory. However, most U.S. defense specialists considered a Soviet invasion to be the least likely threat to U.S. interests there. More likely was a takeover of one or more major oil-producing states by leftist or nationalist internal forces, as occurred in Iran. That prospect would be more difficult for the United States to deal with and would pose sensitive political problems as well.

Africa. Apart from potential threats to Persian Gulf oil, Pentagon officials and members of Congress warned that, in case of a grave U.S.-Soviet crisis, it might become necessary to protect tanker routes around the southern tip of Africa. Such shipments might be prohibitively risky in countries of southern Africa controlled by pro-Soviet governments having access to modern anti-ship missiles that could be fired from airplanes and patrol boats.

Those countries also might endanger U.S. access to minerals, particularly cobalt and chromium, that were critical to U.S. weapons production. More than 90 percent of the world's known chromium ore reserves were located in southern Africa.

Latin America, Caribbean. After the disclosure in 1979 that a Soviet army brigade was stationed in Cuba, the Carter administration was forced to recognize Cuba as a potential military threat. Officials argued that Castro could threaten sea lanes to and from U.S. Gulf Coast ports and send men and supplies to assist revolutionaries in Latin America.

The Reagan administration greatly accentuated fears that Cuba was a major threat to U.S. national security. "In peacetime, 44 percent of all foreign trade tonnage and 45 percent of the crude oil imported into the United States pass through the Caribbean," Weinberger warned in his 1983 defense report. "In wartime, half of NATO's supplies would transit by sea from Gulf ports through the Florida Straits."

Political developments in other Caribbean and Central American countries led the Reagan administration to regard the region generally as the "target of a concerted, Soviet-inspired penetration effort."

Military Planning

The Reagan administration's basic defense priorities were built on those formulated or continued by the Carter administration. Where there were long-standing U.S. interests threatened by unfriendly forces — particularly Western Europe, Japan and South Korea — U.S. ground and tactical air forces were permanently stationed to deter attack. Similarly, naval and amphibious forces had been stationed in the Western Pacific and the Mediterranean since the end of World War II and, intermittently, in the Indian Ocean during the 1970s. In 1979 the United States began to assemble its Rapid Deployment Force — military forces that could be sent quickly to trouble spots around the world.

Soon after taking office, the Reagan administration proposed a general strategy of "horizontal escalation," consisting largely of the application of pressure to peripheral Soviet interests — such as Cuba — in order to gain leverage in areas of more central concern to the Russians, such as Europe. *("Horizontal escalation," p. 148)*

Defending Europe

As of 1983 there was the equivalent of five U.S. Army divisions and 30 Air Force squadrons stationed in Western Europe.

The Reagan administration reaffirmed the major elements of previous U.S. plans for NATO. The immediate goal was to be able to fly five additional U.S. Army divisions and 60 fighter squadrons to Europe within 10 days "of a decision to deploy," perhaps in response to a conspicuous Warsaw Pact buildup or troop movement. Tanks, trucks and other heavy equipment for four divisions already were stored in Europe for their use; thus, only the personnel and lightweight arms and equipment would have to be ferried across the ocean on short notice.

While U.S. forces had been deployed in Europe since World War II, the perception of a growing threat to NATO from the Warsaw Pact induced a reassessment by defense planners of how best to defend Europe.

Maintaining Conventional Strength

As early as the 1950s American and allied military leaders realized that Warsaw Pact conventional forces had outstripped NATO forces in size and strength. In subsequent decades, the imbalance grew worse as the quality of Warsaw Pact weaponry improved and NATO's conventional strength was sapped by decisions to divert greater resources to domestic needs and, during the early- and mid-1970s, by declining economies in many of the West European nations.

Reviving an Old Option. The United States between World War II and the mid-1960s held a preponderance of nuclear weapons, and could hold

Conventional Forces Deployed in Europe

The following table indicates the size of NATO and Warsaw Pact armed forces and selected non-nuclear weapons deployed in Europe as of the first year of the Reagan administration.

Category	U.S. and Other NATO	U.S.S.R. and Other Warsaw Pact	Ratio of Warsaw Pact to NATO Forces
Troops*	2.6 million	4.0 million	1.5:1
Main Battle Tanks	13,000	42,500	3.3:1
Anti-tank Guided Weapon Launchers	8,100	24,300	3:1
Artillery/ Mortars	10,750	31,500	2.9:1
Armored Personnel Carriers	30,000	78,000	2.6:1
Attack Helicopters	400	700	1.8:1
Combat Aircraft	2,975	7,240	2.4:1

* NATO and Warsaw Pact forces deployed in Europe. In the event of a war, some of the Soviet Union's remaining 2.7 million soldiers would join the fighting, as would some of the 1.8 million U.S. troops not stationed in Europe.

Source: North Atlantic Treaty Organization, *NATO and the Warsaw Pact — Force Comparison*, May 1982.

the Soviets at bay by the threat to respond with strategic missiles to any Soviet aggression. But Washington throughout the period relied mainly on its nuclear arsenal to match the Soviet's strength. Once the buildup of Soviet nuclear forces in the mid-1960s made the American nuclear deterrent less credible, the United States began to rely on the so-called "flexible response" doctrine. That strategy was based on a mix of conventional and nuclear arms. Such an arsenal, with a greater variety of both types of weapons, was supposed to give the West greater flexibility in formulating defense tactics for dealing with Soviet threats.

President Reagan reaffirmed the age-old U.S. pledge to retaliate against the Soviet Union with strategic nuclear forces in the event of a Soviet attack on Western Europe. Under the strategy of "flexible response," however, such a threat derived its credibility from the fact that the United States had the option of responding to limited attacks with weapons of less destructive power than those envisaged under the former policy of massive retaliation. This linkage rested on a basic assumption that a threat to escalate a war was more credible, and hence more likely to deter an attack, the smaller the degree by which that escalation would increase the violence.

By this reasoning, if NATO forces were in danger of being overrun by an attack with conventional arms by Warsaw Pact countries, a threat to launch nuclear missiles based in Western Europe against military targets in communist bloc territory would be more credible than a threat of massive retaliation by U.S. ICBMs against Soviet cities.

The same reasoning applied to conventional weapons, and perhaps with greater force as the destructive power of such weapons could more easily be modulated.

Outmoded Tactics. In recent years, there has been considerable debate about the stationing of U.S. forces in Europe: what their role should be and how they should be used. The debate stemmed in part from the fact that U.S. armies historically (although not exclusively) held their ground by wearing opponents down in relentless, predictable campaigns.

Such "wars of attrition" involved few maneuvers by which an opponent might be suddenly surprised and defeated. Rather, an incremental measure of success or failure could be taken at any point in the battle on the basis of territory held or opponents destroyed.

Successful military operations of this kind required vast quantities of weapons with superior destructive power in order to pound the enemy along fixed fronts, as well as the industrial capacity to produce and supply these weapons. This was noted by defense writer Deborah Shapley in a 1982 article in *The New York Times Magazine*. She pointed out that attrition warfare had been practiced in "[t]he closing campaigns of the Civil War, World War I and World War II" in which "United States firepower ... rained down endless rounds of ordnance supplied by the industrial might of the United States."

The basic precepts of attrition warfare still are followed in some quarters of the American military today. However, since the end of World War II it has been an accepted fact that, in any conventional conflict with the Soviet Union, U.S. forces would be outnumbered. In lieu of the vast forces it once employed to overpower an enemy, the U.S. military in the postwar era had to enhance the firepower of its less numerous forces. Some analysts maintained that any current U.S. military strategy based on attrition warfare was bound to be inadequate.

High Technology Fills the Breach

With an eye toward the Soviet Union's large fleet of tanks and its troop superiority in Europe, the Defense Department under Reagan sought to give U.S. forces stationed in the NATO countries additional heavy equipment. And the success of tactical aircraft in the 1982 Falkland Islands war between Britain and Argentina and in Israel's invasion of Lebanon impressed the U.S. Air Force, resulting in a Pentagon decision to upgrade U.S. jet fighters.

Armored Hardware. In his fiscal 1984 report to Congress on the state of military forces, Secretary Weinberger noted that "the Army has embarked on the most extensive modernization and equipping effort in its history." Perhaps the centerpiece of this effort was the development of the new M-1 tank. Although it cost three times as much as the Army's mainstay, the M-60, planners insisted that the M-1 was needed to compete with the Soviet tanks' superior speed and power.

The Army also planned to reinforce its tank-hunting helicopter, the AH-1 Cobra, with the AH-64, also dubbed the Apache, a souped-up model that the Pentagon claimed was "capable of defeating all known or postulated enemy armor." The AH-64 could fight at night, in bad weather and in rough terrain.

The new helicopters were intended to work in conjunction with smaller U.S. Army helicopters that had lasers mounted above their rotor blades. The Army anticipated that these "scout" helicopters would hide behind trees and ridges, sighting their lasers on enemy tanks. The

Apaches then would lob laser-guided Hellfire missiles from several miles away, beyond the reach of the anti-aircraft defenses that would be protecting the Soviet tank columns.

Troop carriers were being redesigned to serve as combat vehicles. The M-113 personnel carrier, the Army's standard troop carrier, was to be replaced by a new one known as the Bradley Fighting Vehicle. Using weapons operated from inside the vehicle, infantrymen would be able to fight from behind five inches of armor alongside tanks and other mechanized weapons.

And to protect its armored and mechanized forces from air attack, the Pentagon planned to improve upon its self-propelled Vulcan anti-aircraft gun. Its new Division Air Defense Gun, known also as DIVAD and Sergeant York, would have greater range and accuracy at night and in bad weather by virtue of its radar-guided missiles. While the Vulcan was a 20mm gun, DIVAD would feature two 40mm cannon.

Tactical Aircraft. The Air Force intended to continue production of its two main fighter aircraft, the F-15 and F-16, through the 1980s. Of the two, the F-15 was designated as the "air superiority" fighter, equipped with a variety of electronic targeting systems to facilitate air-to-air or air-to-surface attacks at night and in bad weather. The Air Force was planning to modernize both planes. New versions of the planes (so-called "E" models) were being equipped for ground attack missions deep in enemy territory. Also being developed were bomber versions of these two aircraft.

The Air Force argued that it needed long-range missiles to wear down Soviet squadrons at a distance because of the Soviets' numerical superiority in fighter planes. For this purpose the F-15 carried a radar-guided, air-to-air missile known as the Sparrow. Funds to develop a new radar-guided missile (called AMRAAM) were requested for fiscal 1984. About half the weight of the Sparrow, the AMRAAM was intended to equip the F-16 as well as the F-15. Through a small, but powerful, computer in each fighter, AMRAAM was intended to make it possible for a single plane to shoot at several targets simultaneously, something not possible with existing radar-guided missiles.

Throughout the 1980s, the Air Force planned to commit large sums for new weapons and electronic equipment to improve the combat effectiveness of its planes against ground targets. One of these was an infrared viewing device, known as the LANTIRN, designed to help pilots navigate and find targets at night and in poor weather. LANTIRN would be complemented by an infrared-guided IIR Maverick air-to-surface missile and would expand the roles of the F-16 fighter and the fixed-wing anti-tank plane, the A-10. Both planes had been equipped with relatively uncomplicated weaponry.

The Move to Simplify

Many defense analysts were skeptical that such sophisticated military equipment and weapons would provide the surest protection for U.S. and allied interests in a war. Washington-based research organizations such as the Heritage Foundation and the Brookings Institution, the Council on Economic Priorities, a public interest research group based in New York, and the military reform group in Congress maintained that U.S. defense and combat planning was being determined by available technology. And costs were being driven up by the very nature of high technology attrition warfare — one-upmanship by hardware. Further, such complex and expensive weapons often failed to perform as advertised, and there was little confidence in military circles that U.S. forces could prevail by relying on these weapons alone.

In a critique of President Reagan's fiscal 1984 defense budget, Sen. Gary Hart, D-Colo., upbraided the U.S. military for defining quality as meaning "increased complexity, high technology for its own sake and competing with the Russians at their own games instead of changing the game on them." He argued that higher quality should mean tactical effectiveness and "not just expensive technology."

Deception and Maneuver. Hart's view had been influenced by the theories of combat advocated by retired Air Force Col. John Boyd. Boyd had argued since the early 1970s that, in defending against an attack by a much larger force, U.S. forces should plan to defeat the enemy by deception and maneuver. The goal was to make an enemy attack disintegrate through lack of coordination rather than by trying to destroy the enemy tank-by-tank or plane-by-plane.

Boyd's theory implied that, up to a point, the number and agility of tanks, planes and ships was more important than the ability of any weapon to destroy its Soviet counterpart one on one.

His theory, therefore, downplayed the combat value of expensive U.S. weapons such as the M-1 tank and the F-15 fighter. It argued that the sophisticated combat capabilities that drove up the cost-per-copy of such weapons would be swamped by the enemy's sheer numbers; the Pentagon never could afford enough of them. Moreover, the mechanical complexity of such weapons meant that only a fraction of the weapons would be combat-ready at any given time.

Proponents of Boyd's views, such as Defense Department analyst Franklin C. Spinney, proposed radical changes in U.S. weapons design. They called for relatively simple designs for U.S. combat planes, which would rely on their numbers and maneuverability to destroy enemy planes in dogfights, rather than on the sophisticated F-15's long-range, radar-guided missiles.

Over-designed Weaponry. Another target of unnecessary complexity in weapons was the M-1 tank. In 1982 Sen. Warren B. Rudman, R-N.H., a member of the Senate Appropriations Defense Subcommittee, suggested accelerating the modernization of existing M-60 tanks instead of relying so heavily on the new one. He calculated that eight M-60s could be modified for the cost of one M-1.

Rudman conceded that the M-1 was in many ways a fine tank despite its frequent need for refueling and troublesome mechanical problems. But compared with the estimated Soviet production rate of 250 tanks a month, the current M-1 production rate of 30 a month "doesn't seem like a great deal," he argued. "There's something to be said for having more armored vehicles."

Similarly, Sen. Barry Goldwater, R-Ariz., noted in 1982 that the Army's AH-64 helicopter was "one hell of a good helicopter. It just costs too much money." By the second half of 1981, the cost of an AH-64 had increased by nearly 40 percent because of inflation, engineering problems and contract disagreements between the Pentagon and the manufacturer, Hughes Helicopter Industries.

Sen. Hart expressed doubts about the helicopter's ability to differentiate between enemy and U.S. tanks in the confusion of battle and cited the lengthy period needed to launch its missiles, during which the aircraft would have to hover or refrain from maneuvering. The result would be a helicopter that was highly vulnerable to anti-aircraft missiles. Hart's alternative budget recommended that the Apache be replaced by the tested and proven A-10 fixed-wing, anti-tank aircraft.

Hart also sought to cancel the Bradley Fighting Vehicle, claiming it was poorly constructed for its task, difficult to transport and unsafe. The vehicle would fail as a troop carrier because it could not accommodate a full infantry squad, while its gun would be ineffective in the battle situations foreseen for it. Also, the armor required to make the Bradley more than just a personnel carrier would have to be removed before it could fit into a C-141 transport plane.

In early 1983 the press reported that the DIVAD anti-aircraft gun had performed poorly in tests against aerial targets. Hart claimed in his alternative defense budget proposal that the gun's radar-guided missiles could easily be foiled by maneuvering targets.

The Army denied the existance of these flaws, yet DIVAD's effectiveness also appeared to be jeopardized by improvements in Soviet weaponry. When DIVAD was designed, Soviet anti-tank helicopters carried wire-guided missiles with a range of about two miles compared with a range of about two and one-half miles for DIVAD's two cannon. But the newest Soviet helicopters carried laser-guided missiles with a range of up to five miles, similar to the range of the Army's AH-64.

Radar Pitfalls. Hart maintained that in its contingency planning for combat against the Soviet air force, the Pentagon relied far too much on long-range, radar-guided missiles, which were very complex and thus likely to break down. They also could be easily decoyed from their targets. Moreover, since the U.S. planes had to broadcast a powerful radar to guide the missiles to their targets, they would be unable to launch a surprise attack; the radar beam would act inadvertently as a homing beacon for Soviet anti-radar missiles.

Hart and others favored short-range missiles, like the U.S. Sidewinder, that home in on the infrared heat from an enemy plane without broadcasting a signal of their approach. Hart also suggested canceling all further procurement of the F-15 fighter and its Sparrow radar-guided missiles and purchasing instead the smaller, non-guided missile F-16 plane. He also proposed to cancel development of the AMRAAM radar missile.

New Tactics for NATO

Besides warfare by attrition, with its reliance on the superiority of individual weapons, U.S. and NATO strategy toward Europe concentrated on holding a fixed front along the border between East and West Germany. This defense plan was influenced by geography, politics and the relative military strength of each side. West Germany encompassed too narrow a strip of land to accommodate the battle technique of defense in depth, trading space for time or trading space for military advantage.

West German leaders were unwilling to plan for war on their own territory, and NATO's strength relative to the Warsaw Pact's was such that it was forced to deploy the bulk of its forces on the front lines. The result was a predictable, and thus vulnerable, defense.

It was this defense policy, however, that the U.S. Army, in cooperation with NATO, sought to improve. During the 1980s, the Army planned to promote among its combat units a new emphasis on force mobility and coordination and greater initiative on the part of individual commanders to anticipate enemy moves. These virtues would be embodied in a new tactical concept known as Airland Battle and its extension into the next century, Airland Battle 2000. The most conspicuous feature of Airland Battle for the early 1980s was a plan to attack behind enemy lines with radar-guided missiles.

Mobility, Coordination, Initiative. Many military leaders regarded the new Army weapons being developed, such as the Bradley Fighting Vehicle and the AH-64 helicopter, as enhancing troop maneuverability. Development of High Technology Light Divisions (HTLDs) — forces that were more mobile than standard heavy U.S. Army divisions, but not to the degree of those assigned to the Rapid Deployment Force — was begun in 1982. The first HTLD was the Ninth Infantry Division at Fort Lewis, Washington.

A key piece of equipment being developed for the HTLDs was the so-called High Mobility Multi-purpose Wheeled Vehicle, also known as the "humvee." In one hypothetical battle plan described in *National Defense* magazine in 1982, "it is visualized that the light vehicles will be transported by helicopters along with HTLD troops so that they can be landed together near enemy objectives. The force would attack, regroup, and move to a designated pickup point for helicopter movement out of the area."

In addition to mobility, Airland Battle entailed a high degree of force coordination — referred to as "synchronization" by the Pentagon. Such coordination was crucial if commanders were to be able to oversee operations on the front lines as well as behind them. Airland Battle 2000, for which more intricate maneuvering and second-guessing of the enemy was anticipated, would rely on even greater coordination.

Airland Battle was touted as an unprecedented scheme for interservice cooperation: the Air Force, for example, would be instrumental in supporting ground troops and carrying out its own behind-the-lines raids. The new plan also would involve significant cooperation with the NATO allies.

Yet the doctrine demanded considerable initiative on the part of individual commanders. Since the Airland Battle plan sought to surprise and disrupt the enemy, on-the-spot decisions, particularly regarding the timing of maneuvers, might be required of combat units cut off from a central command.

Preparing a 'Counterstroke.' The particular tactics envisioned under Airland Battle were drawn up in response to what U.S. military leaders believed would be the Soviet plan of attack. With its massive numerical superiority in troops and military hardware, the Soviet Union long had subscribed to a battle plan employing a series of troop layers, or "echelons," behind its front-line forces. Following an initial probe to test the strength of NATO defenses, second and third waves of Soviet forces would reinforce or replace the preceding units, matching fresh Soviet troops against exhausted NATO forces.

Rather than simply concentrating on holding the front line, NATO strategists pursued plans to neutralize Soviet bloc reinforcements. The result was a strategy calling for simultaneous attacks behind enemy lines. This constituted not merely a static defense but an offensive "counterstroke," to use the Pentagon's term, which was intended to throw the enemy off balance.

The idea received considerable support in the early 1980s from NATO allies, the Reagan administration and some members of Congress, notably Sen. Nunn of Georgia. Not the least of its virtues, according to its backers, was that it would, in the jargon of defense strategy, raise "the nuclear threshold" — the point at which nuclear weapons would be used during a war between the two blocs. With a more effective conventional strategy, NATO might be able to avert early use of nuclear weapons in a conflict with Warsaw Pact forces.

Interdiction by Guided Missiles. The strategy of attacking behind enemy lines would be based on the use of highly sophisticated radar-guided missiles to destroy enemy airfields, armored vehicle concentrations and vital communications and transportation points.

The U.S. "Assault Breaker' missile development program, conducted between 1978 and 1982 by the Defense Advanced Research Projects Agency (DARPA), had spun off a variety of complex weapons, many of them European-made. These included projectiles that break up into individual bombs and fall in a pattern to destroy particular targets such as runways and tank formations.

To guide these missiles, a radar guidance system called "Pave

Mover" was developed in the same period by DARPA. The *Armed Forces Journal* reported in 1983 that the radar system could "locate moving targets as small as a single tank at ranges greater than 150 kilometers." Radar was particularly crucial for the detection of mobile targets that could not be picked up and identified quickly enough by other surveillance techniques. The Army and Air Force shared jurisdiction over these programs, which were incorporated in the Joint Tactical Missile Program (JTACMS) and the Joint Surveillance and Target Attack Radar System (JSTARS) in the fall of 1982.

Tactics and Technology. Although Harold Brown, defense secretary in the Carter administration, said the strategy would help to spawn technological advancements in weaponry, critics of the missile interdiction plan, echoing the debate about tactics vs. technology that had affected other conventional weapons, charged that it was a product of the Pentagon's excessive reliance on technology. Even the proponents conceded that the plan's behind-the-lines interdiction tactic was not a new technique of warfare; the novelty was NATO's technological capacity to carry out the mission.

In 1982 the Pentagon's research and engineering chief, Dr. Richard DeLauer, was quoted by *Armed Forces Journal* as stating that, while new roles and cooperative agreements were anticipated for the military services under the missile strategy, "the technologists will have things well along before the organizational concepts are in order."

Critics on both sides of the technology question attacked the doctrine for ignoring the possibility that the U.S.S.R. might change its plans or that its technology might be up to the task of countering NATO's. Sen. Hart argued that "all of the complex technology weapons and the radar have already failed their tests, and the complex communications systems . . . are likely to fail in combat." Hart went so far as to call the plan a departure from "the Army's . . . adoption of maneuver doctrine," noting that it required centralized coordination of far-flung U.S. forces in preplanned scenarios. Such elaborate coordination, according to Hart, was unlikely to survive the confusion of actual battle.

Naval Expansion

The proffered solution of the Reagan administration for U.S. commitments outside Europe was to expand the naval forces, especially aircraft carriers and amphibious units, and to demonstrate and, if need be, apply power where there was little or no U.S. ground or air strength.

It viewed a Navy buildup as mandatory for U.S. security and global political commitments. These requirements made it necessary for the United States to control the major sea lanes, which in effect meant a large portion of the world's oceans. Navy Secretary John Lehman told the Senate Armed Services Committee in 1982 that the U.S. Navy would have to fight for control of the oceans in the event of war with the Soviet Union: "The growth of the Soviet global navy has eliminated the option of planning for a regionally limited naval war with the Soviet Union."

By the same token, Lehman asserted that a larger Navy would greatly contribute to the administration's goal of having enough naval muscle to mount an offensive against Soviet territory from many sides. That, he said, would "prevent Warsaw Pact concentration of forces in Central Europe by forcing them to defend and distribute their forces against maritime vulnerabilities around the entire periphery of Warsaw Pact territory."

Maintaining a Naval Presence

The Reagan administration emphasized the importance of being able to protect seaborne supply routes against the Soviets or any other hostile forces in regions of vital interest to the United States. But the presumed psychological impact of a dramatic U.S. naval presence also appeared to weigh heavily in the administration's Navy buildup policies.

The Pacific. The U.S. Navy maintained in 1982 that it no longer could plan to switch aircraft carriers from their regular Pacific stations off South Korea and Japan to the Atlantic if an international crisis were to develop there. An expanded Soviet Pacific fleet had more than 80 surface ships, 70 submarines and 100 long-range missile-firing bombers based in eastern Siberia. Accordingly, the Navy argued that the U.S. Pacific fleet had to be large enough to protect Japan, South Korea and the key sea lanes in the Pacific. That meant a force that could attack Soviet air and naval bases near Vladivostok and Petropavlosk.

In congressional testimony, Navy officials warned of the growing Soviet aircraft carrier fleet in the Pacific, particularly that of the carrier *Minsk* — a ship of the *Kiev* class, the largest in the Soviet navy — which joined the Pacific fleet in 1979. It was the second of four carriers planned for the Soviet fleet that was armed with 300-mile-range cruise missiles, helicopters and 10 short-range bombers. (The Soviets completed their third *Kiev*-class carrier in 1982.)

The Navy noted, by comparison, that most of the 13 U.S. carriers were able to carry about four-dozen bombers, compared to the Soviets' 10, and that U.S. planes had a longer range and could carry larger bomb loads. "There's no comparison between the two," one admiral told a Senate subcommittee in 1981, "but in the minds of the Japanese, there is." The implication was that a dependable U.S. naval presence in the region would dispel any perception that the Soviets held the upper hand and would help Japan and other friendly countries to resist Soviet pressure.

The Mediterranean. The Reagan administration maintained that another U.S. carrier fleet was necessary in the eastern Mediterranean to protect ships and planes bound for Israel and to provide support for Turkey and Greece, with occasional carrier reinforcements to support U.S. and European peacekeeping troops in Lebanon. A long-standing U.S. policy decision to keep two carriers in the region at all times was dropped in 1979 after the U.S. Navy transferred one of the ships to the Indian Ocean/Persian Gulf region. But if hostilities broke out in the Middle East, a fleet of at least four carriers would be needed in the eastern Mediterranean, according to U.S. officials.

With the departure of one U.S. aircraft carrier from the Mediterranean in 1979, the U.S. fleet in the region had been weakened dangerously, the administration warned. The Navy was quick to point out that the eastern end of the sea was within easy reach of missile-firing bombers based in the Soviet Union. And the Soviet Mediterranean fleet included missile-firing ships and submarines. Libya, another potential threat to Mediterranean stability, had more than 20 missile-firing naval craft, about 200 modern air-combat fighters and about 150 modern bombers.

Persian Gulf Interests. The Persian Gulf was another region of vital interest to the United States for which the Pentagon had drawn up contingency plans in the event of war, including preparations for sending in a rapid deployment force.

After the Iranian hostage crisis unfolded in 1979, the United States decided to permanently deploy at least one aircraft carrier in the Indian Ocean, and to back it up with a second carrier on a part-time basis. It also deployed a small Marine amphibious unit to the region on a temporary basis. Navy officials pointed out that unless these ships operated from the confined waters of the Persian Gulf itself, carrier-based bombers would have difficulty reaching the major oil fields. Yet the fleet was the only tangible symbol of the U.S. military commitment to the region.

The Caribbean. Cuba was well within range of air bases in the United States, but Pentagon officials insisted that, in the event of hostilities in the Caribbean, the Navy would have to divert a substantial number of ships from the North Atlantic to ensure that ships leaving ports in the Gulf of Mexico would be protected from Cuban air and naval attacks. According to Secretary Lehman, transporting reinforcements from southern U.S. ports to American forces in Europe could be delayed by as much as a month by Cuban harassment.

Modernizing the Navy

The Reagan administration's program to strengthen the Navy had the political advantage of being expressed in a simple slogan: "a 600-ship Navy." The Navy had 479 ships when Carter left office and 514 by late 1982.

Reagan's goal of 600 ships was based primarily on a Pentagon decision to deploy 15 aircraft carriers, four missile-armed battleships and enough amphibious ships to carry a Marine division and one additional brigade (about one-third of a division). The number of additional ships — submarines, cruisers, destroyers, escorts and supply ships — needed to accompany the carriers and battleships would bring the total to something over 600.

By 1983 the Navy had 13 carriers in operation, one battleship that previously had been in mothballs and barely enough amphibious ships for a Marine division. Thus, by contrast to the Carter administration's last five-year plan that called for a total of 80 new ships, the Reagan administration planned to build 124 ships during fiscal years 1984-88.

Aircraft Carriers. At the core of the United States' current naval deployments are aircraft carriers and accompanying ships, units known as carrier battle groups. The tactical aircraft transported by these groups provide the Navy with long-range offensive power.

After many years of Defense Department-congressional wrangling on the optimal size and means of propulsion for the carriers of the future, the Navy succeeded in winning a congressional commitment to construction of three more large, *Nimitz*-class, nuclear-powered aircraft carriers during the next two decades. The *Theodore Roosevelt*, funded by Congress in 1979, will join the fleet in 1987. Two more carriers were approved in 1982 at the urging of the Reagan administration on the basis of Navy estimates that buying two carriers at once would hold down their costs in the long run. These still-unnamed carriers are scheduled to be delivered sometime in the 1990s.

The addition to the fleet of the *Carl S. Vinson* in 1982 brought the total number of operational carriers to 13, and the three new nuclear carriers approved by Congress will mean a fleet of 15 since one of the older ships is to be turned into a training vessel. Congress in 1982 also voted to continue a program of completely rebuilding each of the eight oldest large carriers to give them 15 more years of usable life — the so-called Service Life Extension Program (SLEP).

Battle group deployment depended largely upon the military circumstances at hand. The regular stationing of ground and air units in some of the services, for example, the Army divisions and Air Force squadrons in Europe, was not part of naval operating procedure, which was less oriented to fixed fronts. However, there existed various descriptions of what constituted "normal" Navy deployment.

In 1982 four of the 13 available carrier groups were routinely deployed to meet U.S. military commitments in the Pacific, Mediterranean, and Indian oceans. The remaining carriers were either stationed off the Western and Eastern coasts of the United States, where their crews trained while waiting to relieve other carriers patroling in distant waters or undergoing maintenance in port.

Testifying before the House Appropriations Defense Subcommittee in March 1982, the Navy's director of program planning explained that current peacetime carrier deployment could be expanded to 10 or more battle groups, with two additional carriers each assigned to the Pacific, Mediterranean and North Atlantic in the event of war. With the anticipated 15 carriers, wartime deployment might consist of 13 battle groups, with two more in the Atlantic and one more in the Indian Ocean.

Carrier deployments, however, were subject to frequent adjustments, sometimes on very short notice. In the period since 1979, during which time two carriers were assigned to the Indian Ocean region, one on a part-time basis, additional battle groups occasionally were sent out. After the Israeli invasion of Lebanon in the fall of 1982, eight battle groups were deployed around the globe as extra naval forces were assembled in the eastern Mediterranean.

Cruisers, Destroyers and Submarines. Like naval deployments, the composition of a battle group varies with its mission and whether or not the country is at war. In peacetime, a carrier may be accompanied by one or two guided-missile cruisers (CG-47s), two or three guided-missile destroyers (DDG-51s), two or three other destroyers (DDs) and between one and three nuclear-powered attack submarines (SSNs).

These battle groups would be expanded in a wartime situation, combining as many as four carriers with eight cruisers, eight destroyers and four submarines.

Cruisers and destroyers are perhaps the most versatile ships in the Navy's fleet. They are responsible for protecting carriers from air and sea attacks. In addition to their missions with the carrier battle groups, both may be assigned to protect battleships. The DDG-51s also are used to escort amphibious forces and supply ships assembled in what the Navy calls Underway Replenishment Groups (URGs). Standard destroyers and less powerful frigates are used as convoy escorts.

In its shipbuilding program, the Reagan administration wanted to add to the fleet each year three CG-47 cruisers of the *Ticonderoga* class, which would establish a fleet of 33 cruisers by fiscal year 1988. About half the cost of each of these ships went to its Aegis air-defense system, a powerful, computer-driven radar designed to guide anti-aircraft missiles against attacks of supersonic cruise missiles. The CG-47 carried its own cruise missile as well.

Also equipped with cruise missiles was the smaller DDG-51 *Burke*-class guided missile destroyer, which also carried a smaller version of the Aegis anti-missile system. The shipbuilding program called for more than 60 DDG-51 destroyers by the end of fiscal 1988. These ships were expected to replace some 50 missile-armed destroyers and cruisers due for retirement in the early 1990s. To round out its inventory of supporting attack vessels, the administration sought 37 other destroyers and settled upon 100 as the proper number of attack submarines.

Congress had approved the major acquisitions for this segment of the naval buildup requested by the administration for fiscal 1983, allocating funds for cruisers, destroyers and two submarines.

Cruise Missiles. Despite the Navy's commitment to the future of the carrier, the cruise missile — in which Moscow invested so heavily as a means of checkmating the U.S. carrier fleet — had begun to substantially influence the shape of the Navy's fleet.

In the early 1970s, the carriers along with their air groups were virtually the only ships in the U.S. fleet that could attack a target at any distance. Nearly all other warships were designed to protect the carriers from air or submarine attack.

By the early 1980s, however, cruise missiles the size of torpedoes could be carried on nearly any seagoing ship and could strike sea or land targets hundreds of miles distant. The Navy was determined to take advantage of that flexibility to distribute its offensive power across most of the ships and planes in the fleet.

Reactivating Battleships. A reactivation of mothballed World War II battleships was intended partly to provide heavily armored "platforms" for dozens of cruise missile launchers. And the cruisers and destroyers, designed to protect U.S. fleets against the Soviet cruise missile force, also were to be equipped with long-range cruise missiles.

The Navy in 1981 proposed to take out of retirement four of its old battleships. The reactivated battleships would form the core of the Navy's main attack units other than the carrier battle groups. These were referred to as Surface Action Groups (SAGs). Each SAG was composed of one battleship, one CG-47 cruiser and four DDG-51 guided-missile destroyers.

While the total force of 15 carriers could not be in service until the mid-1990s, when the last of the new carriers would be completed, the Navy argued that, in certain situations, the recommissioned battleships could fill in to form battle groups of respectable power. Their merit lay in their relatively low cost and in the short time needed to modernize them. In response to critics who claimed the ships were obsolescent, the Navy pointed to the battleship's survivability and its ability to provide firepower for amphibious forces.

The first of the converted ships, the *New Jersey*, was recommissioned in December 1982. Congress in that year also funded the conversion of the *Iowa*. The battleships *Missouri* and *Wisconsin* were scheduled for modernization in fiscal years 1984 and 1985, respectively, although Congress in 1982 withheld funds to start work on the *Missouri*.

Other Ships, Missions. To implement an expansion of the amphibious lift capabilities of the Navy and the Marines, the Pentagon sought to augment its inventory of amphibious vessels. In 1982 the Navy had one Marine Amphibious Force (MAF), and defense planners wanted to be able to move a Marine Amphibious Brigade (MAB) as well, increasing lift capacity by one-third. In contrast to other air and sea transports, these amphibious craft allowed Marine Corps units to fight their way ashore against armed opponents.

Shipbuilding plans for 1984-88 called for 13 new amphibious ships, including a new class of helicopter carriers, called LHDs, that would carry about 2,000 Marines, 20-30 helicopters and a class of so-called landing ship docks (LSDs) designed to unload tanks and other combat vehicles on beaches.

The Navy also wanted more multi-purpose ships (AOEs) to act as supply ships for the carriers, oilers (TAOs) to shuttle between forward deployed ships and supply bases, and minesweepers.

Objections to Naval Expansion

There were numerous congressional complaints in 1982 and 1983 directed at Reagan's Navy buildup. And opposition was expressed to the Pentagon's apparent assumption of additional global commitments, particularly in the Persian Gulf.

Members looked upon the latter as a burden-sharing issue involving U.S. allies because the West European NATO countries and Japan were the primary beneficiaries of Middle East oil. Disaffection with the Pentagon's military planning for the Persian Gulf jeopardized support for the Navy's expansion since the permanent deployment of a U.S. fleet in the Indian Ocean was one of the main justifications for the increase. In March 1982 Sen. Ted Stevens, R-Alaska, charged that the naval buildup was intended to protect the supply lines of countries that were unwilling to defend their own interests. "Are we to become the navy of the world?" he asked. *(Burden-sharing issues, p. 165)*

More Smaller Ships? A debate about the likely shape of a future war at sea took place in 1982 when Congress considered the administration's request for expenditures for two additional nuclear aircraft carriers. Echoing a point he had made for years, Sen. Hart insisted that the $3.7 billion cost of one large *Nimitz* would be better spent on three smaller carriers.

In 1978, when President Carter was resisting efforts by the Navy and some members of Congress to build the *Theodore Roosevelt*, Hart had advocated a large fleet of smaller, less powerful aircraft carriers as an alternative. His rationale was that a larger fleet, spread around the globe, could better survive Soviet attacks than a few *Nimitz*-class carriers, even though the *Nimitz* ships were much more powerful.

Hart lost the first round of the carrier battle in 1979. But he continued to criticize the Navy's carrier construction policy. In 1982 he pointed out that the Soviet fleet included 260 submarines and 380 bombers, all equipped with anti-ship missiles. Even one missile, he said, could put a carrier out of action. "How much difference will just two more American carriers really make?" he asked. "We need to disperse our naval aviation onto a significantly larger number of ships — and two is not a significant number," Hart said. In any case, the cost of the big carriers would rule out increasing the carrier fleet beyond 15, he insisted.

Critics of Hart's position responded that Moscow had enough anti-ship missiles to attack a U.S. fleet of any conceivable size. According to the Navy, the only solution was to build ships with enough firepower to defend themselves and enough structural strength to survive combat damage.

Primary Navy Mission. Although Hart insisted that a smaller carrier could carry out all the missions contemplated for a *Nimitz*-class ship, he based that argument on his divergent view of the Navy's proper role in the 1980s and beyond. According to Hart, the Navy's most pressing mission, which would be vital in the event of a war in Europe, was to protect trans-Atlantic convoys against Soviet submarine attacks. Submarine hunting, Hart declared, was an inefficient use of large carriers, with their squadrons of fighters for shooting down airplanes and bombers to strike land targets. Given this premise, smaller carriers and more sub-hunting submarines were a better use of limited resources.

On the other hand, senior defense officials in both the Carter and Reagan administrations emphasized the aerial threat to the Atlantic supply routes. These were well within the range of Soviet missile-armed bombers based near Murmansk, in the northwest extremity of the Soviet Union. Accordingly, the Navy policy was to rely on the large carriers with their medium-range bombers, like the A-6E, and jet fighters, like the F-14 armed with long-range radar missiles, to battle Soviet planes and missiles and to neutralize enemy bases.

In a February 1982 *Washington Post* column, former Under Secretary of Defense for Policy Robert W. Komer attacked this aspect of the Reagan administration's naval policy. He insisted that the underlying reason for the Navy's insistence on large carriers was its more aggressive overall military posture, specifically the threat that such ships represented to Soviet land bases.

"Even if they could survive to launch such an attack," Komer said, "each carrier's offensive power at realistic ranges currently amounts to one puny squadron of 10 A-6 attack jets." Komer dismissed such an attack as "nibbling on [Russia's] maritime flanks."

Despite the criticisms of Reagan's carrier policy, Hart's position was not accepted by the Reagan administration or by a majority in Congress.

Land or Sea? Even among defense analysts who agreed with the administration on military priorities, land-based air power was viewed as a less expensive substitute for large carrier fleets.

Some analysts contended that jet fighters and radar warning planes based in Iceland and Great Britain could head off air strikes against Atlantic shipping from the Soviet's arctic bases.

Even if the United States decided to strike Soviet bases on the Kola Peninsula, where Soviet air and submarine attacks probably would originate, land-based aircraft offered more promise, according to Sen. Nunn, than the Navy's plan to send a large carrier fleet into the Norwegian Sea. "You can't possibly pull those four carriers in toward the Kola Peninsula without a secure Iceland and Norway," he said. "But if you've got a secure Norway and Iceland, why not do it with land-based" airplanes?

Challenging Soviet Interests

Beyond its pledge to confront military threats to U.S. interests around the world, the Reagan administration announced, without much elaboration, a twofold global policy of actively deterring Soviet military pressure and maneuvering or, failing that, minimizing U.S. vulnerability in the face of an actual Soviet attack.

The first element, which Pentagon officials dubbed "horizontal escalation," consisted of a plan to deter Soviet attacks against militarily vulnerable U.S. interests by threatening to retaliate against equally important, and militarily vulnerable, Soviet interests elsewhere.

The second element, termed "simultaneity" by military planners, was based on the Pentagon's assessment that U.S. forces had to be prepared for simultaneous combat on all fronts.

The two concepts constituted the Reagan administration's clearest break with Carter's nonnuclear defense policies and buttressed the administration's plans for naval expansion.

'Horizontal Escalation'

Defense Secretary Weinberger explained the so-called horizontal escalation concept in his 1983 annual report. "We might choose not to restrict ourselves to meeting aggression on its own immediate front," Weinberger said. "A wartime strategy that confronts the enemy, were he to attack, with the risk of our counteroffensive against his vulnerable points strengthens deterrence."

Weinberger subsequently hinted that a vulnerable Soviet point was its potentially fractious empire of satellite countries. But he gave no explanation of how the United States might stir up anti-Soviet elements to divert Moscow from other plans and strategies. Because of U.S. military preponderance in the Caribbean basin, however, some proponents of horizontal escalation hinted of threats against Cuba as one likely application of such a policy

Navy Secretary Lehman, one of the most combative senior defense officials in the Reagan administration, was the leading proponent of horizontal escalation. The Navy's aircraft carriers, ship-launched cruise missiles and Marine landing units were ideally flexible weapons for putting Moscow's interests at risk on all fronts, Lehman asserted. Horizontal escalation was a key element in the administration's commitment to "maritime supremacy."

'Simultaneity'

Senior Reagan officials also touted their so-called simultaneity policy as reflecting a basic difference between their strategy and the Carter administration's. Carter, they argued, was willing to accept a smaller U.S. force than was Reagan partly on the assumption that U.S. forces could be shifted from one theater of hostilities to another, dealing with threats one at at time.

Like horizontal escalation, simultaneity implied that any conventional U.S.-Soviet war would be fought on many fronts at once. But the concept took account of the possibility that a multi-front war could be forced on the United States by Moscow. In that event, Reagan defense planners said, Washington would not have time to shift forces from region to region. For example, Atlantic fleet commander Admiral Harry D. Train Jr. told a Senate Armed Services subcommittee in March 1982 that the Atlantic fleet was big enough only to carry out its assigned missions one at a time. "The forces needed to secure the Caribbean are also needed to ensure the security of the North Atlantic ... [and] the Mediterranean.

"At the beginning of hostilities, some of these forces may be deployed to the Indian Ocean and some in the Mediterranean or Caribbean," Train said. "The choice of the sequence [of battles] may belong to the Soviets."

Policies Questioned

Former Carter defense officials as well as some nongovernment analysts greeted these concepts with profound skepticism. A fundamental criticism of horizontal escalation was that, from the standpoint of U.S. national interests, destruction of peripheral Soviet client states would not offset the loss of Western Europe or Persian Gulf oil.

Robert Komer developed this view in his February 1982 article. He conceded that the Reagan team's planned 600-ship Navy could "sweep the Soviets from the seas and perhaps . . . deal with Soviet surrogates in Cuba, Angola, South Yemen and the like." But suppose "the Soviets responded by utilizing their great conventional force superiority to impose their will on Europe, to seize the Gulf's oil fields or to browbeat Japan and China into neutrality?" Komer asked. "The overall balance of power would turn against us decisively."

In a March 1982 interview in *The New York Times*, Barry Blechman, who served in the State Department during the Carter administration, worried that the only "horizontal" option that would counterbalance a serious Russian provocation was to strike Soviet territory. And "I cannot imagine the Soviet Union absorbing strikes against its own territory without retaliating against American territory," he said.

Withdrawal to the Sea? On Feb. 8, 1982, the day Reagan's fiscal 1983 defense budget was sent to Congress, Komer and several of his colleagues who served in the Pentagon during the Carter years, warned that the administration would not be able to defend NATO adequately and equip the RDF for possible action in the Persian Gulf if it also had to pay for the naval expansion associated with horizontal escalation. "By spending so much on shipbuilding to the neglect of other forces," they said, the Reagan administration seemed "to favor a U.S. withdrawal to the seas, letting the U.S.S.R. control Eurasia."

Komer maintained that Navy Secretary Lehman and Reagan's assistant secretary of defense for international security affairs, Francis J. West, fully intended that "maritime supremacy" should replace the strategy of defending Europe and Persian Gulf oil, partly out of frustration with allied reluctance to maintain adequate conventional forces of their own.

Harold Brown, Carter's defense secretary, offered a similar critique. He argued in a *Los Angeles Times* column that while "[t]he administration's . . . 'offshore' strategy, with its implied concession of the European mainland and Southwest Asia to a predominant Soviet influence" would perhaps save it the trouble of having to defend ungrateful allies, it would "not serve America well."

Despite reports that senior Army and Air Force officials were concerned that their services would be impoverished by the Navy buildup, there was no hint of such fears in their congressional testimony before the Senate Armed Services Committee.

But Gen. Wilbur L. Creech, chief of the Air Force's Tactical Air Command, doubted the feasibility of a horizontal escalation policy. "You can't just conceive of a land war where you're losing, and escalate to sea and somehow it balances," he told the panel in February 1982. A victory at sea would not make up for losing the land war, he emphasized.

Is it Affordable? Sen. Nunn challenged the wisdom of both the horizontal escalation and simultaneity policies by pointing out that even Reagan's large defense increases apparently would not buy a big enough force to carry out that policy. "I can't find any military service that considers itself available to horizontally escalate," he said.

In February 1982 senior military planners for each service told Nunn that the administration's projected five-year defense plan would leave them well short of the forces they would need to have a "reasonable assurance" of carrying out simultaneously all facets of national strategy. The services' "reasonable assurance" force goals were drawn up annually in the Joint Strategic Planning Document (JSPD).

The officials were speaking of the 1981 JSPD, which was based on Carter's policy, not the Reagan plan. But Nunn implied that, if the services fell short of Carter's requirements, they would be even more deficient in the context of Reagan's more ambitious policies.

Since the Reagan budget requests were unlikely to be realized, the horizontal/simultaneity strategy was unaffordable and, therefore, should be abandoned, Nunn maintained. "You're not going to have a continuous, indefinite buildup of [defense] resources to the extent Reagan is proposing."

Setting Priorities. While the administration did not explain in detail the precise link between the size of its proposed force and existing U.S. commitments, it was adamant that no smaller force could do all the necessary tasks. "If Congress decides to cut force structure," Lehman stated at a press conference in March 1982, "they must concurrently face up to cutting commitments. . . . We are no longer going to say, as [previous administrations] have in the past, that we can do more with less. We can only do less with less."

Sen. Nunn acknowledged that the threat to the Soviet Union of the horizontal escalation policy might have some deterrent value. But he charged that the Reagan administration had avoided setting clear priorities among the many U.S. conventional force requirements because of the open-ended nature of the horizontal and simultaneity concepts.

In that case, he warned, the White House would be unable to intelligently allocate congressionally mandated defense budget reductions. "If [the budget] wasn't put together with a sense of priorities, then can it be cut with a sense of priorities?" he asked.

Managing Arms Procurement

By greatly enlarging the defense budget, the Reagan administration was able to buy arms and equipment at a substantially more rapid rate than the Carter budgets had allowed. This applied even to ground and air forces, which did not experience the rapid growth planned for the Navy.

"Compared to the final defense plan of the Carter administration, our plan will provide ground forces with 29 percent more M-1 tanks, 34 percent more fighting vehicles and 25 percent more [anti-tank] attack helicopters," Under Secretary of Defense Fred C. Ikle told a Senate committee in 1982. This policy provided for modernizing the equipment of three and a half more Army divisions than would have been possible under Carter defense spending projections for the same period, he indicated.

The Defense Department under Reagan planned to purchase 4,800 fighters and attack planes for the Air Force between fiscal 1983 and 1987, compared with 4,200 under the last Carter defense plan. Continued production of the F-15 fighter, which Carter planned to end after 1983, accounted for more than two-thirds of the difference.

The F-15, along with the F-16, were the workhorses of the U.S. Air Force.

New Equipment Needs

Reagan's rapid growth in military hardware procurement was set in motion by a variety of forces. Foremost of these was the perceived need to strengthen existing forces by providing them with more advanced weapons and supporting equipment. The production rate was dependent on how much of a speedup was desired. Two salient examples of the administration's new acquisition policy was the proposed procurement of two new aircraft carriers and additional long-range transport planes. Both requests were approved by Congress in 1982.

The administration maintained that the prospect of earlier delivery accounted for the decision to buy more giant C-5 cargo planes instead of the smaller C-17s (formerly the CX), which was conceived expressly for Rapid Deployment Force (RDF) missions.

Replacements. Normally, when a force is being expanded, some of the existing units also must be replaced because of age. For instance, the Reagan plan for a 600-ship Navy was to include 96 cruisers and destroyers armed with long-range anti-aircraft missiles, a 20-ship increase in these two classes. However, because the Navy intended to replace more than 50 older anti-aircraft ships by the early 1990s, the Navy had to build about 70 of these ships to achieve the net increase of 20. If the average warship was good for 30 years of service, the Navy would need to build 20 ships a year to maintain a 600-ship fleet.

Aircraft presented a special case. Unlike ships and tanks, they crashed at a more or less predictable rate during routine training exercises. In 1981 the Navy and Marine Corps estimated they would lose 114 planes. With another 210 planes due for retirement, the Navy needed 324 new planes in fiscal 1982 just to break even.

Improving the Quality. In some cases the primary consideration behind a decision to begin production of a new weapon was to improve the quality of the weapon or to incorporate technological advances rather than to expand the inventory. For instance, some 7,000 M-1 tanks the Army hoped to receive by 1991 would expand its tank fleet from 10,000 to 15,000 (allowing for the retirement in the late 1980s of some obsolete models, including the main battle tank (the M-60). But more critical than expansion of the fleet, according to the Army, was the replacement of the M-60 with the M-1, which, unlike the M-60, was considered superior to the newest tank in the Soviet army.

Stabilizing Procurement

In addition to purely military considerations, the Reagan administration argued that its higher weapons procurement rates would make defense procurement more cost efficient. Pentagon officials maintained that a speedup in weapons procurement would lower the unit cost, attract more contractors and reduce weapons costs generally by increasing competition among arms manufacturers. In the event of prolonged international tension, the larger defense production base would permit a more rapid surge of weapons production.

Increasing Production Rates. A high production rate usually reduces a weapon's cost because contractors can achieve economies of scale. For

Multi-year Defense Contracts: ...

Since 1972 the Defense Department has been required for all practical purposes to buy missiles, planes and other expensive weapons one year at a time, with a separate contract for each year's purchase based on a budget request approved by Congress.

In 1981, however, Congress made an exception: it acceded to a request by the Reagan administration to buy certain aircraft under a multi-year contract as a way of holding down spiraling weapons costs.

Multi-year contracts usually cover the total number of weapons of a given type that the Pentagon expects to buy over a period of several years. Proponents of this approach contend it can reduce weapons costs substantially by allowing contractors to plan more efficient production runs and purchase raw materials and components in large lots at correspondingly lower prices.

Contract Imbroglio

The Pentagon routinely relied on multi-year contracts throughout the 1960s, with impressive, cost-effective results, according to one Navy study. However, Congress ended this practice for large ticket items in 1972 in the wake of one of the most spectacular contract imbroglios of the 1960s. Cost increases and construction delays plagued a $1.097 billion contract with Litton Industries of California to build nine large helicopter carriers; the Navy canceled four of the ships in 1971. An ensuing dispute highlighted the maximum cancellation penalty allowed under the contract — 10 percent of the contract value — which in this case amounted to $109.7 million.

The House Armed Services Committee in 1972 protested that contracts such as these committed the government to large future appropriations over which Congress had no control. Lawmakers refer to such arrangements as "backdoor spending" (technically called contract authority) because it is outside the normal appropriations process. In its consideration of the fiscal 1973 defense

fiscal 1983, the administration planned to acquire certain weapons, including the F-15 and F-16 jet fighters, the AWACS radar plane and the Sidewinder air-to-air missile, at a more rapid rate than had prevailed in the past. This was expected to reduce weapons costs by allowing contractors to buy components in larger, more economical lots and by spreading fixed overhead expenses for a given period over a larger volume of arms and equipment.

Multi-year Contracts. Production contracts covering a period of

... No Panacea for Cost Overruns

authorization, the Armed Services panel had banned contracts with a cancellation ceiling of more than $1 million unless specifically approved by Congress. In 1975 the cancellation ceiling was raised to $5 million, but this still effectively ruled out multi-year contracts for major weapons.

A Viable Option?

Congress, however, has continued to allow multi-year contracts for relatively inexpensive, mass-produced items. In its version of the fiscal 1982 defense authorization bill, the House Armed Services Committee proposed raising the cancellation ceiling to $100 million for proposed contracts covering purchases of a weapon for up to five years. It required certain criteria to be met, including: 1) a likelihood that multi-year contracting would reduce the total cost of the project; 2) a high rate of procurement during the contract period; 3) a low risk of contract cancellation; and 4) a low risk that the item would encounter technical production problems. The final bill incorporated a modified version of the House provision, allowing for a cancellation ceiling of $100 million.

In 1982 the Senate and House Armed Services Committees took another look at the practice of multi-year procurement of major weapons. The Senate committee approved a multi-year plan for the Army's Blackhawk troop-carrying helicopter and other weapons, but added a proviso requiring 30 days prior notice to the committee of any multi-year contract on weapons programs other than the Blackhawk.

The House committee directed its criticism at the Navy, which, the panel said, had proposed multi-year contracts for four planes that would be bought in such small numbers that no real economies of scale could be achieved. The committee disapproved those multi-year proposals and denied all funding for them.

several years, while increasing the immediate costs of the weapons, may yield similar economies in the long run. In 1982 the administration sought to stabilize and reduce the costs of production of such military hardware as Navy oil tankers, NAVSTAR navigation satellites and the Army's Blackhawk troop-carrying helicopter by means of multi-year contracts.

Since the Reagan administration planned to buy some of these weapons in larger numbers than had Carter, lower costs-per-copy would not necessarily lead to a net reduction in the budget requests for these programs. However, for the volume of weapons the Carter administration had expected to purchase, Reagan administration officials claimed the faster production rates and multi-year contracts would have cut the unit cost by more than $3 billion between 1982 and fiscal 1987.

Procurement Faces Budget Cuts

While the weapons portion of the military budget long had been a target of liberal critics of recent U.S. defense policy, concern over the fast pace of Reagan's arms buildup became widespread in Congress by 1982. Senate Budget Committee Chairman Pete Domenici, R-N.M., and his House counterpart, Rep. James R. Jones, D-Okla., were two of an increasing number of prominent conservative and middle-of-the-road members who insisted that the growth in procurement funding had to be slowed.

Cuts in the Pentagon's $90 billion weapons procurement budget request accounted for about half the total congressional reduction in the fiscal 1983 defense appropriations bill. And weapons purchases were targeted for large budget cuts again in 1984. In part, this reflected congressional concern about the projected federal budget deficits in fiscal 1985 and beyond. Unlike appropriations for pay and benefits or operating costs, arms procurement funds require expenditure of money over a period of several years as long-running weapons contracts are fulfilled in stages. Therefore, trimming the procurement budget contributes to a reduction in the deficit in future years as well as in the current fiscal year. *(Budget process terminology, box, p. 16)*

The administration sought to project a sympathetic attitude toward the deficit problem. As evidence of its careful oversight of the weapons procurement process, Deputy Defense Secretary Frank C. Carlucci told the Armed Services committees in 1982 that he and Defense Secretary Weinberger had rejected six of 16 major weapons systems the services wanted to shift from research into production in fiscal 1983.

Procurement Starts and Stops

The most economically efficient and politically feasible time to stop the procurement of an arms programs is in the research and development (R&D) stage, before large expenditures have been committed to prepare an item for production and before the project has amassed political constituencies through the jobs it brings to various states and members' congressional districts.

Cut Now, Save Later. In a February 1983 review of possible budget reductions, the Congressional Budget Office (CBO) considered the effect of terminating three weapons R&D programs. While savings in fiscal 1984 would not be great, the estimated savings in later years was substantial.

The first proposal was to cancel a project under the Army Helicopter Improvement Program (AHIP) to modernize the first 16 of several hundred small observation helicopters designed to aid the new AH-64 Apache attack helicopter in hunting tanks.

Another plan involved the McDonnell Douglas Corporation's C-17 transport plane that was designed to transport large combat equipment to potential overseas trouble spots and to land them on primitive airstrips. The plane was tailored to support the RDF in areas near the Persian Gulf, where there were few large airfields.

Despite much skepticism on Capitol Hill, Congress in 1982 approved an administration request to buy more C-5 transports for the immediate future, but to continue development of the C-17, which the Pentagon wanted as a replacement for the older, and smaller, C-130 and C-141 transports due to be retired in the early 1990s. But CBO warned that the C-17 was too big, and thus too expensive, to replace the smaller planes. Cancellation of the C-17 would save more than $3 billion over five years and billions more in later years, when most of them were to be purchased. *(Contract issue, box, pp. 160-161)*

As for the Navy's plan to replace its fleet of aging destroyers, the CBO warned that cost projections for the DDG-51 might be optimistic. With 60 ships planned, and a production rate reaching five per year by 1988, CBO suggested dropping the program, increasing slightly the production of CG-47s (to four a year instead of three) and developing a new, cheaper ship to replace the vessels becoming obsolete.

Cancellation Costs. While stopping a weapons program early on may save money, arresting a big contract after some development has occurred can be very costly — which accounts for the congressional squeamishness about approving multi-year contracts and high ceilings on cancellation payments to contractors.

One such cancellation was urged in Sen. Hart's alternative defense budget for fiscal 1984. He proposed to rescind the $7 billion, fiscal 1983 appropriation for two additional *Nimitz*-class aircraft carriers and require the Navy to design a much smaller and less expensive ship that would carry anti-submarine planes. Apart from the merits of his idea, Hart's proposal to cancel two ships already under contract faced a major obstacle: a hefty penalty — possibly as high as $1.5 billion, according to House Appropriations Defense Subcommittee Chairman Joseph P. Addabbo, D-N.Y.

Stretching the Buy

Another technique of budgetary restraint involves putting off planned expenditures until future years. "Stretching the buy" — reducing immediate budget costs by buying the same total number of weapons but over a longer period of time — is a time-honored practice of Congress as well as the Defense Department, whose five-year projections of weapons purchases rarely have been realized.

Reagan's actual fiscal 1984 budget request, submitted in January 1983, included several dramatic examples of "stretch-outs" when compared to the 1984 requests that were projected in January 1982 along with the fiscal 1983 budget. The president in 1983 sought procurement of only 720 M-1 tanks instead of the 1,080 projected a year earlier, and a total of 72 F-14 and F-15 fighters instead of the projected 90 planes.

Since lower rates of purchase had prevailed in the past for these weapons, Congress appeared likely to go along with Reagan's request to slow the procurement rate for these and other programs in his defense budget.

Minimum Production Levels. The administration's proposed fiscal 1984 purchase of 48 F-15 fighters was above the annual rates of 36 and 39 planes that were funded the previous two fiscal years, and the Pentagon planned to step up the rate to nearly 100 planes annually by fiscal 1986. The increase was intended partly to equip a planned expansion of the Air Force and partly to replace about 120 jets of 1950s vintage that were assigned to protect U.S. airspace against an enemy bomber attack. But according to the CBO, the F-15's manufacturer, McDonnell Douglas, could achieve an efficient rate of production with only 30 planes per year. The fighter thus was a good candidate for "stretching out."

In another case, the Pentagon's 1984 request for 130 DIVAD anti-aircraft tanks was the same as that projected in the preceding year's budget, and it was some $77 million cheaper. Yet the CBO estimated in October 1982 that the tanks could be produced efficiently at a rate of only 96 tanks per year.

Overhead Costs. In each of the "stretch out" examples described above, contractors' overhead costs would remain relatively fixed but would be spread over a fewer number of weapons each year. Thus the cost-per-copy (and the total cost of the program) likely would go up, even though the appropriation for fiscal 1984 and for each additional year of production would be lower. This policy, therefore, conflicted with one of the Reagan administration's most publicized defense goals: reducing unit costs by stabilizing annual procurement rates at levels that were high enough to be efficient.

Readiness

Cutting the procurement portion of the defense budget was an attractive prospect for members of Congress because the alternative was to cut funding for operations and maintenance of the armed services, including training, which had a direct impact on the combat-readiness of forces in the field.

In the year before Reagan took office, "readiness" — preparedness for combat on short notice — had become an issue of great significance in the Defense Department, in Congress and in the media. The new administration was strongly committed to spending money on defense manpower in an effort to make the all-volunteer system work. Reagan also placed a high priority on a number of unglamorous items that directly affected the ability of combat units to mobilize quickly for war: ammunition, spare parts, routine overhauls and training time.

Precise numbers were secret, but most military observers believed that all the services were far short of the ammunition inventories they would need to fight a protracted conventional war.

One dramatic example was the shortage of air-to-air missiles in the Navy and Air Force. When the carrier *Nimitz* was replaced in the Indian Ocean by the carrier *Eisenhower* in the spring of 1980, it had to transfer some of its Phoenix missiles in mid-ocean to the outgoing ship. Members of the House Appropriations Defense Subcommittee complained that missile stocks were so low that too few of them were fired in training exercises to give servicemen a realistic, combatlike experience.

Sustaining Combat Strength

The Carter administration's budget projection for fiscal 1982 contained additional funds to ameliorate the chronically inadequate spare parts budgets of the past. Like its predecessor, the Reagan administration insisted that the combat readiness of existing units had a higher priority than either equipment modernization or force expansion. But Reagan

In Purchasing Military Hardware . . .

Constituent pressure has been a factor, sometimes an overriding factor, in shaping defense department procurement policies. Contractors peddling weaponry often rely on lawmakers from states where they have factories or subcontractors to protect Defense Department hardware purchases from budget-cutters and defense critics.

In 1981 Rep. Thomas J. Downey, D-N.Y., a member of the House Armed Services Committee from 1975 to 1979, observed in retrospect, "You can identify almost all the members [of the committee] by who they're representing."

Members of Congress say that using defense money to bolster key industries back home is not just a matter of "pork-barrel" politics. They argue that it is important to keep a stable and diverse industrial base available in case the nation needs to mobilize for war. Once an aerospace, shipbuilding or specialty steel company has laid off skilled workers and neglected to modernize, they argue, it loses its competitive edge and its ability to gear up in an emergency.

For example, in 1982 debate over what military transport plane the Air Force should purchase to expand its cargo fleet, the battle lines in Congress were determined as much by state and local concerns as technical merit or cost considerations.

Reagan requested funds that year to begin buying 50 Lockheed C-5 transport planes to join the 77 bought in the late 1960s. But in an unusual effort by a major defense contractor to overturn a Pentagon decision, the Boeing Corp., located in the state of Washington, sought to enlist congressional support for the idea of buying a fleet of 747s instead. Boeing argued that buying second-hand planes owned by the distressed commercial passenger airline industry would provide adequate airlift for the military at far less cost than the acquisition of more giant C-5s, built by the Lockheed Corp. in Marietta, Ga.

Regional Loyalties

On Capitol Hill, the airlift battle was waged primarily by members with a direct constituent interest in the award of the contract. Sen. Sam Nunn, D-Ga., a military specialist on the Armed Services Committee and friend of the Pentagon, obviously was protective of Lockheed's interests. In the House of Representatives, fellow Georgians Ed Jenkins, D, and Newt Gingrich, R, were the leading advocates of the C-5.

Sen. Henry M. Jackson, D-Wash., led the congressional effort in behalf of the Seattle-based Boeing Corp. Jackson, the ranking Democrat on the Armed Services Committee, was supported by Washington's other senator, Slade Gorton, R, and by the state's eight-man House delegation, as well as by members

. . . Members Heed Constituent Interests

from Kansas — another Boeing base — and Missouri, home of McDonnell Douglas Corp. While McDonnell Douglas had been publicly neutral in the legislative battle, congressional sources said the firm hoped that scuttling the C-5 would revive its C-17, another cargo plane the Pentagon was considering for its Rapid Deployment Force.

In May 1982 Jackson convinced the Senate to divert funds earmarked for the C-5s to buy the Boeing 747s. Rep. Norman D. Dicks, D-Wash., tried to repeat Jackson's success in the House, urging procurement of "the most cost-effective commercial wide-body cargo aircraft." But the Boeing coalition had more difficulty there. According to Rep. Jenkins, C-5 supporters had been stunned by their defeat in the Senate and were determined to block a switch to the 747 in the House. Jenkins, whose district included 1,500 Lockheed employees, coordinated a task force of about two dozen mostly Southern lawmakers to lobby other House members in behalf of the C-5, so that if their colleagues voted "against the C-5, [they would] not do so blindly."

Pork Barrel, Executive Favors

Proponents of the C-5 argued that Boeing had sought to rewrite the Pentagon's shopping list in order to help reverse the difficulties it was having selling its passenger planes to U.S. airlines. However, backers of the 747 argued that local economic conditions were a secondary consideration in their support for the plane, albeit one given added urgency by the condition of the industry. "From my boss' point of view, it's a happy coincidence that it's a regional jobs issue," said Terrence L. Freese, legislative assistant to Rep. Dicks. "But it certainly wouldn't hurt at a time when Boeing is laying off people."

Rep. Dicks also went on the offensive, contending that the Pentagon's campaign on behalf of the C-5 was "an unprecedented abuse of a much abused law" against lobbying with congressionally appropriated funds. Rep. Jenkins, when asked about Dicks' charges of impropriety, scoffed, "Norm's suddenly recognized that we were not going to lose the fight lying down. . . . As many times as he's lobbied for Boeing, he's been the champion of that kind of thing."

The House easily rejected Dicks' amendment, 127-289. However, the final version of the defense authorization bill for fiscal 1983 included a directive to the Pentagon to buy three used 747s for Air Force cargo hauling, even though there had been no Reagan administration request for any 747s. Pentagon officials considered this an obvious political gesture toward the Senate position favoring the Boeing planes. As a senior Armed Services member, Sen. Jackson was one of the Senate conferees who negotiated the final version of the weapons authorization bill.

touted the concept of "sustainability" as a significant new commitment to readiness. Under it, the services would be able to carry out combat operations for months at a time rather than weeks.

The new readiness policy reflected the Pentagon's insistence that a military force had to be credible if it were to have a deterrent effect. "Deterrence could easily be weakened if the enemy were misled to believe that he could easily outlast us in a conventional war," Weinberger warned in his 1983 annual report to Congress.

How to Prepare

The Defense Department under Reagan began to emphasize the need to prepare for "industrial mobilization" — the capacity to greatly increase arms production quickly during an emergency and to maintain large stockpiles of weapons and supplies in order to sustain combat units in the field until the new items began rolling off the production lines.

Reagan's defense budgets for fiscal years 1982 and 1983 included marginally higher requests for training, maintenance and spare parts — the raw materials of readiness — than had been projected by Carter. A number of readiness issues came up in the debate on the fiscal 1984 defense budget that served to clarify the imprecise concept of combat readiness in the armed forces:

Personnel. An increase in active duty military personnel totaling 37,300 was projected in the administration's 1984 budget, with the Air Force and Navy getting the lion's share of the increase: 20,000 and 12,000 respectively. This would bring the total U.S. active duty military manpower level to 2,165,000. But because of the large budget deficits, Congress was reluctant to approve additional manpower costs.

The Reagan administration also requested an increase of 28,080 in the number of military reservists assigned to units that drill regularly. Nearly half that increase was for the Naval Reserve, which was to begin receiving more modern anti-submarine frigates as replacements for its fleet of World War II-vintage destroyers. This personnel increase, if approved by Congress, would bring the number of active reservists to 1,030,000.

Operating Tempo. Apart from formal training exercises, the crews of ships and aircraft must have a certain amount of time at sea or in the air simply to maintain proficiency in operating their equipment.

Under the Pentagon budget increases, Air Force crews of fighters and ground attack planes would be able to average 240 hours of flying time annually in fiscal 1984 compared with 210 hours in fiscal 1983. According to Weinberger's fiscal 1984 annual report, Soviet air crews averaged 120 hours per year.

Flying time for Navy air crews, on the other hand, would decline from an average of 288 hours in fiscal 1982 to 240 hours in fiscal 1984. Though this was the same as the Air Force average, some military leaders said Navy pilots needed more experience because of the greater difficulty of operating off aircraft carriers compared to airfields.

The operating tempo of the Navy's surface fleets (measured in "steaming days per quarter") was not disclosed by the Pentagon.

Equipment Condition. In his report to Congress, Weinberger conceded that maintenance backlogs of vehicles, ships and planes — the number overdue for routine overhauls — could not be alleviated in fiscal 1984 because of budget cutbacks.

Although there was an increase in recent years in the number of warships needing to be overhauled, this reflected a change in Navy overhaul policy rather than an increase in the number of ships overdue for maintenance, he indicated.

For maintenance and repairs to defense facilities in fiscal 1984, the Reagan administration planned to increase funding by 15 percent compared to the previous year, an increase the Pentagon said would permit a slight reduction in the backlog of such work.

Substantial increases also were requested for spare parts that wore out frequently and for "consumable" parts, such as spark plugs, that were "used up" in normal operations.

Wartime Stockpiles. Reagan's fiscal 1984 budget included funds to build up the stockpiles of spare parts, ammunition and fuel on which U.S. units could draw on for several months — in the event of an all-out non-nuclear war — while new production lines were started up. But Weinberger conceded there would continue to be shortfalls in the Pentagon's goals through fiscal 1988.

For all kinds of ammunition and bombs — both for training and for reserves set aside for wartime — the requested funding level was raised 30 percent over fiscal 1983, and a 50 percent increase was sought for reserves of spare parts and other equipment needed in wartime.

Squeezing the Readiness Budget

Congressional and executive branch budget cutters often have been tempted to ease the defense budget crunch by holding down funding in a number of accounts that are easily manipulated from year to year. Military readiness expenditures have been conspicuous among these.

Cuts in the 51 percent of the defense budget earmarked for manpower costs and day-to-day operating expenses produce reductions in outlays (actual defense spending) far more easily than reductions in the weapons hardware accounts. Nearly all of the appropriations for military personnel, such as pay and benefits and pensions, and about 81 percent of the appropriations for operations and maintenance, become outlays in the same year, thus producing quick reductions in the administration's defense budget for a given year. *(See also glossary of budget terms, box, p. 16)*

Cutting Stockpiles. In 1982 the Pentagon measured its stockpiles in terms of the number of days they would sustain U.S. forces, given certain assumptions about the rate at which they would be used up in combat. Though most of the actual numbers were classified, the services acknowledged they were substantially short of their goals for most stocks.

The Pentagon's fiscal 1983 budget was intended to provide for increases in ammunition stockpiled in Europe. While defense officials said this would last only 26 or 27 days — compared with a reported 60-day supply in Soviet inventories — members of Congress and others questioned the value of a larger stockpile of U.S. arms and equipment.

Critics observed that the Japanese and European forces, which would be fighting alongside U.S. units in most war scenarios against the Soviet Union and other Warwaw Pact members, had much smaller inventories of wartime supplies. Although he said he approved of increasing U.S. combat endurance as a general idea, Sen. Nunn questioned the efficacy of the plan without allied cooperation, arguing that if allied units ran out of bullets "it becomes irrelevant [that] we have ammunition."

House Armed Services Committee member Les Aspin, D-Wis., claimed that fiscal 1983 defense outlays could have been cut by $3.8 billion merely by slowing the rate at which the administration planned to build up arms stockpiles and improve the war readiness of U.S. forces.

"If the administration saw war looming on the horizon," Aspin said, "the prudent course would be a crash program to build up war reserve stocks of munitions and spare parts." But the administration "is clearly not anticipating a war in the near term," he asserted, since it had not placed U.S. forces in a higher state of alert.

Keeping Up Morale. In 1982 and 1983 the traditional targets for reducing defense spending were not as readily available as they had been in the past. Since the late 1970s, homage to "readiness" had become a staple of congressional speeches on defense. It received particular emphasis from liberals, who criticized the president's decision to speed up funding of weapons procurement at the expense of armed forces readiness. In 1981, for example, Senate Democrats made it a big issue during debate on the fiscal 1982 Defense Department appropriations bill. "We've oversold it, I'm afraid," lamented an aide to one House Democrat, who warned that it might be difficult to make future cuts in the operations and maintenance account, even in projects that were not obviously related to combat-readiness. "Its a sacred cow," he said.

Yet the Pentagon and congressional defense specialists suggested that this loyalty to readiness was appropriate. They cautioned that substantial cuts in those accounts were likely to immediately reduce the combat-readiness of units in the field. Over the long-term, they warned, such cuts would undermine morale and drive out of the services experienced non-commissioned personnel, who already were in short supply.

In the mid-1970s, when Congress was more parsimonious with the defense budgets, the Pentagon and the separate services deliberately cut back on operating expenses, letting tanks and planes sit in repair shops for want of maintenance. This limited the amount of time ships and planes were operational and performing their assigned tasks.

Air Force Chief of Staff Gen. Lew Allen told the Senate Armed Services Committee in 1982 that such reductions were having a severe impact on military morale: "You cannot hide from your people what you're doing," Allen insisted. "You're under-funding their ability to go to war." As a result, Allen said, morale had sagged and experienced personnel had left the service. One example cited by Allen was the reductions in flight time caused by cuts in the fuel account. This, he said, had "seriously antagonized the pilots, . . . and they told us so. Some of them told us by leaving."

Sharing the Defense Burden

Perhaps even more widespread than the controversies over specific weapons issues has been a long-festering complaint in Congress about the burden of the United States' defense commitments to the NATO alliance and Japan. Lawmakers have said repeatedly that the United States had borne an unreasonably heavy share of the cost of defending the vital interests, and even the very security, of its European allies. Washington for many years had extended to them the protection of its costly nuclear umbrella. Moreover, in a more direct and tangible way, the presence of U.S. conventional forces in Western Europe and the Far East provided solid evidence of the long-standing U.S. defense commitment.

By the 1980s, bipartisan coalitions on the House and Senate Armed Services committees and Defense Appropriations subcommittees had become increasingly insistent that Japan and U.S. allies in Europe pay more of the cost of protecting their own security.

More than considerations of abstract equity in sharing costs were involved. Many members argued that the much larger percentage of the U.S. economy being diverted to defense accounted in part for the ability of European and Japanese products to undersell U.S. competitors in world markets.

Specifically, the U.S criticism was directed at the relatively low proportion of national wealth invested in defense by nearly all of the European allies and by Japan. Except for France, which did not participate in the unified NATO command, none of the large NATO countries even approached the annual U.S. investment in defense of nearly 6 percent of its gross domestic product. And few members had consistently met the alliance's 1978 pledge to seek "real" (after inflation) annual defense spending increases of 3 percent.

The real growth rate of Japan's defense budget was much higher than 3 percent, but the share of its national wealth allocated to defense still was very low — less than 1 percent of its gross national product (GNP). *(U.S.-Japanese relations, box, p. 168)*

The burden-sharing issue has posed a dilemma for Democratic and Republican administrations alike. On the one hand, when dealing with Congress, Defense Department officials sought to depict the allies' share as "fair," lest funding for U.S. military efforts be cut in retaliation. At the same time, they continually reminded the allied governments that their defense contributions had not kept pace with their economic growth.

Defense Burden and Economic Conditions

The burden-sharing issue had been exacerbated by disagreements on a number of economic issues:

Particularly galling to some members of Congress was the participation by some NATO members in the financing of a natural gas pipeline between Western Europe and Siberia. The Reagan administration claimed that dependence on Moscow for energy would make the Europeans vulnerable to Soviet economic pressure. Moreover, construction of the pipeline would benefit the Soviet economy and boost its foreign exchange, allowing the Russians to spend more on defense, the administration argued.

Japan, too, was an unduly cooperative commercial partner of the Soviet Union's, in the eyes of the Reagan administration. Japan had sold the Soviet Union a large floating drydock that Moscow had used to maintain the aircraft carrier *Kiev*, the largest ship in the Soviet Pacific fleet.

A more immediate grievance against Tokyo was expressed by Rep. Aspin in *The New York Times* March 14, 1982: "We are putting so much of our capital and our scientific and technical resources into defense, whereas they're putting theirs into Sonys and Toyotas and beating the bejesus out of us in the domestic market."

Similarly, the Senate Appropriations Committee's Defense Subcommittee chairman, Ted Stevens, R-Alaska, was particularly unhappy about the Siberian pipeline deal. "If they [Europeans] feel so secure in their relations with the Russians," he told Defense Secretary Weinberger during a March 2, 1982, defense budget hearing, "then maybe it's time for us to re-examine the number of troops that we have in Europe." Within hours, U.S. Army Gen. Bernard W. Rogers, NATO's senior military commander, was barraged with similar comments by typically pro-Pentagon members of the House Armed Services Committee. They were angry at the European governments' lack of support for various Reagan anti-Soviet policies. "The people over there don't seem to feel as threatened as we think they are," said Rep. William L. Dickinson, R-Ala.

"Maybe it's time to whistle up the dogs and put the chairs in the wagon and tell the troops to go home," Bill Nichols, D-Ala., declared.

Congressional impatience with America's allies came to a head after Washington began to assume the major cost of protecting Persian Gulf oil supplies, which were far more essential to the Europeans than to the United States. *(Details, see Rapid Deployment Force chapter.)*

Congress in 1980 stepped up its efforts to pressure the Pentagon into demanding that NATO members and Japan make a greater contribution to the common defense. This became all the more important because of President Carter's pledge that the United States would unilaterally protect Western oil supplies coming from the Persian Gulf. Said Rep. Robert C. McEwen, R-N.Y., ranking minority member

Defense Burden-sharing Dispute . . .

By the late 1970s, the small sums Japan was spending on the common defense became a source of considerable tension between Washington and Tokyo, particularly in light of Japan's burgeoning economy and large trade imbalance with the United States. "You simply cannot ignore the fact that the two are intertwined," U.S. Trade Representative William E. Brock III said in a 1982 interview. "If they spend less money on defense, they have far more opportunity for investing in support of selected industries, R&D support, lower interest rates and the like that make them more competitive economically."

On the other hand, "We do not believe that action on trade problems resolves our concerns with defense — or vice-versa," said Defense Secretary Caspar W. Weinberger, in a speech at the Japan National Press Club in March 1983.

Japan has maintained a philosophy of pacifism since its defeat in World War II. Its Self-Defense Force contains only about 250,000 troops. Under the 1960 U.S.-Japan Treaty of Mutual Cooperation and Security — which put Japan under the U.S. nuclear umbrella — the United States was allowed to station about 46,000 troops in Japan. The U.S. Seventh Fleet regularly patrolled Japanese coastal waters, and a division of Marines and an Air Force division were based on nearby Okinawa. It cost the United States an estimated $2.4 billion each year to operate these bases in Japan. The Japanese contributed an additional $800 million annually.

The fact that Japan spent less than 1 percent of its gross national product (GNP) annually on defense since the 1960s has not gone unnoticed in Congress. In 1981 Sen. Carl Levin, D-Mich., a member of the Senate Armed Services Committee, and Rep. Clement J. Zablocki, D-Wis., chairman of the House Foreign Affairs Committee, introduced resolutions calling on Japan to increase its defense expenditures to at least 1 percent of its GNP. "Despite their strong economy, the Japanese have shirked some of their defense responsibilities to themselves and to the United States," Sen. Levin told the Senate Nov. 9, 1981.

of the House Appropriations Military Construction Subcommittee: "It seems imperative that these other nations be convinced that they should assume a fair share of this burden. If withholding funds is the only way that we can gain their attention, then so be it."

"In the light of the vast sums being spent in other areas of the world to ensure the security of NATO and the uninterrupted flow of oil, the NATO allies and particularly the German government should expand

... Strains U.S.-Japanese Relations

But some U.S. officials said that focusing on the 1 percent GNP figure was not the best way to influence Japan to assume a greater share of its own defense. "The U.S.-Japanese relationship is essential to both nations and should not be reduced to percentage terms or be threatened by dire consequences should one or both nations not always meet the other's expectations," said then-Rep. Paul Findley, R-Ill. (1961-83), in 1982. Findley and others said the best way to influence Japan was to continue the process of high-level negotiations and consultations on specific issues.

The United States pressured Japan to increase its defense spending primarily because of a reported massive buildup of Soviet forces in Central Asia and the Far East over the last decade. "The Soviet force in Asia is so complex that it may be possible for the U.S.S.R. to reach out with its nuclear might and destroy all the modernized sectors of China . . . within a matter of hours. . . ," said Robert J. Pranger of the American Enterprise Institute in 1982 congressional testimony. "The sheer fall-out from such an attack, of course, could possibly bring havoc to Japan as well."

Although the Japanese displayed less concern about a Soviet threat than did Washington, Japan's prime minister in 1981, Zenko Suzuki, increased defense spending by 7.75 percent, to about $11 billion overall. Japan also agreed to expand its defense commitments by agreeing to defend the sea-lanes (on which its economy is dependent) for a distance of 1,000 miles from the home islands and to protect its own airspace. But most U.S. defense analysts argued that Japan could defend its sea-lanes only if its defense expenditures broke the self-imposed 1 percent ceiling.

Yashuhiro Nakasone, who succeeded Suzuki in November 1982, further emphasized the need to boost Japanese defense spending and shoulder more of the responsibility for its own defense. He even pointed to the need to make Japan an "unsinkable aircraft carrier" in order to defend itself against Soviet bombers. The majority of the Japanese public, however, remained extremely wary of, if not strongly opposed to, such a defense buildup.

their support of our mutual efforts in the defense of Europe," the House Armed Services Committee said in its 1982 report on the fiscal 1983 military construction bill.

That year Congress barred the Pentagon from spending $91 million that had been appropriated to expand the base at Ras Banas on Egypt's Red Sea coast (the base would serve as a jumping-off point for units of the Rapid Deployment Force) until the administration certified that negotiations were under way to ensure that the NATO allies and Japan would offset some of the cost of U.S. efforts to defend the Persian Gulf.

U.S. Troop Reductions

For more than two decades the most persistent burden-sharing issue has involved the cost of stationing U.S. troops in Europe. The cost of maintaining that presence became a controversial issue almost as soon as the North Atlantic Treaty Organization was established in 1949.

By the mid-1960s there was growing sentiment to bring home some of the approximately 300,000 American troops, most of them stationed in West Germany. As the United States became embroiled in the Vietnam War in the mid-1960s, many members began to criticize the NATO allies for not contributing their "fair share" to the defense of Europe.

In 1966 Senate Majority Leader Mike Mansfield, D-Mont. (1953-77), introduced a resolution expressing the sense of the Senate that there should be a unilateral reduction in U.S. troop strength in Europe. Although similar resolutions were introduced in every subsequent congressional session, none was approved.

In 1971 congressional supporters of a cutback changed their tactics. They sponsored an amendment to allocate enough funds only to support 150,000 troops in Europe. Debate was extended, but in the end Congress rejected the amendment and similar proposals.

Legislating Troop Ceilings. Nonetheless, the issue persisted, and in 1982 Congress attached to a defense appropriations bill a provision limiting the number of active-duty U.S. military personnel stationed in Europe to 315,600, the ceiling in effect at the end of fiscal 1982. But the president was permitted to waive that limitation if he declared to Congress that "overriding national security requirements" made such action necessary.

At a Feb. 23, 1983, hearing before his subcommittee, Stevens warned Secretary Weinberger that there was congressional sentiment in favor of incorporating a troop-ceiling provision in the fiscal 1984 Defense Department appropriations bill. Stevens in 1982 had sponsored a move to reduce the number of American troops abroad by 18,900.

Weinberger urged the panel not to support the troop ceiling provision, arguing that some manpower increases might be required by changes in the military balance between NATO and the Warsaw Pact. "The numbers [of U.S. troops] have to depend really on that military situation," he said.

The existing ceiling would be adhered to, Weinberger assured the panel, though that would require the withdrawal of some American soldiers and thus might appear to signal a flagging of the U.S. commitment to Europe's defense.

Stevens maintained that in fiscal 1982, and in the two previous fiscal years, the Pentagon had exceeded its planned deployments to Europe. "The question is, are we going to allow the Department of Defense to increase, increase, increase [the number of troops] without control," he said.

The subcommittee's concern about maintaining the ceiling on American troops was magnified by the panel's impression that periodic U.S. troop increases in Europe were replacing troop withdrawals by other NATO allies. Stevens had complained to Weinberger that since the late 1970s the number of U.S. personnel on the continent had risen by 60,000, while other NATO members had decreased their troop deployments by 58,000.

After the hearing, Stevens suggested to reporters that he was interested in trying to force the administration to take the problem seriously, and was not necessarily against increasing U.S. manpower in Europe. He suggested that a presidential waiver of the troop ceiling in order to add the personnel that would be needed to operate the Pershing II missiles scheduled for deployment beginning in December 1983 would be justified on national security grounds.

But a decision to increase U.S. manpower should be made by the president, Stevens insisted. "It should not be made by an accumulation of thousands of little units, each of which says, 'Give me 10 more men.' "

Deployment Costs and Savings. If Congress became angry enough with its allies in Europe, it might consider removing an Army division (of a total of five division equivalents) deployed on the continent. But according to the Pentagon, merely withdrawing a division would save little if the units were not disbanded.

The Congressional Budget Office (CBO) put the annual savings from disbanding a division at $200 million in operating costs and military compensation in fiscal 1984 and $2.4 billion over five years. However, in the Defense Department's fiscal 1984 budget presentation to Congress, Weinberger disputed the notion that budgetary savings would be achieved through troop reductions. And a rapid withdrawal, he said, would entail added expenditures. Furthermore, Weinberger emphasized that U.S. forces overseas were multipurpose. "While U.S. forces are available to meet any aggression in Europe . . . they must also be able to respond to threats against U.S. security interests in other regions of the world. Thus, even if our NATO commitment were suddenly to disappear, we would not necessarily be able to inactivate a significant portion of the forces now stationed in Europe. . . ."

The report concluded that a troop-cut proposal "should not be considered seriously without reference to the political and military implications . . . and to existing agreements among the Allies. U.S. forces are maintained in Europe directly in support of U.S. political and military interests — not as an act of charity toward our Allies." Substantial withdrawals "would weaken our credibility both with our Allies and with potential adversaries."

"We are not actually in Europe defending them," added Rep. Jack Brinkley, D-Ga., chairman of the House Armed Services Military Construction Subcommittee, during House debate in August 1982 on a military construction authorization bill. "We are in Europe, in NATO, because of the national interest of the United States of America."

NATO Facilities and Troop Support

A forced reduction in the number of U.S. troops in Europe would be so drastic a step that Congress would be more likely to express its unhappiness over the burden-sharing issue through a less draconian approach, such as passing a resolution enumerating the congressional complaints.

In contrast to the troop issue, Congress has expressed its dissatisfaction less dramatically but more effectively on the issue of combat-related military construction projects in Europe, which, members insisted, should be funded by NATO as a whole, not just by Washington, since they supported the common defense effort. In this area, lawmakers had made their displeasure known by voting to withhold approval of such projects. Unhappy members cited various programs calling for deployment of new weapons and improvement in the combat readiness of NATO troop units having an estimated construction cost to the United States of $541 million.

NATO Infrastructure. For years, the congressional defense committees refused to provide funds for ammunition and fuel storage dumps at so-called co-located operating bases (COBs). Under NATO defense plans, these European-owned bases would be used by many of the 60 fighter squadrons Washington could quickly deploy in Europe as reinforcements if a military mobilization became necessary.

Despite pleas from senior U.S. Air Force officers, the committees in 1982 insisted that most COB facilities be funded by NATO's infrastructure fund for jointly financed construction projects. The Pentagon claimed the projects were urgently needed, and it wanted the United States to pay for them to expedite construction since infrastructure funds already were fully committed for the next several years. U.S. expenditures eventually would be recouped from the infrastructure fund, Congress was assured.

The United States provided about 27 percent of the total cost of the infrastructure program, according to the Pentagon. However, decisions relating to infrastructure projects required the unanimous approval of NATO members. Congress in 1982 approved $325 million of the $375 million requested for the annual U.S. contribution to the fund. Although some members commended the program, they complained that it was too small to meet all the construction requirements they felt should be paid for by the alliance. They argued that the allies should increase their collective share of the annual infrastructure budget to offset the cost to the United States of building military facilities in the Indian Ocean and Persian Gulf region.

NATO Troop Relocation Plan. Another source of potential friction between the United States and its allies in Europe was the insistence of the Armed Services committees that West Germany finance construction of a network of new bases that would move three Army brigades — about 20,000 men — from dilapidated and inadequate quarters into modern facilities closer to the borders with East Germany and Czechoslovakia. The old bases, which U.S. forces had occupied since the end of World War II, were located substantial distances from the frontier. Besides the general burden-sharing argument, the defense panels cited two specific reasons why the West German government ought to pay the cost of the relocation, called the Master Restationing Plan (MRP): 1) West German territory could be better defended by U.S. units based closer to the eastern border, and 2) the Bonn government would benefit directly by using the vacated sites for other purposes. The location of some of the old sites in major industrial centers made them valuable tracts of real estate.

Although Congress in 1982 approved the $14.5 million requested for the first major increment of MRP-related construction, the authorization and appropriations committees of Congress emphasized that this was only because those particular projects were needed by U.S. troops whether or not the entire MRP, estimated to cost a total of $1.2 billion, was carried out. In approving the relocation, Congress stipulated that before the funds could be spent the Pentagon would have to notify the appropriations committees that the Bonn government had agreed to "substantially assume the cost of the restationing plan."

Storing Military Equipment. Storing military equipment was another bone of contention in the burden-sharing debate. The Pentagon wanted to store at so-called POMCUS (prepositioned overseas materiel configured in unit sets) sites enough tanks and other heavy equipment for six divisions that could be flown to Europe in the event of a crisis. But in 1982 Congress voted to retain a ban on storing equipment in Europe for more than four U.S. Army divisions. The Defense Department in 1983 resubmitted the request for storing, or "prepositioning," equipment for two additional divisions. Noting that POMCUS was part of the infrastructure program, the Pentagon warned that continued congressional refusal to approve the funding would substantially undermine the other members' contribution to the project.

Congress also refused to allow the Pentagon to spend $44.3 million for a "host nation support" plan to buy equipment to be used in wartime by 93,000 West German reservists assigned to provide transportation, security and supply support for U.S. combat troops. In resubmitting the funding request for fiscal 1984, the Pentagon estimated that the German reservists would cost one-tenth of what it would cost to provide the same capability with U.S. reserve units.

The POMCUS expansion and the joint U.S.-German funding of the host-nation support agreement were part of a package deal under which the United States would expand its plans to quickly come to the aid of Western Europe if threatened, and the European NATO members would provide more support for U.S. troops.

In endorsing both programs, Sen. Nunn said, "We cannot expect to improve allied burden-sharing if we fail to fund our share of key programs designed for that purpose."

Defense Department officials generally supported the idea of getting host nations to provide more assistance, but they were interested primarily in being assured of European support in wartime, not peacetime savings that would result from allied assumption of additional construction or labor costs. One senior Pentagon official acknowledged the divergence of viewpoints. He said the United States was working with the allied governments to nail down agreements to provide wartime logistical support, but "it remains to be seen whether it will reduce peacetime costs as Congress wants."

Assessing the Burden

Some U.S. government officials were of the opinion that congressional criticism of the European allies' burden-sharing commitment was exaggerated and unfair. They pointed out that much of the NATO members' contributions had been indirect, for example, in income foregone by providing infrastructure needs, without requiring dollar outlays.

Appearing before a congressional committee in March 1980, Under Secretary of of Defense Komer noted that the United States accounted for only about half of NATO's real defense effort, when adjusted for European governments' lower personnel costs resulting from a military conscription system that allowed them to pay less for manpower. "When you make an adjustment for that, and calculate pay for their forces at U.S. manpower rates, they are spending just as much as we are, or they are producing just as much online strength as we are," Komer said. The allies "provide all the real estate costs [for bases] free, and real estate is getting to be pretty expensive stuff these days, especially in highly populated countries like Germany and Japan. . . . The allies build the great bulk of the bases."

European NATO members maintained about 3 million troops on active duty, compared to about 2 million for the United States. "If a war was to break out today, West European nations would provide 90 percent of the land forces and 75 percent of the air and naval forces," noted Gen. Rogers in 1982.

In an article in the December 1982 *NATO Review* entitled "Sharing the Defence Burden," Rainer W. Rupp of NATO's economics directorate discussed the problem of assessing the contributions of alliance members. Between 1970 and 1981, U.S. real defense expenditures (after inflation) declined by an average annual rate of 1 percent, while the economy grew by 2.9 percent. That compared to real growth in defense expenditures of 4.2 percent and 2.8 percent for gross domestic product in Belgium; and 2.6 percent (defense) and 2.5 percent (gross domestic product) for West Germany. For the European NATO members as a whole, the percentages were 1.7 percent and 2.5 percent, respectively, according to NATO statistics. However, U.S. defense expenditures per capita were $658 in 1981, more than twice the European NATO average, according to the article.

Defense expenditures as a share of gross domestic product showed that while the U.S. defense share was considerably larger than the NATO-Europe average in 1970-81, the European defense share of gross domestic product increased to 3.7 percent from 3.5 percent while the U.S. share declined to 5.9 percent from 7.9 percent.

"In the final analysis, the concept of burden sharing or equity in defense effort is a highly complex and frequently subjective process," Rupp concluded. "A country's contribution to the defense of the Alliance depends on its economic capacity, its sense of vulnerability, its perception of the threat and a number of other factors such as cultural and historical influences. As countries operate from different perspectives, their defense efforts vary accordingly. The nature and structure of the Alliance, therefore, prevents the production of a mechanical formula for calculating an equitable distribution of the defense burden. Efforts to do so are regularly based on narrow and selective criteria which not only fail to reflect the complexity of the NATO alliance but also distort the relationships implied in membership."

In a March 1982 "Report on Allied Contributions to the Common Defense," Weinberger pointed out that an accurate measurement of the defense burden involved calculations that had to take into account each nation's ability and competing needs. Based solely on quantifiable factors, the United States appeared "to be doing somewhat more than its fair share of the NATO total," providing about 53 percent of the collective military budgets of the allies. The report also found considerable variation among the European governments, due primarily to "the diverging view among the allies of the threat and the resulting differences in opinion about how much defense is enough. . . . Emphasizing social and economic viability as their first priority, many Europeans continue to view the Soviet threat less seriously" than does the United States.

The report concluded, "Ironically, NATO's success in deterring war for more than three decades has undermined the resolve of a generation in Europe that has never experienced the horrors of war."

Chapter 4

U.S. RAPID DEPLOYMENT FORCE

"The U.S.S.R. is pursuing the development of a global, client-state system, which must be viewed in the context of U.S. international security concerns and responsibilities," warned the Joint Chiefs of Staff in its 1983 military posture statement.

"Regional instabilities and Soviet-inspired threats to peace exist in many diverse areas. . . . Conflict involving the Soviet Union could occur anywhere on the globe. U.S. military strategy must concern itself with contingencies in all regions of the world. . . . An essential element of U.S. strategy is the ability to deploy combat ready, well-equipped ground, sea and air forces . . . to wherever needed. Continued investment in airlift and sealift forces to permit such deployment is fundamental to U.S. military strategy."

Concern about a perceived decline in American influence and prestige abroad, coupled with Soviet military and political successes, prompted the Carter administration in the late 1970s to opt for a more assertive U.S. military role overseas, especially in the oil-rich Middle East.

A number of traumatic events between 1978 and 1980 had given a sense of urgency to the creation of a force that could respond rapidly to crises in the Indian Ocean/Persian Gulf region. The revolution in Iran that replaced America's strongest ally in that area, Shah Mohammed Reza Pahlavi, with an anti-American, anti-West Islamic revolutionary regime, raised apprehensions about the security of Persian Gulf oil supplies.

The outbreak of war between Iran and Iraq in September 1980 eroded the region's stability still further. Added to this was the blow to U.S. prestige resulting from the seizure in November 1979 of the American Embassy in Tehran by Iranian militants.

After the invasion of Afghanistan by the Soviet Union in December

1979, Moscow stepped up its naval buildup and military assistance to client regimes in the region, especially South Yemen and Ethiopia.

The 'Carter Doctrine'

Declaring that the Soviet takeover in Afghanistan "could pose the most serious threat to peace" since World War II, President Jimmy Carter, in his 1980 State of the Union address, warned Moscow to stay out of the world's foremost oil exporting region. Any attempt by an outside power to gain control of the area, he said, "would be regarded as an assault on the vital interests of the United States, and such an assault will be repelled by any means necessary, including military force."

Given that decision, however, there remained the problems of how to confront a growing Soviet presence in Southwest Asia without provoking direct retaliation by Moscow and how to strengthen the U.S. position without resorting to an obtrusive military buildup that would place severe strains on the governments in the region.

Although Carter did not specify at what point and under what conditions military force would be used, it was clear that any commitment would entail rethinking existing foreign and defense policies. Some analysts questioned whether the so-called "Carter Doctrine" was a realistic one, given the lack of U.S. access to bases in the region.

To remedy those deficiencies, Carter took several steps: The United States reinforced its naval presence in the Persian Gulf/Indian Ocean and stepped up development of a "quick reaction force." At the same time, the administration sought and eventually obtained use of military facilities at bases in Oman, Somalia, Kenya and Egypt. And the already large U.S. foreign military assistance and weapons sales commitments to Israel, Egypt and Saudi Arabia were increased.

U.S. defense planners had assessed the need for a quick conventional attack capability to counter Soviet incursions and communist insurgencies as early as 1977. But it was not until 1979, after a year of setbacks abroad, that plans for a Rapid Deployment Force (RDF) were disclosed by the Carter administration.

Planning the RDF

The purpose of the RDF, as conceived by the Defense Department, was to provide the United States with an enhanced capability to intervene militarily to protect American interests overseas, particularly in the volatile Persian Gulf region. But it was to have the capability to intervene

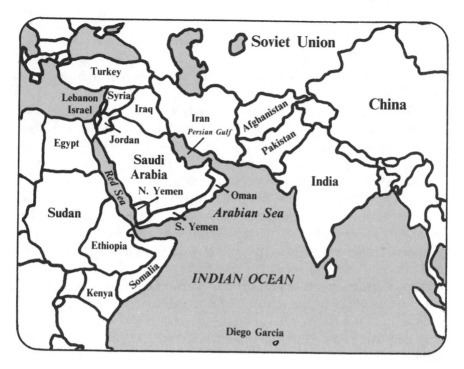

Oil-rich Southwest Asia is the most likely area the U.S. Rapid Deployment Force would be sent to in the event American interests were endangered by Soviet military actions or local instability.

in any part of the world where the United States lacked military facilities.

As Carter's defense secretary, Harold Brown, explained in the Defense Department's annual report for 1980: "The president and I believe that the prospect of renewed turbulence in the Middle East, Caribbean, and elsewhere, and the possibility of new demands on our non-nuclear posture, require additional precautionary actions."

Initial Plans

The Defense Department envisaged that the RDF would provide overall coordination initially for about 150,000 troops and appropriate equipment, stationed in the United States and remote parts of the world, ready to move by air and sea into critical non-European areas. More troops would be available from Army and Marine Corps combat units.

The RDF was structured flexibly so as to meet any contingency.

Marine Corps Lt. Gen. P. X. Kelley was appointed the first head of the RDF. With the assistance of the Joint Chiefs of Staff and personnel at MacDill Air Force Base, Tampa, Fla. (headquarters for the RDF), he devised scenarios to determine which units would be necessary in specific situations.

The Joint Chiefs described the RDF as a "conceptual approach" to readiness that "identifies the number of units from which a task force can be formed, tailored to the specific requirements of a situation." Rather than creating additional units to man the RDF, the force was to be drawn from the existing services. It thus was viewed as an "umbrella" command, drawn primarily from the Marine Corps, the Army's 24th Infantry, 82nd Airborne and 101st Air Assault Divisions and some Navy units. In October 1981 the RDF was chartered as a separate unified command, called the Rapid Deployment Joint Task Force (RDJTF), and made directly responsible to the Joint Chiefs of Staff. In January 1983 the task force structure was upgraded to a Central Command for Southwest Asia, modeled after the existing theater commands in Europe, the Atlantic and the Pacific.

Able to draw on 290,000 military personnel by early 1983, and with plans to substantially increase that number, RDF strength by the mid-1980s was projected to be second only to U.S. conventional forces allocated to Europe.

Buildup Under Reagan

The RDF buildup was pursued even more vigorously after President Ronald Reagan took office. The president believed there was a serious Soviet military threat to the Persian Gulf region and to other unstable areas, the Caribbean in particular, which required an urgent response by his administration.

Reagan's concern about the need to counter perceived Soviet political and military moves in the Middle East and elsewhere was reflected in remarks he made in a Feb. 3, 1981, interview with some daily newspapers. "What I have called for, and what I think is needed as we refurbish our capability," the president told the reporters, "is a presence in the Middle East. . . . What is meant by a presence is that we're there enough to know and for the Soviets to know that if they made a reckless move, they would be risking a confrontation with the United States."

On Feb. 23, 1981, State Department spokesman William Dyess told the press, "We are convinced that the highest priority in that region at this time should be to arrest the deteriorating position of the West vis-à-vis the Soviet Union."

During a March 23 House subcommittee hearing, Richard Burt, director of the State Department's Bureau of Politico-Military Affairs, said the objectives of the administration's Middle East policy were to:

● Demonstrate the ability to counter the influence of the Soviets and their allies.

● Ensure continued Western access to the oil of the Persian Gulf in adequate quantities and at a reasonable price.

● Ensure the continued existence and strength of U.S. friends in the region.

● Continue to work for peace between Israel and its Arab neighbors.

Burt also said the administration viewed the Middle East as part of a larger strategic area "bounded by Turkey, Pakistan and the Horn of Africa." The way to achieve an Arab-Israeli peace, he maintained, was to make the Arabs feel secure against the Soviets. "Only when local states feel confident of U.S. reliability and secure against Soviet threats will they be willing to take the necessary risks for peace," he said.

Forging a 'Strategic Consensus'

Acting on that assumption, the Reagan administration stepped up efforts to supply arms and aid to friendly nations and to seek the cooperation of those governments in the defense of the region. By the spring of 1981 a new policy had emerged, that of seeking a "strategic consensus" in Southwest Asia with nations as diverse as Pakistan, Turkey, Israel, Egypt and Saudi Arabia. As part of its effort to implement that strategy, the administration announced a $3.2 billion economic and military aid/arms sales package for Pakistan and an $8.5 billion arms sales package for Saudi Arabia.

The deal with Saudi Arabia included a Reagan-initiated proposal to sell the kingdom five sophisticated AWACS (Airborne Warning and Control System) radar planes. The administration said the planes would enhance those nations' ability to counter a Soviet threat, while the promise of increased U.S. assistance might in turn make them more receptive to providing bases and other facilities to the United States.

The proposed AWACS sale was severely criticized in Israel, and by pro-Israel members of Congress. The sale was in doubt until the 52-48 Senate roll call on Oct. 28, 1981.

The Israelis claimed the sale of AWACS planes to an avowed

enemy of the Jewish state would pose a grave threat to their security. Opposition in Congress was based both on Israel's worries and concern about introducing such advanced weaponry in such an unstable area of the world. Some lawmakers argued that the administration's policy risked turning Saudi Arabia into another Iran — that is, a country the United States lavished weapons on in the hope that it could act as a "surrogate gendarme" to defend America's strategic interests.

Reagan responded to this concern at an Oct. 1 news conference by saying, "I have to say that, Saudi Arabia, we will not permit to be an Iran. There is no way — as long as Saudi Arabia and the OPEC [Organization of Petroleum Exporting Countries] nations . . . provide the bulk of the energy that is needed to turn the wheels of industry in the Western world — there's no way that we could stand by and see that taken over by anyone that would shut off that oil."

The so-called strategic consensus theory fit in neatly with the Reagan administration's emphasis on competing with the Soviet Union militarily. But it was criticized by numerous Middle East experts. One of those questioning the policy was Robert G. Neumann, a former U.S. ambassador to Saudi Arabia. "The trouble with a strategic conception as a guide for policies is that you look at a region as a piece of territory and you forget there are people living on that territory," said Neumann. "And if those people do not share your perception, what good is it?"

Projected RDF Costs

The Reagan administration's projected RDF program costs for Southwest Asia and other regions amounted to $2.2 billion in fiscal 1984, $2.3 billion in fiscal 1985, $2.5 billion in fiscal 1986, $2.9 billion in fiscal 1987 and $3.6 billion in fiscal 1988, for a total of $13.6 billion. (Carter's fiscal 1981 defense budget had projected a $10 billion multi-year program.)

In presenting the Defense Department's fiscal 1984 budget to Congress, Secretary Caspar W. Weinberger said the RDF effort would continue to focus on Southwest Asia. Potential conflicts in that region encompassed a wide range of situations; thus planning for them would provide a capability covering likely contingencies in other Third World areas as well, according to defense officials. The primary emphasis of RDF efforts would continue to be to enhance the readiness of existing forces by providing better training, mobility and support and improving coordinated command, control and communications.

Challenges to RDF Concept

Devising an effective RDF encountered a number of major problems. Rapid deployment of U.S. forces to the Middle East/ Southwest Asia region was considerably more difficult than sending reinforcements to the NATO countries or even to the Far East, where U.S. troops and materiel already were stationed. (Since the tanks, trucks and other heavy equipment needed to supply four U.S. divisions already were stored at European depots, only the additional troops and relatively light-weight equipment would have to be sent to the NATO theater in an emergency.)

As of 1983 the United States had no base agreements with any of the countries in the Persian Gulf region that allowed it to station combat forces there on a permanent basis in peacetime. A few nations allowed the prepositioning of U.S. military equipment and use of their facilities during crises and to conduct routine training exercises. However, political considerations ruled out a more visible U.S. role.

Thus, Washington could maintain only a limited, sea-based presence in the Persian Gulf. Faced with little or no host support, it was essential for the United States to continue to seek access to facilities in peacetime as well as during crises. In the interim, other means would have to be found to ensure that U.S. forces could rapidly be sent to trouble spots or to areas where events threatened to endanger American interests.

Mobility thus was essential. However, conditions in Southwest Asia presented a logistical nightmare. Once they arrived, American combat forces would have to contend with inadequate to practically nonexistent transportation and communications networks in the region; a harsh climate; and unfamiliar, difficult terrain. For example, supplying sufficient water to troops in the desert posed a considerable challenge, as did transporting equipment through mountainous terrain. An effective command, control and communications network would be particularly difficult to maintain in that area, which is two-thirds the size of the United States. Without access to adequate facilities it would be difficult to protect arriving air transport and ships against Soviet bombers, fighters and submarines.

In its fiscal 1984 budget, the Reagan administration sought the military capability to defend, simultaneously, Southwest Asia, the NATO countries and much of the Pacific region. Its interim goal was to be able to reinforce NATO with six Army divisions, a Marine Amphibious

Brigade and 60 tactical fighter squadrons in 10 days; and to deploy a joint task force and support equipment to Southwest Asia within six weeks.

However, a major problem confronting those plans, according to the Pentagon, was the fact that most of the RDF forces also had missions in other theaters. Because much of the U.S. conventional force was designed for combat in Europe, some types of support units were in short supply or did not exist for the kinds of missions envisaged for the RDF. Moreover, if faced with simultaneous crises in NATO and Southwest Asia, the existing U.S. airlift and sealift capability would not be able to deploy forces to both theaters as rapidly as might be necessary.

Access to Foreign Bases

RDF planners were confronted with the fact that the Pentagon had to build a quick deployment force almost from scratch. At the time of the Iranian hostage crisis in 1979 the United States had a very limited military presence in the Persian Gulf; its capacity to move forces rapidly into the area was severely hampered by the distances involved; and it lacked the necessary sea- and airlift capacity to move military equipment and troops.

Soon after the Iranian militants took over the U.S. Embassy, the Carter administration increased the size of its naval fleet in the Indian Ocean and began plans to establish the RDF. Nevertheless, the successful use of any RDF unit depended on having reliable bases in the area. The only U.S. base in Southwest Asia was on the British-owned island of Diego Garcia, in the Indian Ocean some 2,500 miles from the Persian Gulf. Staging a major operation from Diego Garcia, quipped one defense expert, would be like "staging the Normandy invasion from Cape May, New Jersey."

Reluctance of Gulf Nations. Defense planners said the United States needed bases and port facilities closer to the gulf. But attempts to enhance the U.S. strategic position met with resistance. The conservative Persian Gulf kingdoms generally were reluctant to accept foreigners, who often brought with them economic, political and social tensions. And any hint of a new colonialism risked provoking internal dissension and opposition to the existing regimes. There also was concern that a direct U.S. military presence would make the Persian Gulf nations vulnerable to Soviet pressure or provide fertile ground for internal disturbances, even a communist-inspired rebellion. Finally, most governments simply did not want either superpower flexing its muscles in the region.

After protracted negotiations, the Carter administration in 1980 reached agreements with Oman, Somalia and Kenya allowing U.S. access to some of their military bases. But in none of these countries was Washington granted control of fully operating bases. Kenya, the strongest ally of the three, offered facilities at Mombasa, which already was a regular port of call for the U.S. Navy. Oman agreed to permit only limited use of a few airfields. Details of the agreement with Oman were kept secret, however.

Under the arrangements negotiated with the three countries, the facilities were to be used for routine repair and resupply of warships and long-range patrol planes and to provide shore leave for U.S. forces. The facilities in Oman and Somalia remained under local sovereignty but were made available to U.S. units under the negotiated agreements. (In deference to political sensibilities in the region, the administration described the installations as "facilities" rather than "bases.")

Reagan continued Carter's RDF buildup program and policy of increasing U.S. military aid to the region. In 1981 Congress approved the bulk of the administration's fiscal 1982 RDF-related construction requests. Most of the funds sought were for ongoing projects that were to be completed in later years. For most of the projects, the first installment had been made in fiscal 1981, when Congress appropriated $259.2 million. The fiscal 1982 funding included $237.4 million to enlarge the base on Diego Garcia, as well as money to build facilities in Oman ($78.5 million), Somalia ($24 million) and Kenya ($31.8 million), where supplies and equipment could be stored for U.S. forces.

Also approved was $49.6 million for projects at Lajes Air Force Base in the Portuguese-owned Azores Islands, a staging point for planes flying from the United States to the Middle East.

Dispute Over Egyptian Base. Egypt was the fourth country to offer the use of military facilities to the United States. Washington estimated construction costs at Ras Banas, at the southern end of Egypt's Red Sea coast, would reach $1.6 billion. Reagan in 1981 requested $106.4 million to begin upgrading the facility, which he considered crucial to the RDF program.

However, Congress in 1982 sharply pared back the administration's plans at Ras Banas, approving $91 million of the $125.6 million requested in fiscal 1983 for Air Force facilities and none of the $53 million requested for Army facilities.

The House Appropriations Committee cited several grounds for cutting the funds. The panel said the facility had grown too elaborate and expensive. The area's harsh climate and its distance from the Persian Gulf might severely limit its operational value, according to the committee. Moreover, the committee pointed out that Egypt had not formally signed any agreement guaranteeing U.S. access to the site.

The Senate Appropriations Committee, however, declared its wholehearted support for the Ras Banas plan and dismissed the significance of a formal country-to-country agreement. "The committee is satisfied that our present relationship with Egypt fully supports the development of the rear staging based at Ras Banas," said its report.

Congress appropriated $58 million of $117 million requested in fiscal 1983 for facilities at Diego Garcia but none of the $56 million requested for Lajes. The full $30 million requested for Somalia, $8.3 million for Kenya and $60.3 million for Oman were approved.

'Strategic Mobility'

"Strategic mobility is the key to our rapid deployment planning, but our ability to project forces overseas is currently constrained by limited airlift and sealift resources," said Defense Secretary Weinberger in the fiscal 1984 Pentagon budget presentation to Congress. In early 1983 the U.S. inventory of forces available for RDF use included:

- 215 long-range commercial passenger aircraft and 109 commercial cargo aircraft in the Civil Reserve Air Fleet (CRAF);
- 242 dry cargo ships, 173 of which were available by charter or government contract under the Sealift Readiness Program;
- 70 C-5 wide-body cargo jets and 234 C-141 and 218 C-130 cargo planes in the active forces;
- 12 KC-10s, which could operate either as intercontinental refueling tankers or as airlift aircraft.

In addition, the United States had 494 transport helicopters, 8 high-speed SL-7 container ships and 29 cargo ships in the Ready Reserve Fleet available for use within five to 10 days after notification. (By comparison, during the first two weeks of the April-June 1982 crisis between Britain and Argentina in the Falkland Islands, Britain mobilized 29 merchant ships for service in the war zone, 8,000 miles away.)

Quick Deployment Capability

Although sealift would remain the primary means of transporting forces and equipment over a long period, adequate airlift capabilities were critical during the early days of a conflict. However, the number of aircraft available to the RDF fell far short of what it would take to airlift a division to the Persian Gulf. To move an infantry division there would take the U.S. military air fleet an entire month, it was projected. Furthermore, sending the planes needed to handle contingencies in that region would leave other strategic areas unprotected.

C-17 Transport Issue. To improve airlift capability, the Carter administration had requested funds to begin development of a new transport plane, the CX, subsequently renamed the C-17. The CX, capable of carrying an M-1 tank (the main U.S. battle tank) several thousand miles nonstop, was designed to land on the shorter runways that likely would be encountered in the areas where the RDF would be needed. But the new transport would not be available until 1985, at the earliest, and its production would require nearly five times the $81 million requested for fiscal 1981.

In the interim, the administration requested funds to boost airlift capabilities immediately. The budget included funds to strengthen the wings of the giant C-5 transports — extending their period of service to the year 2000 — and improve the C-141s, the backbone of the air transport fleet. The C-141 was to be equipped for mid-air refueling, and its fuselage enlarged. Improvements in the KC 10-A Advanced Tanker Cargo Aircraft (ATCA), a version of the DC-10 jetliner, would enable it to refuel aircraft, such as the C-141, in mid-air. Because the plane could carry a large cargo load, in addition to fuel, six KC-10s could escort a fighter squadron and all its maintenance equipment nonstop from the United States to Southwest Asia in one day. That would avoid the sometimes sticky political issue of refueling in foreign countries along the way.

Congress in 1980 approved requests of $298.4 million to buy six new KC-10A ATCAs, $187.2 million to modify existing C-5s and $49.5 million to modify existing C-141s.

Budget Realities. In 1981 Reagan initially planned to double the amount Carter had requested for RDF and related programs. However, as the nation's economic problems worsened and projections for the fiscal 1982 deficit soared, the administration came under increasing pressure to pare back its defense increases. Proposed cuts of more than $1.3 billion were contained in Reagan's revised request for programs related to the RDF and in U.S. military forces stationed in the Persian Gulf region.

Reagan was forced to reduce his original request of $245.7 million to develop the CX cargo plane. But even his reduced recommendation of $169.7 million was too high for the Senate and House Armed Services committees. The panels were alarmed at the $10 billion price tag of a new C-17 fleet and were barraged with competing proposals by Lockheed Corp., offering to sell more C-5 transports, and by the Boeing Corp., offering some 747 converted cargo planes.

The Air Force, however, insisted that the C-5 was too large to land safely on small airfields in primitive areas, in contrast to the proposed C-17. And the 747, the Air Force argued, could carry heavy equipment only to major air terminals equipped with special unloading equipment, unlike the C-5 and C-17.

Congress was unconvinced of the Air Force's case for the C-17 and approved only $15 million for the program. Another $50 million could be used (with the Armed Services committees' approval) to fund whatever program for new cargo aircraft the Defense Department justified to the panels, whether that involved the C-17, the existing planes or a mix of both types.

Domestic Political Factors. The battle over cargo planes continued in 1982 and was one of the most heavily lobbied pork-barrel defense issues that year. The battle was waged largely by members with a direct constituent interest in which company was awarded the plane contract. The two primary plane manufacturers competing for the deal had weighed in with full-page newspaper ads, touting their respective aircraft, the day before the crucial votes in the House.

Proponents of the C-5 emphasized the plane's unique ability to carry so-called outsize equipment, such as tanks, helicopters and anti-aircraft weapons that could go into action quickly. The 747 could not carry some of the largest items of equipment, and could carry others only if they were partly disassembled.

Supporters of the 747 maintained that the existing C-5 fleet was adequate. They directed their congressional lobbying on the lower cost of the 747. Over a 20-year lifetime, Boeing estimated that a 747 fleet would cost about $12.1 billion to buy and operate, while a C-5 fleet would cost close to $20 billion. The Air Force put the cost difference at only $1 billion, rather than $7.9 billion, insisting that Boeing had omitted several costs.

In the end, Congress approved the administration's plan to procure 50 more C-5s, authorizing $847.5 million to buy the first plane, procure the necessary facilities and equipment and purchase an initial stock of spare parts. At the same time, $1 million was approved to continue development of the C-17. The Defense Department's fiscal 1984 budget included $1.4 billion to buy four C-5s, $246.6 million to strengthen the wings of the present fleet of C-5s and $26.8 million to continue development of the C-17, due to enter service about 1990.

Reagan in 1982 substantially increased his previous year's request for KC-10 midair refueling tankers; Congress approved $795 million, essentially the amount the administration wanted, for the fiscal 1983 share of a multi-year contract to buy 44 of the planes. For fiscal 1984 the administration requested $813 million to procure eight more KC-10s; 24 KC-10s were to be in service by fiscal 1984. The Defense Department expected to have 60 in service by fiscal 1987.

RDF Readiness

By 1982, according to Gen. Robert C. Kingston, RDF commander, the U.S. quick deployment capability had increased considerably. With adequate warning, Kingston said, a tactical fighter unit could be deployed to the Persian Gulf within several hours; an amphibious battalion of 1,800 Marines could be ashore within 48 hours; and an Army airborne brigade of 3,000 troops could be in the region within four days. The remaining two-thirds of an Army combat division could arrive within two weeks, Kingston said. But it would take considerably longer to dispatch heavy equipment and supply reinforcements. Hence, so-called prepositioning programs would be particularly essential in the early stages of a conflict and would have the advantage of having provided a U.S. peacetime presence in the region.

'Prepositioning' Ships. Congress in 1980 had approved $207 million for the first of a new class of large ships that could be indefinitely deployed in international waters, or "prepositioned" in the Pentagon's jargon, for the purpose of serving as floating bases and resupply warehouses. The ships were to substitute for bases in those parts of the world where an American presence might be politically embarrassing to friendly governments. These ships would hold heavy equipment, vehicles and supplies.

Reagan's fiscal 1984 budget request included $444.8 million to charter a fleet of these prepositioning ships and to purchase the Marine Corps combat equipment that would be stored in them. The Pentagon planned to have the first four prepositioning ships in service and ready to resupply a Marine brigade by the end of fiscal 1984. The budget also in-. cluded $253 million to continue operating a makeshift fleet of prepositioning ships anchored at Diego Garcia.

Reagan's fiscal 1984 budget included $56.8 million to add nine more cargo ships to the U.S. reserve fleet of 29 that were kept ready for sea duty on five to 10 days' notice.

Other Units for RDF. Reagan also requested $252.5 million to begin converting eight fast commercial container ships, called SL-7s, so that enough combat vehicles of an Army division quickly could be driven on and off the vessels. Capable of steaming at 33 knots fully loaded, the ships would cut two weeks off the 30 to 35 days required to move a division to the Indian Ocean from the United States.

For fiscal 1984, the administration requested $525.4 million for procurement of a fourth amphibious landing ship dock (called LSD-41) that could land tanks, combat vehicles and Marine Corps units during a military engagement. Prepositioning ships and other air and sea transports in general could take U.S. troops and equipment only to locations under friendly control.

The fiscal 1984 budget continued the modernization and expansion of the Navy's fleet of amphibious ships. For the first of a new class of helicopter carriers, called LHDs, the administration requested $1.38 billion. Like the 12 other helicopter carriers already in the fleet, the ships would carry about 2,000 Marines and the 20-30 helicopters needed to ferry them ashore.

Readiness for What Kind of War?

By 1984 the RDF was expected to have at its disposal three and one-third Army divisions, plus their combat service support, and one and one-third Marine Amphibious Forces, for a total capability equivalent to about four and two-thirds divisions. (The U.S. forces, as noted previously, were not separate RDF units but were assigned simultaneously to other commands. The Army divisions, for example, were simultaneously assigned to NATO.) And about seven Air Force tactical fighter wings (also assigned simultaneously to NATO) were to be available for use by the RDF. The Navy was scheduled to make available up to three carrier battle groups. A total of 130,767 Army, 69,000 Marine, 32,000 Air Force and 52,000 Navy personnel were detailed to the RDF.

"Regardless of their size, configuration, or destination, our rapid deployment forces must be prepared to deploy on a 'moment's notice,' " said Defense Secretary Weinberger. That required the forces to be " 'streamlined' to maximize combat power early in a crisis," and deployment to be " 'rapid' (by improving their equipment and personnel preparedness as well as planning) and 'ready' (by training combat and logistics support units for operations in unfamiliar and widely varying climates and terrain)," he said.

Middle East Focus

To enhance readiness, the Reagan administration authorized a number of combat exercises, both in the United States and in Southwest Asia. Among them was operation Bright Star, a joint exercise conducted in Egypt, Oman and Somalia in late 1981. That exercise, which took place shortly after the Oct. 6 assassination of Egyptian President Anwar Sadat, involved about 6,000 U.S. ground, air and naval forces (the exercise had been increased in size after Sadat's death from a planned level of 1,500). The maneuvers included a drop by the 82nd Airborne over Egypt's western desert and a much smaller exercise involving landings by Marines from assault ships at Oman and Somalia, whose troops participated in the operation. A handful of B-52s from North Dakota flew to Egypt, dropped bombs on test ranges and returned to the United States.

A year later, another exercise, called Jade Tiger, was conducted in Oman, Sudan and Somalia. That one involved Air Force F-15 interceptors and AWACS radar planes, Navy carrier-based aircraft and Air Force B-52s to simulate enemy aircraft. Joint operations also were carried out with Omani Army troops. The Defense Department planned to conduct one exercise (either a Bright Star type or a communications exercise) in the Persian Gulf annually. In alternate years, a division-size exercise in the United States was planned.

Who is the Enemy?

An issue that was fundamental to the RDF's readiness involved the kind of Middle East war in which U.S. troops were to be trained to fight. Senate Armed Services Committee Chairman John Tower, R-Texas, and the chairman of the panel's Sea Power Subcommittee, William S. Cohen, R-Maine, and others maintained that, rather than sending U.S. forces to the region to counter an overt Soviet incursion, the emphasis should be on deterring and, if necessary, fighting regional wars or leftist or nationalist insurgencies that threatened U.S. and allied access to the region's oil supplies.

U.S.-Soviet Balance of Forces . . .

Geographical factors remained important considerations in comparing U.S. and Soviet military capabilities in the Indian Ocean/Persian Gulf region. The Soviet Union borders Iran and is only 650 miles from the head of the Persian Gulf. From their bases in occupied Afghanistan, the Soviets are only 300 to 400 miles from the Strait of Hormuz — through which much of the Persian Gulf's oil is shipped.

The distance to the gulf from bases in the United States obviously is much greater. U.S. planes would have to fly more than 8,000 miles and U.S. ships would have to steam about 12,000 miles around Africa or about 8,000 miles through the Suez Canal.

In its *Strategic Survey* for 1981-82, the London-based International Institute for Strategic Studies summarized the forces then available to the United States and the Soviet Union in that region of the world and concluded that "Soviet capabilities to project military force over long distances, while growing, remained distinctly inferior to those of the United States."

The Soviet forces available for operation in Southwest Asia were deployed in the southern Military Districts of the U.S.S.R. They consisted of 29 divisions, more than 800 tactical aircraft and about 400 helicopters. (About 105,000 Soviet troops were in Afghanistan as of early 1983.)

The closest Soviet equivalent to the U.S. Rapid Deployment Force was the U.S.S.R.'s airborne force — seven line divisions of about 7,300 men each. The Soviet Naval Infantry was small by comparison to the U.S. Marine force, comprising five regiments of about 2,000-2,500 men each. The Soviet airlift fleet also was smaller. The Soviets' Indian Ocean fleet numbered about 30 ships.

The United States had one aircraft carrier battle group continuously stationed in the area, as well as a Marine amphibious unit that was positioned part time in the Indian Ocean. Thirteen supply ships stocked with enough fuel and equipment to keep a 12,000-man unit operating for 30 days were stationed in Diego Garcia.

Two air bases in Soviet-occupied southern Afghanistan "not only placed much of the Persian Gulf region within range of Soviet tactical aircraft but

The original RDF plan was ill-suited to local problems not involving overt Soviet action, they argued. Such local upheavals could develop too quickly to permit a large U.S. force to step in at the invitation of a friendly government and deter a *coup d'etat* or other threat. A very mobile deployment force was needed since domestic and regional

. . . In Persian Gulf/Southwest Asia

shortened the air route to more distant Soviet client states, such as South Yemen or Ethiopia.

In a crisis, the Soviet's bases in Afghanistan also would give the U.S.S.R. a route to the Arabian Sea, which would only involve overflying the poorly defended Baluchistan area of Pakistan," according to the London-based institute, which added, "Even if the Soviet Union is judged unlikely to attack the oil-producing regions of the Persian Gulf, she will continue to enjoy the advantages of relative proximity to that region. That proximity also means that she is likely to regard Western efforts in the region less as efforts to insure oil supplies than as measures which increase the military weight of the West in a region near to the Soviet Union."

The study said the capabilities of America's European allies in the Persian Gulf region were limited. With 20 ships, France had the third largest force in the Indian Ocean. During the 1980 war between Iran and Iraq, France deployed a five-ship minesweeping force to the Arabian Sea. The 3,500 French marines and legionnaires based at Djibouti, on the east coast of Africa at the Gulf of Aden, constituted the largest Western intervention force close to the Persian Gulf. France also maintained several other units earmarked for possible use in the Middle East.

In 1980 Britain established a surveillance patrol in the Gulf of Aden that consisted of two major combatant units plus a tanker and support ship. When the Iran-Iraq war broke out in September of that year, Britain had at least six ships operating in or near the Indian Ocean.

Pakistan possessed more than 22 divisions, but most of those were infantry units reserved for threats from the Soviet Union or India. However, Pakistan maintained a large military advisory group in Saudi Arabia that could be increased.

Turkey had about 23 divisions, but they too were primarily infantry units and were ill-equipped and below full strength. However, Turkey had about 100 modern jet aircraft and hundreds of older planes. Turkish bases would be important for any air operations against the Soviet Union itself.

politics had blocked the basing of U.S. forces in the gulf states, they pointed out. In any case, U.S. bases in that region might exacerbate the very nationalist pressures that endangered U.S. interests, they argued.

Tower and Cohen both favored a greater emphasis on Marine amphibious forces, which would not rely on local land bases and would be equipped to shoot their way ashore against military opposition. And a large amphibious landing fleet in the region would provide skittish U.S. allies "a greater presence over the horizon — one that they can feel and not see," Cohen said in 1982 testimony before a congressional committee. For Saudi Arabia and other nations this would ease the political problem of being too closely tied to Washington. On the other hand, assault units could intervene in regional or internal conflicts quickly enough to deter some revolts. If the situation got out of hand, they could intervene despite local military opposition, a point usually left unsaid by Tower and Cohen.

The administration pointed out that RDF plans all along had included a "forcible entry" option, relying on Marines. "We must be able to open our own doors," Marine Commandant Gen. Robert H. Barrow told the Senate Defense Appropriations Subcommittee in March 1982. "That's the *raison d'être* of my service."

But Tower and Cohen insisted that the Pentagon budget would not have enough money both for equipment designed for Marine landings and equipment designed for an uncontested landing by a larger force.

According to Cohen, the increased emphasis on an assault-oriented RDF was a factor in the Reagan administration's decision to buy more C-5 transport planes instead of the proposed C-17.

Future Shape of the RDF

By 1983 some observers were arguing that creation of an RDF in the Persian Gulf was superfluous in light of the global oil glut. At a Feb. 2, 1983, hearing before the Senate Energy and Natural Resources Committee, Energy Secretary Donald P. Hodel said the strategic priority of the region had decreased because the potential for another oil embargo was "far less" than it had been in recent years. "If you look at the [likelihood of] an interruption of oil from . . . the Persian Gulf, it is a much smaller percentage now than it has been for years," he said. Hodel also noted that Mexico had replaced Saudi Arabia as the largest foreign oil supplier to the United States.

Nonetheless, it was generally argued that the United States should plan for any eventuality in the Persian Gulf, including the need for military action.

Some critics argued that any RDF plan for the gulf region risked military disaster by relying on airborne and seaborne reinforcements for forces stationed at U.S.-owned or -controlled bases in the Southwest

Asian/Indian Ocean area. However, Congress in 1982 praised the Reagan administration for shifting its emphasis from trying to develop a capability that could confront a large-scale Soviet invasion to the kind of quick deployment force that could cope with local threats to U.S. interests without relying on the use of local bases. According to the Senate Armed Services Committee, local threats were far more likely to arise.

Some officials warned that a rapid deployment capability might make U.S. intervention around the world more likely. According to Harold Brown, Carter's defense secretary, the United States needed "to be somewhat cautious to see that the pendulum doesn't swing too far back the other way, to the point where we begin to believe that military strength can solve all of our international problems."

Most criticism, however, was heard from those who felt the RDF could not handle serious kinds of contingencies. They argued that it merely addressed the problem of transporting U.S. ground forces into trouble spots, without seriously considering what they would do when they got there. In the view of military analyst Jeffrey Record, the RDF was too lightly structured to respond adequately to contingencies in the Middle East, where U.S. troops might face "numerically superior Soviet-model client armies of heavy forces whose tactical mobility and firepower, even battalion for battalion, far exceed that now possessed by either U.S. Army or Marine light forces."

"Given existing doubts about the nature of the threat, the reception [that would be given] an American presence in the area, the willingness of Western Europe to cooperate and U.S. military capacity, a strategy that places U.S. ground forces in the Persian Gulf should not be undertaken without a thorough national and congressional debate," wrote former Under Secretary of State David D. Newsom in 1981. "In the meantime, the presence of America's substantial fleet should be maintained and its readiness strengthened."

"The Soviet invasion of Afghanistan upset the regional geopolitical equation, but this does not mean that the Soviet Union is the primary threat to Western interests in the Persian Gulf," wrote Christopher Van Hollen, a former deputy assistant secretary of state, in the Summer 1981 issue of *Foreign Affairs*. "An exclusively anti-Soviet military approach can be dangerously destabilizing if pressed with excessive zeal in the politically volatile Persian Gulf region."

The possibility of overt Soviet seizure of Middle East oil fields was, according to Van Hollen, "near the bottom of the threat list. The most likely challenges to Western interests will come from wars between regional states, transborder incursions, civil disturbances, oil embargoes or production cuts."

According to Van Hollen, most of the gulf states viewed the RDF "as a threat to their oil resources, rather than as a protector of their national integrity. Moreover, the inevitable escalation in demands for logistical support ... carries the risk of imposing intolerable political strains on the four states — Egypt, Kenya, Oman and Somalia — which have granted the United States military facilities." He concluded that "a small, highly mobile force, based at sea and supplied by sea, might be superior to the ungainly Rapid Deployment Force."

Chapter 5

MANAGING TODAY'S ARMED SERVICES

More than 2,100,000 men and women currently serve on active duty in the United States military forces. If an emergency befell the nation close to 1,000,000 more could be mobilized, with varying degrees of speed, from the reserve elements of the land, sea and air forces.

More than 1,000,000 civilians are employed by the Defense Department throughout the world to back up the U.S. military establishment.

Of those forces on active duty, about 25 percent at any given time are deployed overseas — military headquarters, combat units, military assistance groups and other formations — to support U.S. security interests and treaty obligations. Commitments are embodied in the NATO alliance, the ANZUS treaty with Australia and New Zealand, the seven-member Southeast Asia treaty, the Rio de Janeiro treaty linking 22 Latin American countries and the United States, and bilateral treaties with the Philippines, Japan and South Korea. Commitments similarly are lodged in presidential declarations, most notably that made by President Jimmy Carter in 1980 pledging the defense of the Persian Gulf, if necessary, to ensure access to the region's vital oil supplies.

The Defense Department spent $182.9 billion to maintain and strengthen the armed forces in fiscal 1982. In fiscal 1983, it expected to spend $208.9 billion.

Military Buildup Objectives

After two years of success with its military buildup, altered only minimally by Congress, the Reagan administration found itself in deep controversy over the scale and speed at which the expansion should continue. The controversy was rooted in the country's economic hard times and widespread alarm about the prospect of widening federal deficits during the years the buildup of military production — and thus of heavy Pentagon spending — would be hitting its stride.

Disagreements arose specifically over how much more money should be spent and how many men and women should serve in uniform. Personal costs, though declining as a percentage of the defense budget, still ate up more than 40 percent of military expenditures. The administration had no intention of slowing down the buildup, though Congress might make alterations. In any case, Reagan already had achieved many of the defense objectives he considered his first priority upon taking office. Whatever the pace of future expansion, it would take off from the high base established in the first years of his presidency.

The administration, said Defense Secretary Caspar W. Weinberger, had to perform a "double duty." "First, we have had to act quickly to increase the basic readiness and sustainability [in combat] of our forces, so that we could meet an immediate crisis if one arose. At the same time, we ... [had to] make up for lost years of investment by undertaking the research and development and force modernization [expanded purchases of new weapons and equipment] needed to meet threats that may arise in the future."

Weinberger's own report card showed that the first aim — that of immediate improvements in readiness and in personnel — was "partially accomplished" with the big additions the administration and Congress made to the fiscal 1981 and 1982 budgets. The foundations for the longer-term modernization, he maintained, were laid in the fiscal 1983 budget — and were threatened, in his view, by the growing resistance in Congress — even among many Republicans — to his proposed 1984 spending plan.

If the congressional critics found some weapons requests of doubtful value — either their cost or performance — as they sought ways to reduce or stretch out Pentagon expenditures, Weinberger answered that, indeed, not all weapons and equipment met all the specifications that would be desired. And some that had been years in development had cost too much, he conceded. He yielded no further, however. All the requests he had made to Congress were needed, he insisted. In the long run, there would be improvements in development and production. But "in the short run, we cannot face an adversary with weapons that are still on the drawing board."

In making the hard choices, it generally was recognized that certain defense requirements were immutable: No one wanted to disregard any

U.S. treaty obligations; no one seriously wanted the nuclear deterrent to develop cracks; no one wanted American combat units to field inferior weapons.

But on these and many connected questions there was fierce debate over what was sufficient to meet the military's requirements. Were so many U.S. troops needed in Europe? Should Japan stop sheltering under the American wing and provide more of its own defense? Could the active forces be held at current strength while the reserves were increased and better supplied with modern arms? For worldwide mobility, should more expensive C-5 aircraft be bought, as planned, or should there be a switch to fast sealift forces? Was the B-1 bomber needed, or could the Strategic Air Command wait for development of the so-called Stealth, or radar-evading, bomber?

As viewed by the United States, the "threat" — a military term describing an assessment from which planning of conventional and nuclear forces proceeds — lay chiefly in the power of the Soviet Union and in its perceived willingness to use that power when opportunities arose. The threat doubtless was exaggerated from time to time as the administration pressed its "rearm America" programs on Congress. On the other hand, no one contended the threat presented by the communist bloc was diminishing.

Organization of the Armed Services

The structure of the military forces of the United States can be viewed in two ways:

Traditional Concept

The traditional picture the words "military forces" conjure up is that of an Army, a Navy and Marine Corps and an Air Force. The services in fact tend to view themselves in this "parochial" way, to paraphrase President Dwight D. Eisenhower. The "unification" of the forces under the National Security Act of 1947 put all the services under the direction of a new Cabinet officer, the secretary of defense. But that law did not "merge" them; this, indeed, was expressly forbidden by that act.

In proposing his defense reorganization plan of 1958, President Eisenhower noted ironically that the law retained "traditional concepts of separate forces for land, sea and air operations" but simultaneously called for "their integration into an efficient team of land, naval and air forces."

Eisenhower's solution, as approved by Congress, was to preserve "the traditional form and pattern of the services" — the Army, Navy, Marines and Air Force — Congress would have had it no other way — but to establish the "unified" commands that today are the cutting edge — the fighting elements — of the United States' defense establishment.

These units of land, sea and air forces — the regional commands: the U.S. Pacific Command and the U.S. European Command, for example — are responsible to the secretary of defense, not to any individual service or its secretary.

Functional Forces

The other way, therefore, to view the armed services is on a functional basis. This is the way they are viewed by the defense secretary's office and by the Joint Chiefs of Staff, the top military body, comprising the chairman (currently Gen. John W. Vessey, Jr.) and the chiefs of the military services.

Nobody wears a Defense Department uniform, as distinct from an Army or a Navy uniform, and nobody is recruited or commissioned into one of the unified commands, such as the Pacific Command, rather than into an individual service. But that is the way the forces are organized to fight — in integrated, operational commands with assigned missions.

To cite a pertinent example: An outbreak of hostilities in the Persian Gulf area would bring the new U.S. Central Command into play. This organization was created in January 1983, replacing the former Rapid Deployment Joint Task Force, with responsibility to plan for Southwest Asian contingencies. Such contingencies became a major focus of administration endeavors to improve combat readiness for operations in remote, Third World areas. *(Details, see Rapid Deployment Force chapter.)*

Before the collapse of the shah's regime in Iran and the Soviet invasion of Afghanistan in 1979, there were periodic U.S. naval sorties into the Indian Ocean but no preparations for swiftly moving forces into that vital oil-producing region. By 1983, however, the Pentagon could point to 17 cargo ships stationed in the area, loaded with equipment and supplies for an amphibious brigade of 12,500 Marines as well as the weapons and supplies needed for Army and Air Force units that would arrive by air if there were a crisis. A measure of the extent of this effort, as envisioned by the Reagan administration, was that supplies for 45,000

Marines were scheduled to be stored (prepositioned) aboard ships in the region by 1986.

The Central Command, thus far, was distinct from it larger and more traditional counterparts having permanently assigned land, sea and air units. But the U.S. military high command had assembled a rather imposing list of forces that would be "on call" for the Central commander-in-chief. As enumerated by the Pentagon, these included: three Army combat divisions and Ranger and Special Forces (Green Beret) units; 23 Air Force fighter and bomber squadrons; three aircraft carrier task forces; and Marine amphibious outfits totaling 60,000 men.

As Weinberger had stated, "Our strategy [in the Persian Gulf area] is to be prepared to insert sufficient forces rapidly enough to deter a Soviet invasion of the region." This had a ring of getting there first with the least or, at any rate, not with a massive military effort. The administration's theory was that neither superpower would want to risk a direct confrontation there; thus, the one that got there first — and displayed a willingness to hold the ground — would hold the aces.

Forces for Many Wars

Weinberger's formal pronouncements on strategy in general have taken on a calmer and more realistic aspect. He speaks now of "inhibiting" rather than "halting" Soviet expansion.

Weinberger in 1981 warned about the possibility of war in Central Europe, the Persian Gulf, Africa, East Asia or Central America. "We may have to deal with more than one conflict at a time," the defense secretary warned. To many observers, including members of Congress, this was looked upon as a sort of fight-everywhere-at-once strategy, an idea reinforced by Weinberger's companion expressions on what came to be known as horizontal escalation: "If we are forced into war, we must be prepared to launch counteroffensives in other regions and try to exploit the aggressor's weaknesses wherever they exist." *("Horizontal Escalation," p. 148)*

It was this sort of official concern about boundless emergencies and threats that resulted in defense calculations that to do the job the armed forces might require $750 billion more over five years than the $1.6 trillion program the administration had formally requested. However, military officials were not espousing anything like that kind of buildup.

The caveats about war possibly spreading and being prolonged continued to be expressed by Reagan administration officials. But in his

1983 defense posture report to Congress, Weinberger articulated strategy in more plausible terms:

"In responding to an enemy attack, we must defeat the attack and achieve our national objectives while limiting — to the extent possible and practicable — the scope of the conflict. We would seek to deny the enemy his political and military goals and to counterattack with sufficient strength to terminate hostilities at the lowest possible level of damage to the United States and its allies."

Trying to limit the scope of a war and to end it at the lowest possible level of damage seemed, on the face of it, a different matter from "horizontal escalation" and fighting on multiple fronts.

The Regular Forces

Just as the combat forces are organized functionally in unified commands to carry out national strategy, the entire military establishment and its civilian work force are organized — and displayed for budgetary purposes — on functional lines.

The categories are: strategic nuclear forces, which have provoked most of the defense debate in and outside Congress but required just 10.26 percent of the total defense appropriations sought by the Pentagon for fiscal 1984; general purpose forces, all the tactical land, sea and air formations, for which approximately 40 percent of the budget request was devoted; intelligence and communications; airlift and sealift; National Guard and reserve forces; research and development; central supply and maintenance; training and medical; and administration. Military and civilian personnel and budgets are distributed throughout the individual services and defense-wide organizations to carry out these functions.

The Reagan administration's defense team arrived on the scene with ambitious plans for expanding the military roster by 250,000 men and women over several years, in large part to go with envisioned increases in the number of combat units. In the fiscal year that already was in progress (1981) it quickly added 10,000 persons to the Carter administration's base figure of 2,065,000 then on active duty.

For reasons that had nothing to do with the draft-free, all-volunteer force concept, but rather with budgetary restraints, military planners had to rein in their original hopes. In a recession period, with military pay substantially boosted after years of falling behind, the forces were able to recruit the number and types of persons they thought were needed. But

Draft Registration Kept

Reversing a stand he took during the 1980 presidential campaign, President Ronald Reagan on Jan. 7, 1982, ordered the continuation of mandatory military draft registration for 18-year-old men. The registration requirement had been reinstated by President Jimmy Carter in January 1980, ostensibly as a response to the Soviet invasion of Afghanistan.

During the campaign, Reagan had cited estimates that peacetime registration would reduce by only a few days the time needed to call up draftees in case of war. But presidential counselor Edwin Meese III cited new estimates that registration could speed the start of conscription by about six weeks. In a statement read to reporters by Meese, Reagan said the decision "does not foreshadow a return to the draft."

Meese denied that the Polish situation played any role in the decision, but anonymous White House sources were reported as saying the president did not want to signal a softening of the U.S. stance toward Moscow by ending registration. Polish authorities, backed by the U.S.S.R., had imposed martial law the previous December.

Congress, with an eye on rising military costs in other areas, held down the Pentagon's manpower goals. That was likely to prevail again in fiscal 1984. The trend as of early 1983 was toward holding the forces at their current strengths.

Manpower Ceilings

The congressionally authorized manpower level for the end of fiscal year 1983 stood at 2,127,000, a figure already reached by March 31. If Congress voted to accept a freeze on further increases in the active duty manpower level, as introduced in the House, the Reagan gain over the Carter base figure would stand at 62,000 since mid-1981.

Weinberger wanted to add 38,000 more in fiscal 1984 and had plans for a further 48,000 increase in fiscal 1985, which would raise total manpower to 2,213,000. He complained in May 1983 that the then-projected freeze would "reverse the major gains" in increasing combat readiness made in the previous two years and would deny the services the manpower needed to operate the increasing numbers of ships, aircraft, cruise missiles and other weapons, and to perform adequate maintenance and training.

Increases in the active military roster under Reagan occurred chiefly in the Navy (15,000 added in two years) and the Air Force (22,000 added) as naval, aircraft and missile forces were expanded and the manning of existing units was improved. As Reagan's goal of a 600-ship Navy moves toward realization, further increases in Navy personnel were likely. Marine and Army manpower remained fairly stable, though the Army picked up slots for combat troops as its needs for trainees declined.

The individual service manpower strengths in fiscal 1983 were: Army — 782,000; Navy — 555,000; Marines — 199,000; Air Force — 592,000.

If one calculated manpower strength through the functional organization of the military, only 97,000 men were assigned to the strategic nuclear forces, while the tactical land, sea and air forces and the airlift and sealift units claimed 1,007,000. Most of the remaining military personnel served in intelligence, communications, research and development, and the host of supporting activities such an organization required.

It should be noted that as many as 84,000 military members at any time were in transit from one assignment to another, and in 1983 13,000 were patients or prisoners and 227,000 were students, cadets and trainees.

Civilian Work Force

The Defense Department's employment of civilians grew from 1,019,000 in fiscal 1981 to 1,056,000 in fiscal 1983. The Pentagon's large civilian bureaucracy was needed to support the 2-million-strong armed forces. Civilians help to administer the vast weapons and related research and development and procurement programs, maintenance, health care (the Pentagon operated 161 hospitals throughout the world), accounting and management of the enormous amounts of money needed to finance the military, and many other more mundane jobs. Weinberger contended that if Congress imposed a freeze on military manpower it might require hiring more than the 16,000 additional civilians he already had proposed in the fiscal 1984 defense budget.

The Reserve Forces

In the years immediately after the military draft ended, from 1974 through 1978, the strength of the reserve forces plummeted. The pressure of potential conscription for active service no longer was an incentive to volunteer for the reserves. Monetary inducements, compared to the opportunities then existing in the private sector, were not very effective. Manpower declined by 137,000, bottoming out at 788,000.

However, with the aid of an enlistment and re-enlistment incentive program, and the faltering economy a contributory factor, the military reserves in 1979 began to prosper. Manpower strength climbed steadily to its present level of 1,002,000. And the Pentagon's manpower agency was optimistic that the trend would continue; its goal was 1,030,000 in fiscal 1984 and 1,068,000 in fiscal 1985.

Hand-in-hand with the reserves' recruitment successes there had come an increasing share of responsibility for the military's missions. Lawrence J. Korb, the assistant secretary of defense for manpower, reserve affairs and logistics, reported in 1983 that the reserves constituted 50 percent of the combat capability and two-thirds of the support for the country's conventional military forces.

"In the event of a conflict," according to Korb, "the individuals and units of the Guard and Reserve will deploy with the active forces." Therefore, they had to be as capable and professional as the active forces.

The planned strengths of the Selected Reserve (organized reserve military units, which would be the first to back up regular forces in a war) for fiscal 1983 were:

> Army National Guard — 417,000.
> Army Reserve — 268,500.
> Naval Reserve — 105,800.
> Marine Corps Reserve — 105,800.
> Air National Guard — 101,800.
> Air Force Reserve — 66,600.
> Total — 1,002,300.

The cost of the reserves' various incentive programs — enlistment and re-enlistment bonuses, educational assistance and student loan repayment programs — grew from $47 million in fiscal 1981 to a projected $95 million in fiscal 1984. The Defense Department's annual outlays for equipping and otherwise supporting the reserves were fairly constant in recent years: $10.6 billion in fiscal 1982, $11.4 billion in fiscal 1983 and $11.6 billion projected for 1984.

If success was the word for the Selected Reserve, the status of the Individual Ready Reserve (IRR) was less clear-cut. The Ready Reserve represented a pool of previously trained manpower, available to fill understrength units and to replace casualties in the first days of a conflict.

Its average strength in recent years was slightly more than 400,000, far below any estimates of what was needed during a war.

One partial solution to the manpower problem that was being proposed by the Reagan administration was to extend the current six-year military service obligation to eight years. Service members serve out the obligated years beyond their active duty periods in the IRR. Also, bonuses were being proposed by the Pentagon for direct enlistment into the IRR, with initial training in the Army, and for re-enlistment in the IRR after the obligated periods ended. The only benefit of IRR membership today, said Korb, was the chance for quick call-up in time of war, and that is "not a sufficiently attractive inducement to cause many IRR members to re-enlist."

Women in the Military

In the 1970s, according to a new Pentagon publication, "Military Women in the Department of Defense," the number of uniformed women increased more than 350 percent, to a total of 150,000.

"The increase was spurred primarily by social pressures for equal opportunity, with particular emphasis on utilization of women in non-traditional skills," the publication said. "Unfortunately, little effort was made during this period to empirically determine the best way to utilize women based on skill, mission and readiness requirements."

It was felt that a lot of women were given jobs less challenging and rewarding than they had expected, such as changing tires on 10-ton trucks or repairing tank turrets. Expanding the numbers of women in the services was widely seen not only as responding to social pressures but as a key element in making the all-volunteer military force successful in its troubled early years at the end of the Vietnam War. Subsequently, some women left, and some migrated back into more traditional clerical and administrative positions. The medical field within the services remained a major attraction for women.

The publication looked upon the 1980s as starting a new phase for women, one in which all the services were designating "more clearly defined requirements" for them. "These requirements are being developed based on the proven capability of women in manning specific military requirements."

Between 1980 and 1982, the number of women in the services increased by 27 percent, to 190,000; this figure included more than 25,000 officers. Women made up about 9 percent of the active-duty force, compared with 4 percent a decade ago. The total number was expected to grow over the coming years, but the percentage of women in the services probably would not.

Korb noted that servicewomen were clustered in mid-to-lower grades. They had entered in relatively large numbers in the early 1970s and, therefore, had less service time on the average than men. But in the next few years, said Korb, "the experience and grade distribution of military women will approximate more closely that of military men."

Major Military Units

With their concentration on short-term combat readiness and longer-term modernization, the Reagan defense planners were able to realize significant increases in the manning and equipping of existing formations, but they were less successful in increasing the number of combat units. As against the administration's rhetoric about "windows of vulnerability" and new strategies for deterring nuclear and conventional war, William E. Kaufmann concluded, in an extensive study for the Brookings Institution, that "the programs themselves are familiar and fit into the traditional mold of U.S. defense policy." Kaufmann for many years was a Defense Department consultant and author of its annual defense posture reports.

In the latest of those reports, no longer Kaufmann products, there was a reduction in land-based strategic nuclear forces from fiscal 1982 to 1984, as older Titan missiles and B-52 bombers were phased out and newer model replacements were being readied. There was some increase in tactical air squadrons and a substantial growth in the size of the fleet.

The following figures document the number of units expected to be operational in fiscal 1984, starting Oct. 1, 1983 (pluses or minuses in parentheses show changes from fiscal 1982; otherwise the numbers are the same for both years):

Strategic Forces:

> Titan intercontinental ballistic missiles — 34 (-18).
> Minuteman ICBMs — 1,000.
> B-52 bombers, C, F and D models — 0 (-75).
> B-52 G and H models (the newest versions) — 241.
> FB-111 bombers — 56.

211

Poseidon submarine-launched ballistic missiles — 496.
Trident SLBMs — 120 (+72).
Air defense interceptor squadrons: active Air Force — 5; Air National Guard — 10.

General Purpose Forces:

Combat divisions: active Army — 16; Army Reserve — 9 (+1); active Marine Corps — 3; Marine Corps Reserve — 1.

Attack and fighter aircraft squadrons: active Air Force — 81 (+1); Air Force Reserve — 43 (+2); active Marine Corps — 28; Marine Corps Reserve — 8; active Navy — 63 (+3); Navy Reserve — 10.

Naval forces: active fleet combatants — 443 ships (+4); fleet auxiliaries, naval reserve and other — 96 ships (+2); strategic missile-carrying submarines and support ships — 42 (+2).

Airlift and sealift: 328 (+13) C-5, C-141 and KC-10 aircraft for strategic (intercontinental) airlift; 218 active Air Force C-130, and 305 (+1) Air Force Reserve and National Guard C-130 and C-123 aircraft for tactical (intra-theater) airlift; 36 (+1) active fleet tanker, cargo and stores ships; 36 (+3) chartered tankers and cargo ships; 189 (+8) ships in the National Defense Reserve Fleet.

Force Deployment

"We continue to strengthen our forces deployed on the homelands of our traditional allies in Europe and East Asia and to prepare for new contingencies in Southwest Asia," Weinberger said in assessing administration achievements in its first two years. Forward deployment — to be near potential foreign trouble spots in order to deter Soviet bloc threats or aggressive moves and to be able to react swiftly to them — has been the essence of U.S. strategy for more than 30 years. According to defense strategists, the peace prevailing in Europe and the northern Pacific was convincing evidence of the success of that strategy, which throughout the postwar era was backed by the sanction of the nuclear weapon.

The Reagan administration maintained the general, long-established pattern of military deployments while undertaking to beef up the deployed forces themselves.

Forces in the United States

In the continental United States, where the bulk of the nation's military power was concentrated, there were (as of 1983):

● Army — 10 airborne, helicopter air assault, armored, mechanized and infantry divisions, three separate brigades and an armored cavalry regiment.

● Marine — two Marine Amphibious Forces, one in California and one in North and South Carolina; each consisted of a combat division and a supporting air wing.

● Air Force — nine strategic missile wings, 18 bomber wings (an aircraft wing nominally has three squadrons), five interceptor squadrons, 38 fighter squadrons, three reconnaissance squadrons, nine tactical airlift squadrons, six strategic airlift wings and six tanker wings.

● Navy (major units) — Atlantic Fleet: seven aircraft carriers, 105 surface combatant ships, 28 amphibious ships and 83 submarines. Pacific Fleet: six carriers, 88 surface combatants, 31 amphibious ships and 44 submarines. Both fleets contributed units to U.S. operations in the Indian Ocean, where a nominal presence consisted of an aircraft carrier battle group and an amphibious unit.

Forces Overseas

By far the largest concentration of U.S. military power outside the United States is in West Germany, where 256,000 uniformed men and women were stationed in large formations as of 1983. They received the latest military equipment, and in adequate quantities. The forces maintained in the United States and the adjacent waters were geared to reinforce the overseas units as circumstances warranted.

When the Defense Department took its roll call at the end of 1982, it counted about 528,000 service members stationed overseas. The primary locations and numbers serving were:

West Germany — 256,000.
Other European stations — 67,000.
Near Europe aboard ships — 33,000.
South Korea — 38,000.
Japan, including Okinawa — 51,000.
Other Pacific stations — 15,000.
In the Pacific aboard ships — 33,000.
Miscellaneous foreign stations — 34,000.

Congress at the end of 1982 froze military manpower in Europe at existing levels, ostensibly to induce Europeans to make greater defense efforts of their own. The Pentagon urged Congress to lift the ceiling as it prepared to deploy Air Force ground-launched cruise missiles and Army Pershing II missiles in NATO countries. *(Details, see Role of Conventional Arms chapter.)*

Outside the continental United States, the Army deployed four armored and mechanized divisions, two border-patrol armored cavalry regiments, three separate brigades from U.S.-based divisions, and a multitude of supporting units in West Germany; an infantry brigade in West Berlin; an infantry brigade in Alaska; a brigade in Panama; an infantry division in Hawaii; and an infantry division in South Korea.

The Marines headquartered an amphibious force of one division and one air wing on Okinawa, with elements of the division located in Hawaii and units of the air wing stationed on the Japanese home islands.

Major units of the Air Force outside the continental United States consisted of 28 fighter, two reconnaissance and various airlift squadrons in Europe; an interceptor squadron in Iceland; two fighter squadrons and an airlift squadron in Alaska; and 10 fighter, one reconnaissance and two airlift squadrons in the Pacific area, including South Korea.

Force Readiness

"As a defensive power which has global interests and which faces varied threats, the United States must be ready to go to war quickly if necessary," the Defense Department said in defending its 1984 budget requests. "This requires first-rate and highly trained personnel and well-maintained weapons and equipment.... Great progress is being made."

The administration could argue that establishing the all-volunteer military force on a solid working basis was its major achievement in defense. Pay was boosted almost 20 percent in two years, after being raised almost 12 percent in the Carter administration's last year. The services consistently had met or exceeded their recruiting goals. Re-enlistments were running very high. Education and experience levels were improving; this has become a necessity for those service members handling complex, modern weapons. Units were more fully manned. Spare parts bins were beginning to fill up. Ammunition stocks were growing.

"The number of fully or substantially ready major active units has increased by almost one-third during the term of this administration," Weinberger asserted in his 1983 military posture report.

In 1982, 86 percent of first-term enlistees were high school graduates — those most likely to succeed in military careers — compared with 68 percent in 1980. About 68 percent of service members eligible to re-enlist did so in 1982, compared with a 1980 figure of 55 percent.

In addition, training picked up as major sums were allocated for that purpose. An example the Pentagon liked to cite was the increase in Air Force tactical aircraft crew flying hours — from 13 a month in 1978, to 15 in 1980, to 17 in 1982, and to a planned 20 in 1984.

There was a parallel attack on the problem of keeping equipment in working order. The number of ships overdue for overhaul has been halved since 1979, and the Army expected to eliminate its depot maintenance backlog.

Problems with arms and personnel persisted, which was hardly surprising in an organization the size of the U.S. military. The Army's new M-1 tank continued to suffer maintenance problems, and weapons experts sought to establish the right stockpile levels for parts. The Air Force complained about shortages of spare parts for aircraft. The Navy had shortages of the more sophisticated weapons and continued to lose highly trained, much-needed persons, particularly nuclear power specialists.

It was feared that the Reagan administration might be inviting serious personnel problems by its decision to withhold a general pay raise in fiscal 1984. Many members of the military forces likely would react by charging that the White House was breaking a commitment to keep pay comparable with that in the civilian sector.

Some pro-defense members of Congress could be expected to seek enactment of at least part of a 7.6 percent pay boost the administration had in mind before it decided in its fiscal 1984 budget to freeze wages — one of the few options it thought it had for making large savings in defense spending in the year ahead. At the same time, Congress seemed determined to reduce requested funds for operations and maintenance in the services, which could adversely affect readiness depending on how the reductions were allocated.

Manpower Costs

"There is no job in the civilian community that compares to being a solider," the Army's official magazine "Soliders," once pointed out. Many skills were similar, but there was a big difference: "The solider must always be prepared to perform under combat conditions and be prepared to lay his or her life on the line." And there were other demands, such as family separations, frequent moves, field duty and extra duties.

But if the demands were unique, said the magazine, so was the unique array of benefits. It mentioned pay raises and tax-free allowances, commissary and post exchange savings, free medical care, no requirement for contributions to health insurance and pension funds, travel, recreation, housing, educational opportunities and 30 days of paid annual leave, starting with the first year.

Selective re-enlistment bonuses went as high as $16,000. An "old sergeant" could make $20,000 to $25,000 a year in base pay, before counting in the allowances for quarters and various types of special pay. A lieutenant colonel with 16 years service received base pay of about $35,000. Bonuses of all sorts were available for use as tools to lure servicemen and women into the specialities where they were needed most.

Personnel costs, and all those associated benefit costs implied in the "Soldiers" magazine list, represented a very large proportion of the total defense budget. This had been the case especially since the early 1970s when the basic policy decision was made to abandon the draft in favor of an all volunteer armed force. With volunteers, the government no longer could, in effect, operate a defense establishment in which much of the work in the armed services was performed cheaply.

In another of its functional arrangements of the military budget, the Defense Department broke down its $274.1 billion appropriations request for 1984 as follows:

Military personnel — $47.9 billion.

Retired pay — $16.8 billion.

Operations and maintenance — $74 billion.

Procurement — $94.1 billion.

Research, development, test and evaluation — $29.6 billion.

Military construction — $6 billion.

Family housing — $2.8 billion.

Other — $2.5 billion.

Of the Pentagon's fiscal 1984 appropriations request, an estimated $238.6 billion, if approved by Congress, would be spent during that year. When outlays for personnel costs, including civilian salaries, were extracted from those functional categories and toted up, the Defense Department calculated that spending on military personnel comprised 42.2 percent of all defense spending.

This percentage had been even higher in the years before the Reagan administration dramatically raised the procurement and operating accounts.

Key Dates in U.S. Defense Policy, 1977-83

1977

Jan. 18. Soviet President Leonid I. Brezhnev says the U.S.-Soviet 1974 Vladivostok agreement on strategic nuclear weapons should be ratified.

Jan. 27. The White House announces that newly elected President Jimmy Carter will seek an early resumption of strategic arms limitation talks (SALT II).

March 9. The Senate confirms Paul C. Warnke as chief U.S. arms control negotiator by a 58-40 vote after four days of debate during which critics charged he advocated large defense cuts and unilateral constraints on U.S. weapons development.

March 30. The Soviet Union rejects the initial U.S. SALT II proposals, submitted by the Carter administration, that called for a freeze on new weapons systems, a freeze on advanced missiles and a ban on mobile missiles. The proposals called for reductions below those agreed upon at Vladivostok.

May 18. NATO defense ministers agree to a 3 percent increase in defense spending over five years.

May 20. The SALT stalemate ends, with the United States and the U.S.S.R. agreeing on a framework for negotiations and general principles.

June 30. Carter announces his decision to cancel production of the B-1 bomber and, instead, to equip existing B-52s with cruise missiles.

Dec. 6. The House votes against rescinding funds for the B-1.

Dec. 16. The SALT talks recess. Both sides say significant progress has been made.

1978

Feb. 1. The Senate insists on dropping funds appropriated for the B-1 bomber.

Feb. 2. Defense Secretary Harold Brown urges a defense buildup, citing a "standoff or stalemate" in U.S.-Soviet strategic strength and warning that the Soviet military position had improved.

Feb. 22. The House agrees to rescind all funds for the B-1.

Oct. 22-23. The SALT talks resume; disagreements persist over the Soviet Backfire bomber, the range of U.S. cruise missiles and the number of multiple independently targeted re-entry vehicle (MIRV) warheads allowed each side.

1979

April 5. Defense Secretary Brown formally launches SALT II ratification drive, despite the fact that the treaty is not yet completed. He gives assurances that the United States has "essential equivalence" with the Soviet Union.

May 16. NATO ministers officially endorse the draft SALT treaty.

June 8. The White House announces Carter's decision to approve full-scale development of the MX land-based intercontinental missile.

June 18. Carter and Brezhnev sign the SALT II treaty in Vienna.

June 28. France formally endorses SALT II.

July 9. The Senate Foreign Relations Committee opens hearings on the SALT treaty.

July 11. The Joint Chiefs of Staff formally endorse the treaty in testimony before the Foreign Relations Committee.

July 26. Gen. Alexander M. Haig Jr., former NATO commander, recommends that the Senate delay its approval of SALT II until "flaws" in the treaty are corrected.

July 31. Former Secretary of State Henry A. Kissinger links his support for SALT II to substantial increases in defense spending.

Sept. 7. Carter announces his decision to base the MX missile on a "race-track" system in which the missiles would move at random to avoid their destruction in the event of a Soviet nuclear attack.

Nov. 9. The Senate Foreign Relations Committee votes 9-6 to recommend approval of SALT II.

Dec. 12. NATO defense ministers announce agreement on a "two-track" policy that includes deployment of U.S. Pershing II intermediate-range nuclear weapons and ground-launched cruise missiles in Western Europe, coupled with endorsement of U.S.-Soviet negotiations to reduce or eliminate intermediate-range nuclear weapons deployed in Europe.

Dec. 13. Congress passes a defense appropriations bill providing $670 million requested by Carter for initial development of the MX missile.

1980

Jan. 3. Carter formally asks the Senate to postpone indefinitely further consideration of the SALT II treaty following the Soviet Union's invasion of Afghanistan on Dec. 27, 1982.

May 6. The administration drops the so-called race-track basing plan for the MX missile in favor of a "linear" system that it says will save space and money.

May 14. The MX easily survives attempts by liberal members of the House to block or delay it.

The House backs restoration of B-1 funding by a margin of 3-to-1.

Aug. 20. In a speech at the Naval War College, Secretary Brown outlines a new nuclear strategy (Presidential Directive 59) that emphasizes military flexibility to allow for limited nuclear strikes against Soviet military targets. He warns of a growing vulnerability of U.S. forces, particularly the land-based Minuteman ICBMs, in a Soviet nuclear attack.

Aug. 20. Defense Department officials reveal that a so-called "stealth" radar-evading plane is under development.

Aug. 26. Congress passes a defense bill authorizing $300 million for research and development and $75 million for initial procurement of a new manned bomber: either the B-1, a variant of the B-1, a modified FB-111, or a completely new plane.

1981

May 4. Secretary of State Haig says the United States is ready to begin talks with the U.S.S.R. on eliminating intermediate-range nuclear weapons in Europe.

Sept. 24. The United States and the U.S.S.R. announce that talks will begin Nov. 30 on the intermediate range weapons.

Oct. 2. Reagan announces a five-part, $180 billion, long-term plan to improve U.S. strategic forces. The plan includes an MX missile deployment plan — placing 20-40 MXs in existing hardened missile silos as an interim basing system — production of B-1 bombers, production of Trident submarines and development of a Trident II missile, improved command, control and communications systems and improved anti-missile defenses.

Nov. 18. Reagan announces a four-point arms control plan for Europe: 1) cancellation of planned U.S. deployment of intermediate-range nuclear forces in return for Soviet dismantling of their existing intermediate-range missiles aimed at Western Europe; 2) U.S.-Soviet discussions "as soon as possible" on reducing long-range missiles and bombers; 3) a reduction in Soviet conventional forces in Europe; 4) a U.S.-Soviet conference on reducing the risks of surprise attack.

Nov. 30. U.S.-Soviet talks on Intermediate Range Nuclear Forces open in Geneva. Participants foresee a long negotiating process.

Dec. 15. Congress passes a defense appropriations bill that bars use of funds to harden existing Minuteman silos for use as a basing mode for the MX; it also orders the administration to select a long-term MX basing mode by July 1983.

1982

Feb. 10. Reagan rejects a Soviet intermediate-range weapons proposal made public Feb. 9. The proposal would have allowed deployment of Soviet SS-20 missiles, but not U.S. Pershing IIs.

March 16. Brezhnev announces a unilateral halt in deployment of new Soviet missiles in Europe. The United States rejects the move as a propaganda ploy.

March 30. A proposal to freeze nuclear weapons deployment by both the Soviet Union and the United States at existing levels is endorsed by 58 senators.

April 6. In a speech at the International Club in Washington, Secretary of State Haig rejects a nuclear freeze and a "no-first-use" of nuclear weapons declaration by the United States.

May 9. In a speech at Eureka College, Reagan offers to begin strategic arms reduction talks (START) and outlines an initial negotiating proposal.

May 18. Brezhnev responds favorably to Reagan's offer but rejects his specific proposals as one-sided. Brezhnev also calls for an immediate nuclear freeze.

June 10. NATO ministers endorse START talks.

June 12. A peace rally in support of a nuclear freeze in New York's Central Park attracts more than 500,000 persons.

June 15. Soviet Foreign Minister Andrei A. Gromyko relays Brezhnev's pledge of no-first-use in a speech to the U.N. General Assembly. The White House discounts the pledge.

June 22. The Pentagon rejects recommendations made by a blue-ribbon panel established by Defense Secretary Caspar W. Weinberger for an airborne MX basing plan.

June 29. The initial phase of President Reagan's START arms reduction talks begins in Geneva.

Aug. 5. In a victory for the administration, the House votes 204-202 to reject a strong nuclear freeze resolution. A modified version acceptable to Reagan is adopted.

Sept. 20. The London-based International Institute for Strategic Studies says the balance of nuclear power in Europe "is distinctly unfavorable to NATO and is becoming more so."

Sept. 30. U.S.-Soviet talks on intermediate-range nuclear weapons reopen after a two-month suspension.

Oct. 6. The second round of the START talks begins in Geneva.

Nov. 22. Reagan warns of a growing Soviet nuclear threat in a major address to the nation and announces his decision to base the MX in a closely spaced "dense pack" plan. Members of Congress are skeptical of the plan.

Nov. 26. The Soviet Communist Party newspaper *Pravda* says U.S. deployment of the MX in a "dense pack" arrangement would violate the SALT II treaty. The Reagan administration denies the charge.

Dec. 7. The House votes to delete $988 million to procure the first five MX missiles. (The Senate votes Dec. 17 to restore the funds, but with the proviso that the money not be spent until a basing plan is approved. The final version, cleared Dec. 20, contains $2.5 billion for MX research and development, but no money for procurement of the first missiles, and requires the president to report on his choice of a basing system on or after March 1, 1983.

Dec. 13. The U.N. General Assembly approves nuclear test ban and nuclear freeze resolutions.

Dec. 21. Yuri V. Andropov, who became the leader of the U.S.S.R. upon Brezhnev's death Nov. 10, 1982, offers to reduce the number of Soviet intermediate-range missiles aimed at Western Europe to 162, the number deployed by France and Britain. The offer is immediately rejected by the United States, Britain and France.

1983

Jan. 16-18. Soviet Foreign Minister Andrei Gromyko visits West Germany as part of a campaign to persuade the German government to oppose deployment of Pershing IIs and cruise missiles.

Jan. 27. Talks on intermediate-range forces resume after being recessed Nov. 30, 1982.

Feb. 2. The third round of START, recessed in December 1982, opens.

Feb. 10. Vice President George Bush completes a 12-day visit to seven Western European nations as part of a White House public relations effort to solidify support for deployment of the Pershing II and the Reagan administration's so-called zero option plan for eliminating all intermediate-range missiles in Europe.

March 6. In what is widely viewed as a major test for NATO's so-called two-track policy, approved in December 1979 *(see Dec. 12, 1979, entry)*, Chancellor Helmut Kohl's Christian Democratic Party is returned to office in national parliamentary elections. Kohl endorses the policy, while his opponent in the elections, Social Democrat Hans-Jochen Vogel, is critical of it.

March 8. As the House Foreign Affairs Committee approves a nuclear "freeze" resolution, Reagan warns, in a speech to the National Association of Evangelicals, that "a freeze would reward the Soviet Union for its enormous and unparalleled military buildup."

March 12. In an interview with *The Washington Post*, Kohl expresses the belief, widely held by West European governments, that Reagan's "zero option" proposal, while the optimal solution, is not attainable.

March 23. In the first of a series of major speeches on defense policy, Reagan defends his record $280.5 billion defense budget request and again warns of the Soviet military buildup. At the end of his nationally televised address he describes a "vision of the future" that foresees a defense against nuclear attack by new anti-missile missiles on the Earth and in space.

March 28. The seventh successful Pershing II test flight occurs, with 12 more planned before the missiles are deployed.

March 30. In a televised White House speech, Reagan announces modifications in the "zero option" plan. The scaled-back proposal calls for equal limits on U.S. and Soviet intermediate-range nuclear weapons on a global basis. He says "zero option" remains the final goal.

March 31. Reagan expands on his arms control policies in an address before the Los Angeles World Affairs Council. He restates his belief in the need to continue the U.S. defense buildup and defends his START and intermediate-range weapons proposals.

April 2. Soviet Foreign Minister Gromyko dismisses as "unacceptable" Reagan's modified IRBM proposal and says there is "no chance" it could serve as the basis for an agreement. NATO governments generally reacted favorably to Reagan's March 30 proposal.

April 11. An 11-member blue-ribbon panel established by Reagan Jan. 3, 1983, recommends that 100 MX missiles be deployed in existing

Minuteman missile silos while the United States develops a new, smaller missile that would be mobile and invulnerable to Soviet attack. According to the panel, formally known as the President's Commission on Strategic Nuclear Forces, the smaller missile could become the keystone of a new approach to stabilizing the nuclear balance between U.S. and Soviet nuclear forces.

April 19. Reagan approves the commission's proposal and submits it to Congress. Under legislation passed in 1982, Congress had until mid-June to approve a resolution providing the funds for the basing recommendation.

May 3. Culminating a two-year effort, the U.S. Roman Catholic Bishops vote 238-9 to adopt a pastoral letter condemning first use of nuclear weapons and calling for "immediate, bilateral and verifiable" agreements to halt the testing, production and deployment of new nuclear weapons.

May 3. Soviet leader Yuri Andropov says Moscow is prepared to reach an agreement with the United States on limiting the number of nuclear warheads, as well as launchers, in the European theater to the existing NATO levels (including French and British forces). He also says that Moscow "will be compelled to take measures in reply" if the United States goes ahead with plans to deploy IRBMs in Europe. Reagan calls Moscow's proposal "encouraging."

May 4. The House, by a vote of 278-149, approves a non-binding nuclear "freeze" resolution calling on the United States and the U.S.S.R. to negotiate an immediate, mutual and verifiable freeze on the production, development and deployment of nuclear weapons. Reagan administration supporters succeed in adding an amendment that would end the freeze if a mutual weapons reduction agreement were not achieved within "a reasonable, specified period of time."

May 12. In letters to influential members of Congress, Reagan commits himself in general terms to a "build-down" approach to nuclear arms control proposals. That plan would require each country to reduce the overall size of its nuclear arsenal as it deployed new weapons. Reagan also endorses the development of relatively small, single-warhead ICBMs that was recommended April 11 by the President's Commission on Strategic Forces.

Following Reagan's pledge, two congressional panels approve the use of some fiscal 1983 appropriations to implement the new MX basing plan.

May 24-25. Reagan wins a solid victory in Congress on his MX policy. The House May 24 and Senate May 25 approve resolutions to allow funds to be used to convert existing Minuteman silos to hardened MX launching sites and to conduct MX test flights. The House resolution (H Con Res 113) is approved 239-186; the identical Senate measure (S Con Res 26) is passed by a vote of 59-39. During the debates, several members in each chamber warn the White House that their continued support for MX depends on the administration's adherence to the arms control recommendations made by the President's Commission on Strategic Forces.

June 8. Reagan announces changes in the U.S. negotiating position at the strategic arms reduction talks (START) in Geneva. The proposed ceiling of 5,000 on the number of strategic missile warheads to be allowed each side is retained, but the proposed ceiling on the number of missiles themselves would be increased from 850 to an unspecified figure, thus requiring a less radical cut in the existing Soviet missile force.

Glossary of Common Defense Terms

Anti-Ballistic Missile (ABM). A weapons system for intercepting and destroying ballistic missiles. Also called ballistic missile defense (BMD).

Ballistic Missile. A self-propelled missile that is guided in its ascent and follows a ballistic trajectory, part of which is outside the Earth's atmosphere.

Binary Chemical Weapon. A shell or warhead filled with two chemicals of relatively low toxicity that mix while the device is being delivered to the target; the chemical reaction produced when they mix becomes a supertoxic chemical warfare agent, such as nerve gas.

Biological Weapons (BW). Living organisms, or infective material derived from them, which are intended for use in warfare to cause disease or death in man, animals or plants, and the means of their delivery.

Conventional Weapons. Weapons not having mass destruction effects. Non-nuclear weapons. *(See also Weapons of Mass Destruction.)*

Countervailing Strategy. Also referred to as counterforce strategy. An attack directed against military targets as well as vital industrial and command centers for the purpose of persuading an adversary that no plausible outcome of a confrontation could result in success by the adversary.

Cruise Missile. A missile that can fly at very low altitudes (and can be programmed to follow the contours of the terrain) to minimize radar detection. It can be air-, ground- or sea-launched and can carry a conventional or a nuclear warhead.

Enhanced Radiation Weapon (ERW). *(See Neutron Weapon.)*

Fallout. Particles contaminated with radioactive material as well as radioactive nuclides, descending to the Earth's surface following a nuclear explosion.

First-Strike Capability. The capability to destroy within a very short period of time all or a very substantial portion of an adversary's strategic nuclear forces.

Flexible Response Capability. The capability to react to an attack with a full range of military options, including use of small, or "limited," nuclear weapons.

Intercontinental Ballistic Missile (ICBM). Ballistic missiles with a range in excess of 5,500 kilometers.

Intermediate-Range Nuclear Weapons. The U.S. designation for long-range and medium-range theater nuclear weapons. *(See also Theater Nuclear Weapons.)*

Kiloton (Kt). The measure of the explosive yield of a nuclear weapon equivalent to 1,000 metric tons of trinitrotoluene (TNT) high explosive. (The bomb detonated at Hiroshima in World War II had a yield of about 12-15 kilotons.)

Launcher. The apparatus used to launch a missile. ICBM launchers are land-based launchers that can be either fixed or mobile. SLBM launchers are missile tubes built into submarines.

Medium-Range Nuclear Weapons. Soviet designations for long-range theater nuclear weapons. *(See also Theater Nuclear Weapons.)*

Megaton (Mt). The measure of the explosive yield of a nuclear weapon equivalent to one million metric tons of trinitrotoluene (TNT) high explosive.

Multiple Independently Targeted Re-entry Vehicles (MIRV). A portion of a strategic ballistic missile designed to carry a number of nuclear warheads and to re-enter the Earth's atmosphere in the last phase of its trajectory. With a MIRVed missile, each of the warheads can be directed at a separate target.

Mutual Assured Destruction (MAD). A concept of reciprocal deterrence that rests on the ability of the countries having nuclear weapons to inflict intolerable damage on one another after surviving a nuclear first strike.

Mutual Reduction of Forces and Armaments and Associated Measures in Central Europe (MURFAAMCE). The subject of negotiations between the NATO and Warsaw Pact countries begun in Vienna in 1973. Usually referred to as the mutual (balanced) force reduction (M(B)FR) talks.

National Technical Means of Verification. Electronic and optical devices, including satellites, radar and radio receivers, with which each country can monitor the other's compliance with an arms limitation treaty.

Neutron Weapon. A nuclear explosive device designed to maximize the radiation effects and reduce blast and thermal damage.

Nuclear Weapon. A device that is capable of releasing nuclear energy in an explosive manner and which has a group of characteristics that are appropriate for use for warlike purposes.

Payload. The warhead of a ballistic missile, along with the compartment or final stage carrying it; the weight of such a load. *(See also Throw Weight.)*

Re-entry Vehicle (RV). A portion of a strategic ballistic missile designed to carry a nuclear warhead and to re-enter the Earth's atmosphere in the last phase of the trajectory.

Second-Strike Capability. The ability to survive a nuclear attack and to launch a retaliatory blow powerful enough to inflict intolerable damage on the enemy. *(See Mutual Assured Destruction.)*

Strategic Arms Limitation Talks (SALT). Negotiations between the Soviet Union and the United States, initiated in 1969, that sought to limit the strategic nuclear forces, both offensive and defensive, of both sides. A SALT I treaty was signed by President Richard M. Nixon and Soviet President Leonid I. Brezhnev on May 25, 1972, and approved by the Senate Sept. 14, 1972. A SALT II treaty was signed by President Jimmy Carter and Brezhnev on June 18, 1979. The treaty was never approved by the Senate. President Carter formally shelved the treaty indefinitely on Jan. 3, 1980, after the Soviet Union invaded Afghanistan.

Strategic Arms Reduction Talks (START). Negotiations between the United States and Soviet Union, initiated by President Ronald Reagan and begun in Geneva June 29, 1982, aimed at reducing the number of long-range ballistic missiles deployed by each of the superpowers.

Strategic Nuclear Forces. ICBMs *(see separate entry)*, submarine-launched ballistic missiles (SLBMs), air-to-surface ballistic missiles (ASBMs) and bomber aircraft having intercontinental range (the U.S. B-52s and proposed B-1).

Tactical Nuclear Weapons. Nuclear weapons designed for battlefield use, along with tanks, guns and combat troops. The enhanced radiation weapon, the so-called neutron bomb (actually a warhead or artillery shell) is an example.

Theater Nuclear Weapons. Also referred to as intermediate-range nuclear weapons. Nuclear weapons having a range of less than 5,500 kilometers (km). Often divided into longer-range (over 1,000 km.; for instance, the so-called Eurostrategic weapons) and shorter-range (up to 200 km.) weapons. The latter also are referred to as tactical or battlefield nuclear weapons.

Throw Weight. The total weight of re-entry warheads, MIRV aiming devices and penetration aids carried by a missile. *(See also Payload.)*

TNF Negotiations. Negotiations on theater nuclear forces (TNF) between the United States and the U.S.S.R., begun Nov. 30, 1981, in Geneva, aimed at reducing deployment of those weapons in the NATO and Warsaw Pact countries.

Warhead. That part of a missile, torpedo, rocket or other munition that contains the explosive or other material intended to inflict damage.

Yield. The released nuclear explosive energy expressed as the equivalent of the energy produced by a given number of metric tons of trinitrotoluene (TNT) high explosive. *(See also Kiloton and Megaton.)*

Selected Bibliography on Defense Policy

Books

Barnaby, Frank, and Thomas, Geoffrey, eds. *The Nuclear Arms Race — Control or Catastrophe?* New York: St. Martin's Press, 1982.

Berman, Robert P., and Baker, John C. *Soviet Strategic Forces.* Washington, D.C.: The Brookings Institution, 1982.

Betts, Richard K. *Cruise Missiles and U.S. Policy.* Washington, D.C.: The Brookings Institution, 1982.

——. *Surprise Attack.* Washington, D.C.: The Brookings Institution, 1982.

Binkin, Martin. *Youth or Experience?: Manning the Modern Military.* Washington, D.C.: The Brookings Institution, 1979.

Binkin, Martin, and Eitelberg, Mark J. *Blacks and the Military.* Washington, D.C.: The Brookings Institution, 1982.

Blechman, Barry M., ed. *Rethinking the U.S. Strategic Posture.* Cambridge, Mass: Ballinger Publishing Co., 1982.

Boston Study Group. *The Price of Defense: A New Strategy for Military Spending.* New York: Times Books, 1979.

Branch, Hans Guenter, and Clarke, Duncan L. *Decisionmaking for Arms Limitation in the 1980s: Assessment and Prospects.* Cambridge, Mass.: Ballinger Publishing Co., 1982.

Broadhurst, Arlene Idol, ed. *The Future of European Alliance Systems: NATO and the Warsaw Pact.* Boulder, Colo.: Westview Press, 1982.

Brown, Harold. *Thinking About National Security.* Boulder, Colo.: Westview Press, 1983.

Burns, Richard D. *SALT Nonproliferation and Nuclear Weapons-Free Zones: An Introduction to Nuclear Arms Control and Disarmament.* Los Angeles: California State University, Center for the Study of Armament and Disarmament, 1979.

Buteux, Paul. *Strategy, Doctrine, and the Politics of Alliance: Theatre Nuclear Force Modernisation in NATO.* Boulder, Colo.: Westview Press, 1983.

Canan, James. *War in Space.* New York: Harper & Row, 1982.

Clark, Ian. *Limited Nuclear War.* Princeton, N.J.: Princeton University Press, 1982.

Coffey, Kenneth J. *Manpower for Military Mobilization.* Washington, D.C.: American Enterprise Institute for Public Policy Research, 1978.

Collins, John M. *U.S. Defense Planning: A Critique.* Boulder, Colo.: Westview Press, 1983.

———. *U.S.-Soviet Military Balance.* New York: McGraw-Hill Book Co., 1980.

Davis, Jacquelyn K., and Pfaltzgraft, Robert L., Jr. *The Atlantic Alliance and U.S. Global Strategy.* Cambridge, Mass.: Institute for Foreign Policy Analysis, 1982.

Feld, Werner J., and Wildgen, John K. *NATO and the Atlantic Defense: Perceptions and Illusions.* New York: Praeger Publishers, 1982.

Foreign Policy Association. *SALT II: Toward Security or Danger? A Balanced Account of the Key Issues in the Debate,* New York: 1979.

Freedman, Lawrence. *The Evolution of Nuclear Strategy.* New York: St. Martin's, 1983.

George, Alèxander L. *Managing U.S.-Soviet Rivalry: Problems of Crisis Prevention.* Boulder, Colo.: Westview Press, 1983.

Goodpaster, Andrew J.; Elliott, Lloyd H.; and Hovey, J. Allan, Jr. *Toward a Consensus on Military Service.* Elmsford, N.Y.: Pergamon Press, 1982.

Goodwin, Geoffrey. *Ethics and Nuclear Deterrence.* New York: St. Martin's Press, 1982.

Gray, Colin S. *The MX ICBM and National Security.* New York: Praeger Publishers, 1981.

Grayson, Benson Lee. *Soviet Intentions and American Options in the Middle East.* Washington, D.C.: National Defense University Press, 1982.

Greenwood, Ted. *Making the MIRV: A Study of Defense Decision Making.* Cambridge, Mass.: Ballinger Publishing Co., 1975.

Hanks, Rear Adm. Robert J., (Ret.). *The U.S. Military Presence in the Middle East: Problems and Prospects.* Cambridge, Mass.: Institute for Foreign Policy Analysis, 1982.

Hoeber, Francis P. *Slow to Take Offense: Bombers, Cruise Missiles, and Prudent Deterrence.* Washington, D.C.: Georgetown University Center for Strategic and International Studies, 1977.

Holloway, David. *The Soviet Union and the Arms Race.* New Haven, Conn.: Yale University Press, 1982.

Huntington, Samuel P., ed. *The Strategic Imperative: New Policies for American Security.* Cambridge, Mass.: Ballinger Publishing Co., 1982.

Jasani, Bhupendra, ed. *Outer Space: A New Dimension of the Arms Race.* London: Taylor & Francis, 1982.

Johnson, Maxwell Orne. *The Military as an Instrument of U.S. Policy in*

Southwest Asia: The Rapid Deployment Joint Task Force, 1979-1982.
Boulder, Colo.: Westview Press, 1983.

Laird, Melvin R. *People, Not Hardware: The Highest Defense Budget Priority.* Washington, D.C.: American Enterprise Institute for Public Policy Research, 1980.

Leites, Nathan. *Soviet Style in War.* New York: Crane, Russak & Co., 1982.

Lewis, William J. *The Warsaw Pact: Arms, Doctrine, and Strategy.* Cambridge, Mass.: Institute for Foreign Policy Analysis, 1982.

Mandelbaum, Michael. *The Nuclear Question.* Cambridge, Mass.: Harvard University Press, 1980.

Nakhleh, Emile. *The Persian Gulf and American Policy.* New York: Praeger Publishers, 1982.

Nathan, James A., and Oliver, James K. *The Future of United States Naval Power.* Bloomington: Indiana University Press, 1979.

Neidle, Alan F., ed. *Nuclear Negotiations: Reassessing Arms Control Goals in U.S.-Soviet Relations.* Austin, Texas: Lyndon B. Johnson School of Public Affairs, 1982.

Nerlich, Uwe, ed. *Soviet Power and Western Negotiating Policies.* 2 vols. Cambridge, Mass.: Ballinger Publishing Co., 1982.

Nuclear Weapons: Report of the Secretary-General of the United Nations. Brookline, Mass.: Autumn Press, 1981.

Olive, Marsha McGraw, and Porro, Jeffrey P., eds. *Nuclear Weapons in Europe.* Lexington, Mass.: Lexington Books, 1983.

Platt, Alan, and Weiler, Lawrence D., eds. *Congress and Arms Control.* Boulder, Colo.: Westview Press, 1978.

Record, Jeffrey. *NATO's Theater Nuclear Force Modernization Program: The Real Issues.* Cambridge, Mass.: Institute for Foreign Policy Analysis, 1982.

Reichart, John F., and Sturm, Steven R. *American Defense Policy.* 5th ed. Baltimore: The Johns Hopkins University Press, 1982.

Scoville, Herbert Jr. *MX: Prescription for Disaster.* Cambridge, Mass.: MIT Press, 1981.

Scowcroft, Brent, ed. *Military Service in the U.S.* New York: Prentice-Hall, 1982.

Smoke, Richard. *War: Controlling Escalation.* Cambridge, Mass.: Harvard University Press, 1978.

Tahir-Kheli, Shirin, ed. *U.S. Strategic Interests in Southwest Asia.* New York: Praeger Publishers, 1982.

Talbott, Strobe. *Endgame: The Inside Story of SALT II.* New York: Harper & Row, 1979.

Taylor, William J., Jr., and Maaranen, Steven A. *The Future of Conflict in the 1980s.* Lexington, Mass.: Lexington Books, 1983.

Taylor, William J., Jr.; Olson, Eric T.; and Schrader, Richard, eds. *Defense Manpower Planning: Issues for the 1980s.* Elmsford, N.Y.: Pergamon Press, 1981.

Thompson, E. P. *Beyond the Cold War: A New Approach to the Arms Race and Nuclear Annihilation.* New York: Pantheon Books, 1982.

Thompson, W. Scott, ed. *National Security in the 1980s: From Weakness to Strength.* San Francisco, Calif.: Institute for Contemporary Studies, 1980.

Tucker, Robert W., and Wrigley, Linda, eds. *The Atlantic Alliance and Its Critics.* New York: Praeger Publishers, 1983.

Articles

"The Arms Control Debate." *Atlas,* July 1979, pp. 31-36.

Ball, R. "Nuclear Weapons: Suppose We Froze?" *Fortune,* May 17, 1982.

Barkenbus, Jack N. "Whither the Treaty?" *The Bulletin of the Atomic Scientists,* April 1980, pp. 37-39.

Barlow, Jeffrey G. "Western Europe and the NATO Alliance." *Journal of Social and Political Studies,* Spring 1979, pp. 3-15.

Beck, M. "Defending the United States." *Newsweek,* Dec. 20, 1982.

Bertram, Christoph. "The Implications of Theater Nuclear Weapons in Europe." *Foreign Affairs,* Winter 1981/82.

Bowden, James A. "The RDJTF and Doctrine" (Rapid Deployment Joint Task Force). *Military Review,* November 1982.

Bundy, McGeorge; Kennan, George F.; McNamara, Robert S.; and Smith, Gerard. "Nuclear Weapons and the Atlantic Alliance." *Foreign Affairs,* Spring 1982.

Burt, Richard. "The Cruise Missile and Arms Control." *Survival,* January/February 1976, pp. 10-17.

Butterfield, F. "Anatomy of the Nuclear Protest." *The New York Times Magazine,* July 11, 1982.

Cameron, Juan. "It's Time to Bite the Bullet on the Draft: Both in Number and in Quantity, Volunteer Forces are Inadequate to Meet a Real Emergency." *Fortune,* April 7, 1980, pp. 52-54.

Canan, James W. "A U.S. Scenario for Fighting a Mideast War." *Business Week,* February 25, 1980.

____. "The Pentagon's New Plan for Mideast Defense." *Business Week*, February 19, 1979.

Cohen, E. A. "Why We Need a Draft." *Commentary*, April 1982.

Cohen, Richard E. "SALT II: Selling the Treaty to the Senate." *National Journal*, July 16, 1979.

"Combat Readiness for a Deterrent Strategy." *Armed Forces and Society*, Winter 1980, pp. 169-312.

"Controversy Over Proposed Draft Registration: Pro and Con." *Congressional Digest*, April 1980, pp. 99-128.

"Controversy Over the MX Missile: Pro and Con." *Congressional Digest*, November 1980, pp. 259-288.

Dean, Jonathan. "Beyond First Use." *Foreign Policy*, Fall 1982.

Dougherty, Russell E., and Hatfield, Mark O. "Should the United States Build the MX?" American Enterprise Institute, *Foreign Policy and Defense Review*. No. 6, 1980.

Fairlie, H. "What the Falklands Teaches Us." *New Republic*, July 12, 1982.

Fallows, J. "America's High Tech Weaponry." *Atlantic*, May 1981.

____. "Civilianization of the Army." *Atlantic*, June 1981.

Feld, Bernard T. "A Mutual Freeze." *The Bulletin of the Atomic Scientists*, May 1982.

____. "The Hands Move Closer to Midnight." *The Bulletin of the Atomic Scientists*, January 1980.

Flint, J. "Hard Truths about Swords and Plowshares." *Forbes*, Dec. 20, 1982.

Freedman, Lawrence. "NATO Myths." *Foreign Policy*, Winter 1981-82.

____. "SALT and NATO." *Ditchley Journal*, Autumn 1979, pp 36-43.

Frye, Alton. "How to Fix SALT." *Foreign Policy*, Summer 1980, pp. 58-73.

Gordon, Michael R. "Rubles for Defense: Are the Soviets Really Outspending the Pentagon?" *National Journal*, April 11, 1981.

Gray, Colin S. "NATO Strategy and the 'Neutron Bomb.'" *Policy Review*, Winter 1979, pp. 7-26.

Gray, Colin S., and Payne, Keith. "Victory is Possible." *Foreign Policy*, Summer 1980, pp. 14-27.

"Guns vs. Butter." *Business Week*, Nov. 29, 1982, pp. 68-74.

Halperin, Morton H. "Keeping Our Troops in Europe." *The New York Times Magazine*, Oct. 17, 1982.

Hart, G. "What's Wrong With The Military." *The New York Times Magazine*, Feb. 14, 1982.

Hoffmann, Stanley. "NATO and Nuclear Weapons: Reasons and

Unreason." *Foreign Affairs*, Winter 1981/82.

Isaacson, Walter. "The Winds of Reform: Runaway Weapons Costs Prompt a New Look at Military Planning." *Time*, March 7, 1983, pp. 12-30.

Jacobsen, C. G. "Soviet-American Policy: New Strategic Uncertainties." *Current History*, October 1982.

Jenson, John W. "Nuclear Strategy: Differences in Soviet and American Thinking." *Air University Review*, March/April 1979, pp. 2-17.

Jervis, Robert. "Why Nuclear Superiority Doesn't Matter." *Political Science Quarterly*, Winter 1979/1980, pp. 617-633.

Jones, D. C. "What's Wrong With Our Defense Establishment." *The New York Times Magazine*, Nov. 7, 1982.

Kahn, H. "Thinking about Nuclear Morality." *The New York Times Magazine*, June 15, 1982.

Kaiser, Karl; Leber, Georg; Mertes, Alois; and Schulze, Franz-Josef. "Nuclear Weapons and the Preservation of Peace." *Foreign Affairs*, Summer 1982.

Keeny, Spurgeon M., Jr., and Panofsky, Wolfgang K. H. "MAD Versus NUTS." *Foreign Affairs*, Winter 1981/82.

Klare, M. T. "Army in Search of a War" (Rapid Deployment Force). *Progressive*, February 1981.

Lee, John M. "An Opening 'Window' for Arms Control." *Foreign Affairs*, Fall 1979, pp. 121-140.

Lodal, Jan M. "Finishing START." *Foreign Policy*, Fall 1982.

Luciano, Peter J. "Sealift Capability: A Dwindling Defense Resource." *Defense Management Journal*, Third Quarter 1982.

Maynes, Charles William. "Old Errors in the New Cold War." *Foreign Policy*, Spring 1982.

McGrath, Peter. "Where to Cut Defense." *Newsweek*, Dec. 20, 1982.

Mearsheimer, John J. "Why the Soviets Can't Win Quickly in Central Europe." *International Security*, Summer 1982.

Megill, William K. "The Deployment of Pershing II to Europe — Some Implications." *Military Review*, Dec. 1980, pp. 58-66.

Nacht, Michael. "ABM ABCs." *Foreign Policy*, Spring 1982.

"The Nuclear Freeze Proposal: Pro and Con." *Congressional Digest*, Aug./Sept. 1982, pp. 195-224.

Nunn, Sam. "Those Who Do Not Serve in the All-Volunteer Armed Forces." *Journal of the Institute of Socioeconomic Studies*, Autumn 1979, pp. 10-21.

Paine, C. "Nuclear Combat: The 5-Year Defense Plan." *The Bulletin of the Atomic Scientists,* November 1982.

Payne, Keith B. "Deterrence, Arms Control and U.S. Strategic Doctrine." *Orbis,* Fall 1981.

Powers, Thomas. "Choosing a Strategy for World War III." *Atlantic,* November 1982.

Ramazani, R. K. "Security in the Persian Gulf." *Foreign Affairs,* Spring 1979, pp. 821-835.

Richelson, Jeffrey T. "Soviet Responses to MX." *Political Science Quarterly,* Fall 1981, pp. 401-410.

Robinson, C. A., Jr. "Tactical Weapons Effort Slowed 2 Years." *Aviation Week and Space Technology,* Oct. 26, 1981.

Schemmer, Benjamin F. "NATO's New Strategy: Defend Forward, But Strike Deep." *Armed Forces Journal,* November 1982.

Seybold, Calvin C. "Mutual Destruction: A Deterrent to Nuclear War?" *Military Review,* September 1979, pp. 22-28.

Shapley, Deborah, "The Army's New Fighting Doctrine," *The New York Times Magazine,* Nov. 28, 1982.

Shreffler, R. G. "The Neutron Bomb for NATO Defense: An Alternative." *Orbis,* Winter 1978, pp. 959-973.

Sigal, Leon V. "Warming to the Freeze." *Foreign Policy,* Fall 1982.

Smith, H. "How Many Billions for Defense?" *The New York Times Magazine,* Nov. 1, 1981.

Smith, R. J. "High Cost Lemons in the U.S. Arsenal." *Science,* April 17, 1981.

Sonnenfeldt, Helmut. "Russia, America and Detente." *Foreign Affairs,* January 1978, pp. 275-294.

Specter, Michael. "Is the Volunteer Army a Failure?" *Nation,* June 19, 1982.

Steinbruner, John D. "Nuclear Decapitation." *Foreign Policy,* Winter 1981/82.

Taylor, Maxwell D. "Changing Military Priorities." *AEI Foreign Policy and Defense Review,* No. 3, 1979, pp. 2-13.

"Tomorrow's Infantry: More Lethal and Much Swifter." *Business Week,* Oct. 18, 1982, pp. 189ff.

Turner, S. "Toward a New Defense Strategy." *The New York Times Magazine,* May 10, 1981.

Turner, S., and Thibault, G. "Preparing for the Unexpected: The Need for a New Nuclear Strategy." *Foreign Affairs,* Fall 1982.

Ulam, Adam B. "Reality and U.S.-Soviet Relations." *New Leader,* Jan. 10, 1983.

Ullman, Richard H. "The Euromissile Mire." *Foreign Policy,* Spring 1983.

"U.S. Air Force in Europe: Special Report." *Aviation Week and Space Technology,* June 7, 1982.

van Voorst, L. Bruce. "The Critical Masses." *Foreign Policy,* Fall 1982.

Velocci, Tony. "Battle Doctrine for the 21st Century." *National Defense,* November 1982.

Government Documents

Gellner, Charles R. *U.S.-Soviet Negotiations to Limit Intermediate-Range Nuclear Weapons.* Congressional Research Service. Library of Congress. Washington, D.C.: Government Printing Office, 1982.

Joint Chiefs of Staff. *United States Military Posture, Fiscal Year 1984.* Washington, D.C.: Government Printing Office, 1983.

Report of the President's Commission on Strategic Forces, April 1983. Washington, D.C.: Government Printing Office, 1983.

U.S. Congress. Congressional Budget Office. *Costs of Manning the Active-Duty Military, May 31, 1980.* Washington, D.C.: Government Printing Office, 1980.

——. *SALT II and the Costs of Modernizing U.S. Strategic Forces, September 1979.* Washington, D.C.: Government Printing Office, 1979.

——. *U.S. Sea-Based Strategic Force: Costs of the Trident Submarine and Missile Programs and Alternatives, February 1980.* Washington, D.C.: Government Printing Office, 1980.

——. *The Selective Service System: Mobilization Capabilities and Options for Improvement.* Washington, D.C.: Government Printing Office, 1978.

——. *Shaping the General Purpose Navy of the Eighties: Issues for FY 81-85, January 1980.* Washington, D.C.: Government Printing Office, 1980.

U.S. Congress. House. Committee on Armed Services. *Weapons Acquisition Policy and Procedures: Curbing Cost Growth.* Report of the Special Panel on Defense Procurement Procedures. Feb. 12, 1982. Committee Print No. 13.

U.S. Congress. House. Committee on Armed Services. Subcommittee on Military Personnel and Compensation. *Defense Manpower Policies and Problems among Member Countries of NATO.* Presentation by members of the Subcommittee on Manpower and Personnel of the North Atlantic Assembly. May 5, 1981. Washington, D.C.: Government Printing Office, 1982.

U.S. Congress. House. Committee on Foreign Affairs. *Report on a Resolution Calling for a Mutual and Verifiable Freeze on and Reductions in Nuclear Weapons and for Approval of the SALT II Agreement.* July 19, 1982. Washington, D.C.: Government Printing Office, 1982.

U.S. Congress. House. Committee on Foreign Affairs. Subcommittee on International Security and Scientific Affairs and the Subcommittee on Europe and the Middle East. *Overview of Nuclear Arms Control and Defense Strategy in NATO. Hearings, Feb. 23-March 22, 1982.* Washington, D.C.: Government Printing Office, 1982.

U.S. Congress. House. Committee on Government Operations. Subcommittee on Environment, Energy and Natural Resources. *Will U.S. Nuclear Attack Evacuation Plans Work? Hearing April 22, 1982.* 97th Cong., 2d sess. Washington, D.C.: Government Printing Office, 1982.

U.S. Congress. Joint Economic Committee. *The Persian Gulf: Are We Committed? At What Cost?.* 97th Cong., 1st sess. Washington, D.C.: Government Printing Office, 1981.

U.S. Congress. Joint Economic Committee. Subcommittee on Economic Goals and Intergovernmental Policy. *The Defense Buildup and the Economy.* Feb. 17, 1982. Washington, D.C.: Government Printing Office, 1982.

U.S. Congress. Office of Technology Assessment. *The Effects of Nuclear War.* Montclair, N.J.: Allanheld, Osmun & Co., 1980.

———. *MX Missile Basing.* June 1981. Washington, D.C.: Government Printing Office, 1981.

U.S. Congress. Senate. Committee on Appropriations. Subcommittee on Defense. *Hearings on Department of Defense Appropriations for Fiscal Year 1983, March 2-25, 1982.* Washington, D.C.: Government Printing Office, 1982.

U.S. Congress. Senate. Committee on Armed Services. *Europe and the Middle East: Strains on Key Elements of America's Vital Interests.* April 23, 1982. 97th Cong., 2d sess. Washington, D.C.: Government Printing Office, 1982.

U.S. Congress. Senate. Committee on Armed Services. Subcommittee on Strategic and Theater Nuclear Forces. *Strategic Force Modernization Programs. Hearings, Oct. 26-Nov. 13, 1981.* Washington, D.C.: Government Printing Office, 1981.

U.S. Congress. Senate. Committee on Foreign Relations. *Crisis in the Atlantic Alliance: Origins and Implications.* 97th Cong., 2d sess. Washington, D.C.: Government Printing Office, 1982.

———. *NATO Today: The Alliance in Evolution.* April 1982. 97th Cong., 2d sess. Washington: Government Printing Office, 1982.

———. *Nuclear Arms Reduction Proposals. Hearings, April 29-May 13, 1982.* Washington, D.C.: Government Printing Office, 1982.

U.S. Congress. Senate. Committee on Foreign Relations. Subcommittee on European Affairs. *SALT II: Some Foreign Policy Considerations.* 96th Cong., 1st sess. Washington, D.C.: Government Printing Office, 1979.

U.S. Department of Defense. Directorate for Management Information Operations and Control. *Selected Manpower Statistics.* Washington, D.C.: 1980.

U.S. Department of Defense. *Soviet Military Power.* Washington, D.C.: Government Printing Office, 1983.

U.S. General Accounting Office. *The Congress Should Act to Establish Military Compensation Principles: Report to the Congress by the Comptroller General of the United States, May 9, 1979.* Washington, D.C.: Government Pring Office, 1979.

———. *Improvements Needed in Army's Determination of Manpower Requirements for Support and Administrative Functions: Report by the U.S. General Accounting Office, May 21, 1979.* Washington, D.C.: Government Printing Office, 1979.

Weinberger, Caspar W. *Annual Report of the Secretary of Defense to the Congress, Fiscal Year 1984.* Washington, D.C.: Government Printing Office, 1983.

INDEX

A

ABM (anti-ballistic missile) systems - 29, 55, 67-68
   Treaty (1972), 46-47
Addabbo, Joseph P. (D-N.Y.) - 158
   B-1 bomber - 106
   MX missile - 92, 106
Afghanistan
   Soviet bases - 192-193
   Soviet invasion - 22, 61, 120, 179, 180, 198
Africa
   Soviet involvement - 12, 118
   Strategic issues - 128
Air Force
   Aircraft - 5, 21, 100, 105-106, 132, 133, 152, 190
   Expansion - 122
   General purpose forces - 211
   MX missile - 86
   NATO defense role - 137-138, 139
   Overseas forces - 184, 213
   Personnel - 162, 163, 208
      Training - 214, 215
   Rapid deployment forces - 194, 195, 204, 205
   Reserve - 208, 209
   U.S.-based forces - 212, 213
Airborne Warning and Control System. *See* AWACS.
Aircraft
   AWACS planes - 67, 68, 154, 183-184
   Bombers - 99, 101
      A-10 tank-hunter - 37-38
      B-1 bomber - 11, 12, 18, 20, 21, 26, 27, 33, 65, 70, 99-100, 102, 104, 105, 106, 217, 218
      B-52 bomber - 100, 102, 106-107
      Backfire bomber (U.S.S.R.) - 21, 74, 217

Cargo planes - 5, 157, 188, 189, 190-191
   Helicopters - 132-133, 135, 155, 157, 188
   Lobbying for contracts - 38
   Procurement objectives - 133, 142-143, 152, 513, 157-158
   Stealth plane - 99, 105-106, 219
   Tactical fighters - 11, 105, 132, 133-134
   V/STOL planes - 15
Aircraft carriers, nuclear-powered - 21, 23, 33, 37, 122, 142-143, 157
   Small vs. large - 146-147
Allen, Gen. Lew - 165
AMRAAM missile - 133
Anderson, John B. - 26
Andropov, Yuri V. - 46, 76, 221, 223
Anti-Ballistic Missile (ABM) Treaty (1972) - 46-47
ANZUS alliance - 201
Appropriations. *See* Defense spending.
Arab-Israeli War (1973) - 12
Armed Services
   Active strength - 206-208
   Combat readiness - 214-215
      Costs, 215-216
   Combat units - 211-212
   Functional forces - 204-205
   General purpose forces - 206
      Units - 211
   Personnel - 201
      Expansion - 207-208
      Pay raises - 24-25, 28
      Women - 210-211
   Reserve forces - 208-209
   Structure - 203-204
   Troop deployment
      Overseas - 129, 213-214
      United States - 212-213

O, P, Q